THE EFFECTS OF NEWSPAPER-TELEVISION CROSS-OWNERSHIP ON NEWS HOMOGENEITY

William T. Gormley, Jr.

Poynter Institute for Media Studies
Library

MAY 26 '87

Institute for Research in Social Science
The University of North Carolina
Chapel Hill

1976

© WILLIAM T. GORMLEY, Jr. 1976
ALL RIGHTS RESERVED

Second Printing, 1977

LIBRARY OF CONGRESS CATALOG CARD NUMBER: 76-21859

ISBN: 0-89143-065-2

This study was prepared with the support of the John and Mary Markle Foundation under Grant 1-0-107-5210-MY-265. Any opinions, findings, conclusions, or recommendations expressed herein are those of the author and do not necessarily reflect the views of the John and Mary Markle Foundation.

ACKNOWLEDGMENTS

Many people have cared enough to criticize my work, and I have benefited from their concern. I am reminded of how Carl Albert improved his oratory. As a youth, Albert delivered speeches in the company of a friend, who honed Albert's skills by heckling him, yanking his necktie, untying his shoelaces, and throwing sand at him. It is a pleasure to know people who will throw sand at you as long as your lungs hold out.

I owe a special debt to Professor Duncan MacRae, the chairman of my doctoral dissertation committee. Professor MacRae has not merely observed the forest and its trees; he has brought to my attention the bark on the trees and the firmament above the forest. His ability to decompose and restructure my arguments has enabled me to move in unexpected directions. His critical evaluations of my chapters have been so insightful that I almost wish I had several more chapters to write.

I am also deeply grateful to the other members of my dissertation committee--John Adams, Thad Beyle, William Keech, and Frank Munger. They provided me with many thoughtful criticisms and suggestions and raised numerous provocative questions. Their contributions were substantial and I consider myself fortunate to have had such an excellent committee.

I am happy to acknowledge other debts. Ben Bagdikian and Angell Beza advised me on questionnaire survey techniques. David Price strengthened my discussion of the policy-making process. Jack Hoadley, David Kovenock, George and Stuart Rabinowitz, William Reynolds, and Richard Rockwell patiently answered methodological questions. Dan Nimmo helped to place my findings in perspective. And Scott Keeter, Donald Shaw, and Carl Van Horn threw sand at me as often as possible.

Several other people aided me in various ways. Professor Munger arranged for me to work in comfortable quarters at the Institute for Research in Social Science. Elizabeth Fink, John Leonarz, and Mary Warnock taught me the intricacies of grant management. Sandy Branscomb, Barbara Higgins, and Pat Sanford rendered my dissertation suitable for publication. Poppy Anderson, Garry Ballance, Ken Brantley, Frank Buhrman, Scott Keeter, and John Tankel did an excellent job of coding. And William Denton, Dan Levy, and Rose Spalding chauffered me to and from the Raleigh-Durham airport so that I could do my field work. I don't know how many situation comedies they missed on my account.

I could not have conducted my research without the assistance of numerous news directors, managing editors, and reporters. I appreciate the willingness of these journalists to take time out of their busy schedules to communicate with me. What I have learned about intermedia relations is due largely to their kindness and candor.

Finally, I would like to thank the John and Mary Markle Foundation for their generous financial support and for their confidence in someone as young as myself.

TABLE OF CONTENTS

I   MEDIA PLURALISM AND MESSAGE PLURALISM IN A DEMOCRACY   1

       Effects of Similar Issue Emphasis   3
       Effects of Story Overlap   6
       Pack Journalism and News Homogeneity   10
       Wires, Networks, and News Homogeneity   11
       Newspaper Chains and News Homogeneity   14
       Cross-Media Ownership and News Homogeneity   17

II   CROSS-MEDIA OWNERSHIP AND THE POLICY-MAKING PROCESS   23

       Prelude to a Decision   23
       The F.C.C. Decides   31
       Bounded Rationality Model   36
       Pluralist Politics Model   39
       Symbolic Politics Model   42
       Implications of Three Models   46
       Mass Media Coverage of the F.C.C.'s Decision   49
       Aftermath of the F.C.C.'s Decision   53

III   METHODOLOGY   56

       Mailed Questionnaires   57
       The Effects of Cross-Ownership on Intermedia Relations . .   59
       A Stratified Sample of 10 Cities   66
       Data-Gathering in 10 Cities   67
       Checking the Reliability of Questionnaire Data   71
       Coding the Data   74
       Controls for Story Overlap Comparisons Within Cities . . .   75
       Controls for Story Overlap Comparisons Across Cities . . .   80
       Effects of Cross-Media Ownership on Similarity of Issue
          Emphasis   85

IV   THE SPECTRUM FROM COMPETITION TO COOPERATION   90

       The Professional Vacuum   93
       Non-Interventionist News Executives   94
       The Views of News Executives   95
       The Urge to Compete   100
       The Urge to Cooperate   105
       Effects of Cross-Ownership on Intermedia Relations   111
       The Sharing of Carbons   112
       Hiring Patterns   118
       News Organization Location   121
       Conclusion   126

V	EFFECTS OF CROSS-MEDIA OWNERSHIP ON STORY OVERLAP	128

Within-City Story Overlap Comparisons Involving Jointly
  Owned Media Which Share Carbons 130
Within-City Story Overlap Comparisons Involving Jointly
  Owned Media Characterized by Cross-Employment (From
  the Newspaper to the Television Station) 135
Within-City Story Overlap Comparisons Involving Jointly
  Owned Media Located Within the Same Complex of
  Buildings 142
Within-City Story Overlap Comparisons Involving Jointly
  Owned Media Lacking Particular Ties 147
Lessons of Within-City Comparisons 152
Overall Effects of Cross-Ownership on Story Overlap 153
Direct vs. Indirect Effects of Cross-Ownership on Story
  Overlap 158
Effects of Different Combinations of Cross-Ownership-
  Related Variables 162
Explanatory Power of Cross-Ownership-Related Variables vs.
  Non-Cross-Ownership-Related Variables 165
Effects of Cross-Ownership on Intermedia Relations, by
  City Size 167

VI	EFFECTS OF CROSS-OWNERSHIP ON ISSUE TREATMENT AND STORY TREATMENT	173

Effects of Cross-Ownership on the Willingness of Television
  Stations to Editorialize 175
Effects of Cross-Ownership on Issue Ranking Similarity . . . 182
Effects of Cross-Ownership on Agenda Composition Similarity 188
Scientific vs. Journalistic Approaches 194
Possible Links Between Cross-Ownership and Story Treatment . 199
An Unresolved Question 204

VII	PUBLIC POLICY RECOMMENDATIONS	206

The Case for Divestiture 208
The Case Against Divestiture 213
Ethics and Policy Choice 217
A Critical Evaluation of the F.C.C.'s Cross-Ownership
  Decision 220
Rulemaking vs. Case-by-Case Approaches 227
A Proposed Rule 232
Supplementary Proposals 241
Conclusion 246

APPENDIX A 249

APPENDIX B 255

APPENDIX C 259

APPENDIX D 261

APPENDIX E 264

A SELECTED BIBLIOGRAPHY 265

LIST OF TABLES AND FIGURES

Tables

Table 1. Next-Day Coverage of F.C.C. Decision on Cross-Media Ownership by 18 Newspapers Which Own a Local T.V. Station . . 51

Table 2. Characteristics of Newspaper-Television Monopolies and Matched Pairs 60

Table 3. Effects of Cross-Ownership on Carbon-Sharing, Controlling for the Number of T.V. Stations Per City 65

Table 4. Effects of Cross-Ownership on Cross-Employment, Controlling for T.V. News Staff Size 65

Table 5. News Media in the Sample 70

Table 6. Effects of Cross-Ownership on News Organization Location, Controlling for City Size 73

Table 7. Simple Correlations of Four City Size Variables With Story Overlap 84

Table 8. Top Ten Issues for News Media in the Sample 86

Table 9. Simple Correlations of Four City Size Variables With Issue Ranking Similarity 87

Table 10. Simple Correlations of Four City Size Variables With Agenda Composition Similarity 89

Table 11. Crosstabulation of Cross-Ownership by Carbon-Sharing . . 113

Table 12. Crosstabulation of Cross-Ownership by Cross-Employment 119

Table 13. Crosstabulation of Cross-Ownership by News Organization Location 122

Table 14. Story Overlap Comparisons Involving Jointly Owned Media Which Share Carbons 131

Table 15. Story Overlap Comparisons Involving Jointly Owned Media Characterized by Cross-Employment (From the Newspaper to the Television Station) 136

Table 16.	Story Overlap Comparisons Involving Jointly Owned Media Located Within the Same Complex of Buildings	142
Table 17.	Story Overlap Comparisons Involving Jointly Owned Media Lacking Particular Ties	147
Table 18.	Effects of Cross-Media Ownership on Story Overlap, Controlling for the Log of T.V. Market Size (Unweighted Sample)	154
Table 19.	Effects of Cross-Media Ownership on Story Overlap, Controlling for the Log of T.V. Market Size, T.V. News Audience Share and Newspaper Circulation Share (Unweighted Sample)	156
Table 20.	Effects of Cross-Media Ownership on Story Overlap, Controlling for the Log of T.V. Market Size (Weighted Sample)	157
Table 21.	Indirect Effects of Cross-Ownership on Story Overlap	162
Table 22.	Effects of Cross-Ownership-Related Variables on Story Overlap, Controlling for the Log of T.V. Market Size	163
Table 23.	Variance in Story Overlap Explained by the Log of T.V. Market Size and Four Cross-Ownership-Related Variables	165
Table 24.	Variance in Story Overlap Explained by the Log of T.V. Market Size and Four Variables Not Caused by Cross-Ownership	168
Table 25.	Relationship Between Cross-Ownership and Carbon-Sharing, by City Size	169
Table 26.	Relationship Between Cross-Ownership and Cross-Employment, by City Size	170
Table 27.	Relationship Between Cross-Ownership and News Organization Location, by City Size	172
Table 28.	Crosstabulation of Cross-Ownership by Editorializing	178
Table 29.	Effects of Cross-Media Ownership on Editorializing, Controlling for City Size, Frequency, Network Affiliation, and T.V. News Staff Size	179
Table 30.	Relationship Between Cross-Ownership and Editorializing, by City Size	181
Table 31.	Effects of Cross-Ownership on Issue Ranking Similarity, Controlling for City Size, T.V. News Audience Share, and Newspaper Circulation Share	184

Table 32. Effects of Local Cross-Ownership on Issue Ranking Similarity, Controlling for City Size, T.V. News Audience Share, and Newspaper Circulation Share 185

Table 33. Issue Emphasis on Hypothetical Newspaper and T.V. Station With Identical Issue Ranking, Different Agenda Composition 189

Table 34. Issue Emphasis of Hypothetical Newspaper and T.V. Station With Identical Agenda Composition, Different Issue Ranking 190

Table 35. Effects of Cross-Ownership on Agenda Composition Similarity, Controlling for Log of City Size, T.V. News Audience Share, and Newspaper Circulation Share . . 192

Table 36. Effects of Local Cross-Ownership on Agenda Composition Similarity, Controlling for Log of City Size, T.V. News Audience Share, and Newspaper Circulation Share . . 193

Table 37. Newspaper-Television Monopolies 226

Table 38. Effects of Cross-Ownership on Four Variables Which Limit Diversity, in Cities with One Local Television Station 234

Table 39. Effects of Cross-Ownership on Four Variables Which Limit Diversity, in Cities with Two Local Television Stations 235

Table 40. Effects of Cross-Ownership on Four Variables Which Limit Diversity, in Cities with Three Local Television Stations 236

Table 41. Effects of Cross-Ownership on Four Variables Which Limit Diversity, in Cities with More than Three Local Television Stations 237

Figures

Figure 1. Relationship Between Slice of Newscast Analyzed and Raw Story Overlap Score: Rock Island Argus and WHBF-TV 77

Figure 2. Relationship Between Average Number of Stories Per Day Per Newspaper and Average Story Overlap Score Per Newspaper 83

Figure 3. Causal Model: Effects of Cross-Ownership-Related Variables on Story Overlap 160

Figure 4. Cumulative Effects of Cross-Ownership on Four Variables Which Limit Diversity, by Number of Local T.V. Stations Per City 239

I

MEDIA PLURALISM AND MESSAGE PLURALISM
IN A DEMOCRACY

In a democracy, the public must be well-informed about the issues of the day, important socioeconomic trends, the performance of public officials, and the qualifications of candidates for public office. Otherwise, "self-government" becomes a myth--an exercise in self-deceit. Madison recognized this danger: "Knowledge will forever govern ignorance. And a people who mean to be their own governors must arm themselves with the power knowledge gives. A popular government without popular information or the means of acquiring it, is but a prologue to a farce, or a tragedy, or perhaps both."[1]

To argue that public vigilance is a virtue in a democracy is not to suggest that all citizens must demonstrate an extreme interest in politics. Rather, it is to argue, as Duncan and Lukes have put it, that "men ought to play some part in politics for their own good and for the good of society."[2] It is not clear how large the "attentive public" should be.[3] However, it is essential that the attentive public--however

_____

[1] James Madison, quoted in William Rivers, The Adversaries: Politics and the Press (Boston: Beacon Press, 1970), p. 8.

[2] Graeme Duncan and Steven Lukes, "Democracy Restated," in Frontiers of Democratic Theory, ed. by Henry Kariel (New York: Random House, 1970), p. 211.

[3] A number of scholars have contended that some apathy is functional in a democracy. See, for example, Bernard Berelson, Paul

large it may be--should have access to a wide variety of information about public affairs.

The success of a democracy, of course, depends not only on the public's level of knowledge but on the public's judgment as well. It is not enough that the public be well-informed. The public must also be able to decide wisely which policy problems are more important than others, which solutions are better than others, and which candidates for office are more deserving than others. There is no way to guarantee that the public will be wise. However, a fundamental democratic assumption is that popular wisdom flourishes in a society where diverse ideas and opinions flow freely.

In "Areopagitica," Milton articulated a strong case in favor of diversity in public discourse: "Since therefore, the knowledge and survey of vice is in this world so necessary to the constituting of human virtue, and the scanning of error to the confirmation of truth, how can we more safely and with less danger scout into the regions of sin and falsity than by reading all manner of tractates and hearing all manner of reason?"[4] John Stuart Mill shared a similar commitment to diversity: "Truth . . . is so much a question of the reconciling and combining of opposites that very few have minds sufficiently capacious and impartial to make the adjustments with an approach to correctness, and it has to

---

Lazarsfeld, and William McPhee, Voting (Chicago: University of Chicago Press, 1954), pp. 305-323; also see Lester Milbrath, Political Participation (Chicago: Rand McNally, 1965), pp. 142-154. For a critique of these arguments, see Jack Walker, "A Critique of the Elitist Theory of Democracy," American Political Science Review (June 1966), pp. 285-295.

[4] John Milton, "Areopagitica," in John Milton: Complete Poems and Major Prose, ed. by Merritt Hughes (New York: The Odyssey Press, 1957), p. 729.

be made by the rough process of a struggle between contestants fighting under hostile banners."[5]

As Almond and Verba have noted, "Democratic competence is closely related to having valid information about political issues and processes and to the ability to use information in the analysis of issues and the devising of influence strategies."[6] The extent to which citizens have valid information and are able to use the information wisely depends not only on their sense of civic competence but on the information and opinions which are made available to them by the mass media. In modern society, the mass media play a crucial role in providing the public with political information and in nurturing the pursuit of truth. In fact, the mass media's role is so important that Cater has referred to the press as "the fourth branch of government."[7] By making information and viewpoints about the conduct of public affairs available to citizens, and by transmitting feedback from citizens to political elites, the mass media have helped to make democracy work. As the mass media have grown in importance, they have come to deserve greater scrutiny, since the messages which the mass media transmit are partially determined by characteristics of the mass media themselves.

Effects of Similar Issue Emphasis

One of the more routine—and more significant—powers of the mass media is the ability to influence the public's perception of the relative

---

[5] John Stuart Mill, On Liberty, ed. by Alburey Castell (New York: Appleton-Century-Crofts, Inc., 1947), p. 47.

[6] Gabriel Almond and Sidney Verba, The Civic Culture (Boston: Little, Brown and Company, 1965), p. 57.

[7] Douglass Cater, The Fourth Branch of Government (New York: Vintage Books, 1965), p. 13.

importance of various issues. As Cohen put it, the press "may not be successful much of the time in telling people what to think, but it is stunningly successful in telling its readers what to think about."[8] As McCombs and Shaw have noted, there is evidence that the mass media can "set the agenda" for the public by influencing the salience of public attitudes toward different political issues. McCombs and Shaw reached this conclusion after discovering an extremely high correlation between the aggregate agenda of a sample of North Carolina voters and the aggregate agenda of the mass media to which those voters were exposed during the 1968 Presidential campaign.[9] Extending these discoveries, Becker and McLeod found that Democrats who regarded the Honesty and Vietnam issues as very salient in the 1972 Presidential campaign were more likely to favor McGovern.[10] In short, citizens' agendas may affect their political behavior.

If the mass media merely reflected underlying social realities, the mass media's agenda would not be of much interest. However, as Funkhouser has shown, the mass media's emphasis on various issues over time bears only a weak relationship to the "actual" importance of these

---

[8] Bernard Cohen, The Press and Foreign Policy (Princeton: Princeton University Press, 1963), p. 13.

[9] Maxwell McCombs and Donald Shaw, "The Agenda-Setting Function of Mass Media," Public Opinion Quarterly (Summer, 1971), pp. 176-187.

[10] Lee Becker and Jack McLeod, paper presented at the Conference on Agenda-Setting, S.I. Newhouse School of Public Communications, Syracuse, N. Y., October 27, 1974.

issues over time, as measured by social indicators.[11] Although journalists frequently inveigh against "news management" by government officials, the fact remains that the primary "news managers" in the U.S. today are the journalists themselves. It is the very nature of their business to cover some stories and not cover others, to emphasize certain issues and not emphasize others.

In a society glutted by problems, controversies, and crises, public opinion about the relative importance of various issues matters a great deal. Because the public's perception of the relative importance of different issues depends heavily on the news the public receives, those who control the flow of news wield considerable power. In Schattschneider's words, "He who determines what politics is about runs the country, because the definition of the alternatives is the choice of conflicts, and the choice of conflicts allocates power."[12]

When two news organizations emphasize the same issues, citizens may be adversely affected by overexposure to one set of priorities. Lacking a genuine basis of comparison, citizens cannot effectively judge the merits of a single set of priorities. The fate of media consumers in such a situation is akin to that of voters in an election where there are no apparent issue differences between the candidates.

---

[11] Funkhouser's measures of the importance of issues over time were based primarily on data obtained from Statistical Abstracts of the United States. For example, Funkhouser measured the changing importance of inflation by looking at changes in the purchasing power of the dollar. See G. Ray Funkhouser, "The Issues of the 60's: An Exploratory Study in the Dynamics of Public Opinion," Public Opinion Quarterly (Spring, 1973), pp. 62-75.

[12] E. E. Schattschneider, The Semi-Sovereign People (New York: Holt, Rinehart and Winston, 1960), p. 68.

Unable to choose on the basis of issue differences, voters have little reason to think about the issues. Unable to choose on the basis of differences in issue emphasis, media consumers have little reason to wonder whether the issues being emphasized by a particular news organization deserve that amount of emphasis. Key's lament is as true of media consumers as it is of voters: "Fed a steady diet of buncombe, the people may come to expect and to respond with highest predictability to buncombe."[13] Thus, as a consequence of similar issue emphasis by two news organizations, the public may come to regard some issues as being more important than they actually are, other issues as being less important than they actually are.

Effects of Story Overlap

A news organization's decision to cover one story rather than another can be as significant for the course of public policy as a decision to emphasize one issue more than another. Publicity is vital if an event or development is to be transformed into an issue. As Cobb and Elder have suggested, events and developments often serve as "triggering devices" which create issues.[14] However, events and developments are unlikely to trigger anything unless they are dealt with by at least one news organization. For this reason, an event or development must become a story before it can lead to the emergence of an issue.

---

[13] V. O. Key, Jr., <u>The Responsible Electorate</u> (New York: Vintage Books, 1966), p. 7.

[14] Roger Cobb and Charles Elder, <u>Participation in American Politics: The Dynamics of Agenda-Building</u> (Boston: Allyn & Bacon, Inc., 1972), p. 84.

A story frequently involves a public policy problem or possible solution. Consequently, a news organization's failure to cover a particular story may deprive citizens of knowledge concerning a problem or opportunity for some time. Even if the problem or opportunity is eventually publicized, the delay may be fraught with significance. Whether a city council candidate's views on zoning become known before or after a local election can be important. Whether the details of a university expansion plan become known before or after construction begins can be important. Whether a health or safety hazard becomes known before or after a tragedy occurs can be important. Thus, a news organization's failure to cover a particular story may keep a problem or opportunity from being brought to light early enough for citizens or political elites to take timely action.

Story coverage is so closely related to the publicizing of problems and opportunities that decisions to cover some stories instead of others have considerable political significance. Unless at least one news organization focuses on a problem or opportunity, it is unlikely to be placed on what Cobb and Elder have called "the systemic agenda" or "all issues that are commonly perceived by members of the political community as meriting public attention and as involving matters within the legitimate jurisdiction of existing governmental authority."[15] Furthermore, unless an item is on the systemic agenda, it is unlikely to be placed on what Cobb and Elder refer to as "an institutional agenda" or "the set of items explicitly up for the active and

---

[15] Ibid., p. 85.

serious consideration of authoritative decision-makers."[16] Thus, the mass media play a crucial role in the very early stages of the policy-making process--a role which Easton has described as "gatekeeping."[17]

Due to limitations of time, space, and manpower, the number of stories covered by a newspaper or a broadcasting station (especially the latter) is relatively inelastic. Consequently, the more that news organizations cover the same stories, the greater the number of stories that will be condemned to obscurity.[18] Whether intentional or not, attention to the same problems and opportunities by the mass media has the effect of keeping other problems and opportunities off the systemic agenda--at least in the short run. These neglected problems and opportunities might otherwise have been dealt with in a timely fashion by the political system.

Story overlap can be harmful in still another way. When a newspaper and a broadcasting station cover the same stories, this appears to have a depressing effect on the knowledge level of the public. In Zanesville, Ohio, where local broadcasting stations ran fewer "exclusive" stories than local broadcasting stations in two cities comparable in size and education level, Stempel found that the public was less well informed than the public in the two comparable cities.[19] To the extent

---

[16] Ibid., p. 86.

[17] David Easton, A Systems Analysis of Political Life (New York: John Wiley & Sons, Inc., 1965), pp. 133-137.

[18] The extent to which a newspaper and a broadcasting station (or other news organizations) cover the same stories may be referred to as story overlap.

[19] Guido Stempel, III, "Effects on Performance of a Cross-Media Monopoly," Journalism Monographs (June 1973), pp. 12-13.

that a newspaper and a television station cover the same stories, persons exposed to both will receive redundant information. On an average day, a substantial number of Americans read a newspaper and watch television news.[20] The Stempel study suggests that these Americans learn less when the newspaper and the television station cover the same stories.

It is possible to exaggerate the virtues of message pluralism in the mass media. After all, some people do not read a newspaper and watch television news; rather, they do one or the other. There are probably some stories so important that everyone ought to know about them. There are probably some issues so important that everyone ought to know how important they are. Identifying an appropriate level of news homogeneity is extremely difficult because the needs of heavy media users and light media users are different. In general, persons who are exposed quite a bit to the mass media are well served by message pluralism in the mass media. On the other hand, persons who rely primarily on one news medium for their news should probably be able to learn about certain important stories and issues by attending to that news medium alone.

If two news organizations independently determine that a story is worth covering or that an issue is worth emphasizing, some media consumers may benefit from such news homogeneity. However, news organizations do not always make their choices independently. Several sources

---

[20] According to a national survey conducted for the Newspaper Advertising Bureau in 1971, 36% of the American people both read a daily newspaper and watch television news on a typical day. See "A National Survey of the Content and Readership of the American Newspaper," published by the Newspaper Advertising Bureau, New York, N.Y., December 1972.

of news homogeneity have nothing to do with the independent news judgment of journalists.

Pack Journalism and News Homogeneity

Reporters and editors often practice "pack journalism" and succumb to the "herd instinct." News organizations may emphasize the same issues because reporters reach a consensus about the relative importance of issues in conversations with other reporters or because editors experience less cognitive dissonance if they know that other editors are emphasizing the same issues. News organizations may cover the same stories because reporters fear they will be rebuked by their editors if the competition runs a story which they neglect, because reporters find it easy to cultivate the same sources as other reporters, or because editors have been similarly socialized and have come to believe that stories which are timely, proximate, and involve conflict are more newsworthy than other kinds of stories.[21]

If journalists, by virtue of their training, are better equipped than other citizens to decide what is newsworthy, there may be nothing wrong with news homogeneity which results from similar training experiences. However, to the extent that journalists cover the same stories and emphasize the same issues as a matter of convenience, or caution, or as a knee-jerk reaction to what their colleagues are doing, the public interest is not being served by such news homogeneity. In his

---

[21] In a study of the news selection practices of television news editors, Buckalew found that stories characterized by conflict, proximity, timeliness, and the availability of film were selected 95% of the time. See James Buckalew, "News Elements and Selection of Television News Editors," Journal of Broadcasting (Winter, 1969-1970), pp. 47-54.

study of statehouse reporters in Wisconsin, Dunn found ample evidence of pack journalism. Reporters monitored each other's work, traded information, bounced ideas off one another, and tended to write the same stories as their colleagues. In the words of one newsman Dunn interviewed, "Reporters go around in circles chasing each other."[22] Even reporters for elite newspapers practice pack journalism, as Sigal discovered, in his study of the New York Times and the Washington Post. As Sigal put it, "On the beat, as in the newsroom, reporters do not work alone, but in groups; and in the course of events, the group subtly molds individual values into group judgment."[23]

Wires, Networks, and News Homogeneity

Due to obvious economic constraints, very few newspapers or broadcasting stations can afford to have their own correspondents in the nation's capital or in news centers around the world. And yet, the growing importance of the federal government and international relations has sparked a public interest in "instant" communications about national and world affairs--an interest which weekly magazines cannot completely satisfy. In response, newspapers and broadcasting stations have tried to serve their readers and viewers by establishing relationships with wire services and broadcasting networks.

By 1970, approximately 68% of all U.S. daily newspapers were members of the Associated Press and approximately 50% of all U.S. dailies subscribed to United Press International. In the same year, over

---

[22] Delmer Dunn, Public Officials and the Press (Reading, Mass.: Addison-Wesley Publishing Company, 1969), p. 30.

[23] Leon Sigal, Reporters and Officials: The Organization and Politics of Newsmaking (Lexington, Mass.: D. C. Heath & Company, 1973), p. 39.

3,000 U.S. broadcasting stations were members of the Associated Press and over 3,000 U.S. broadcasting stations subscribed to United Press International.[24] Individual newspapers and broadcasting stations can, of course, run some wire service stories and discard others. Indeed, recent technological developments permit the easy editing of wire service copy. Nevertheless, the two major wire services have a profound influence on the pool of national and international news stories which most newspapers and broadcasting stations have at their disposal. In Emery's words, the wire services "have contributed mightily to the excellence" of the mass media, but they have become "one of the common denominators of a standardized journalism."[25]

If the power of the wire services is diluted by the ability of editors to select which wire stories to run, the power of the three major television networks is not similarly restricted. In practical terms, the impact of the networks is diluted only when affiliated television stations decide which network stories to include in their late evening newscasts. Although network affiliates have the option of refusing to air a particular early evening newscast, they lose considerable advertising revenue when they do so and they also run the risk of losing their network affiliation if they do so too often.[26] According to A. C.

---

[24] Edwin Emery, *The Press and America: An Interpretative History of the Mass Media* (Englewood Cliffs: Prentice-Hall, Inc., 1972), p. 481. Since the Associated Press is a cooperative, news media are "members" of AP, "subscribers" to UPI.

[25] *Ibid.*, p. 465.

[26] The networks rarely resort to such extreme retaliation, but it does happen. In March 1976, for example, CBS deprived KXLY-TV (Spokane, Washington) of its CBS affiliation, primarily because KXLY had failed to run a number of CBS programs. See "Split in Spokane," *Broadcasting* (March 15, 1976), p. 90.

Nielsen figures, approximately 50 million U.S. adults watch some network television news on an average day, and approximately 81 million watch network television news sometime during the week.[27] Alarmed by the power of the networks, Joseph Coors founded Television News, Inc., to reduce the dependence of television stations on CBS, NBC, and ABC. At its peak, Television News, Inc. was providing daily news feeds to 80 television stations, but TVN discontinued that service on October 31, 1975 when it became apparent that the news service was not making a profit.[28]

An individual network brings the same stories into millions of American homes every evening. Furthermore, the networks tend to cover the same stories. As Lemert discovered in a content analysis of the networks' week-day evening newscasts, nearly 70% of the stories covered by one network were also covered by at least one of the other two on the same evening.[29] Pack journalism undoubtedly accounts for some of this news homogeneity, but an additional factor is that all three networks are influenced by similar financial and logistical constraints. As Epstein has noted, the networks can afford to maintain camera crews in only a handful of cities--New York, Washington, D.C., Chicago, and a few others. By sending camera crews to Oshkosh or Kalamazoo, the

---

[27] Benjamin Bagdikian, "Newspapers: Learning (Too Slowly) to Adapt to Television," Columbia Journalism Review (November/December 1973), p. 47.

[28] "T.V.N. to Stop Its News Feeds," Broadcasting (October 6, 1975), pp. 49-50.

[29] James Lemert, "Content Duplication by the Networks in Competing Evening Newscasts," Journalism Quarterly (September 1974), pp. 238-244.

networks can cover stories there, but this is extremely expensive. In addition to paying transportation costs, the networks must pay for the costs of transmitting stories via special cables whenever they desert their regular headquarters for more remote locales. As a result, all three networks tend to cover a disproportionate share of stories originating in a few very large cities.[30] The networks are also reluctant to send a reporter out on a wild goose chase, with a cameraman and producer in tow, since this is expensive and time-consuming if no story materializes. Consequently, all three networks delight in covering "low-risk" stories such as congressional committee hearings or the Secretary of State's press conferences. By virtue of covering the same stories, the networks may give emphasis to the same issues as well.

Newspaper Chains and News Homogeneity

The number of daily newspapers in the U.S. has declined from a total of 1,942 in 1930 to a current total of 1,768.[31] Under financial pressure, newspapers have collapsed as a result of increases in the cost of newsprint, crippling strikes and demands for higher wages, and losses of advertising revenue to television. While there were competing (separately owned) daily newspapers in 288 cities in 1930, there are competing dailies in only 58 cities today.[32] In some cities served by two jointly owned daily newspapers, the newspapers have maintained separate news and editorial staffs. However, in others, the news and/or

---

[30] Edward Jay Epstein, *News From Nowhere* (New York: Random House, 1973), pp. 206-208.

[31] These figures have been obtained from Emery, *op. cit.*, p. 621 and *Editor and Publisher International Yearbook 1975*.

[32] Emery, *op. cit.*, p. 621.

editorial staffs have been merged.

Concomitant with the decline in the number of daily newspapers has been the growth of newspaper chains and mass media conglomerates. In 1935, 63 chains owned 328 daily newspapers. Currently, 157 chains own 879 daily newspapers, or approximately 50% of all dailies.[33] The Frank Gannett Company alone owns 54 newspapers, one television station, and two radio stations. The New York Times owns 11 newspapers, one television station, and one AM-FM combination. Cox Enterprises include 10 newspapers, five television stations, nine radio stations, and such publications as Floor Covering Weekly and Industrial Machinery News.[34]

After counting the mass media "monopolies," "baronies," "empires," and "conglomerates" in the U.S. today, Nicholas Johnson was sufficiently alarmed to call for action: "If we are serious about the kind of society we have undertaken, it is clear to me that we simply must not tolerate concentration of media ownership--except where concentration creates actual countervailing social benefits."[35] Certainly, the concentration of mass media ownership has grown to the point where a few conglomerates wield an enormous amount of potential power. To the extent that message pluralism depends on media pluralism, newspaper chains and mass media conglomerates pose a threat to diversity.

---

[33] Ibid., p. 629.

[34] These figures have been obtained from Broadcasting Yearbook 1975.

[35] Nicholas Johnson, "The Media Barons and the Public Interest," The Atlantic (June 1968), p. 49.

Thus, a key question is whether mass media concentration has a homogenizing effect on the flow of news or opinion in the mass media.

Where a newspaper chain has its own news service, membership in a chain is the functional equivalent of membership in the Associated Press. Like AP members, chain members have the option of running or not running stories furnished by the chain's home office. The Scripps-Howard chain, with newspapers widely dispersed in different states, provides national and international news stories to member newspapers. The Frank Gannett Company, which owns a number of New York state newspapers, provides national, international, and state news stories to member newspapers. In general, Bagdikian is probably correct that chains have done for the newspaper business what Howard Johnson's has done for the restaurant business.[36] Although a Scripps-Howard newspaper in Memphis may differ in important respects from the Scripps-Howard newspaper in Cleveland, the two will have similar news outputs to the extent that they use the same Scripps-Howard news service stories.

Chain ownership also contributes to opinion homogeneity when the chain's home office dictates editorial policy to member newspapers. The Lindsay-Schaub chain in Illinois, for example, furnishes editorials endorsing candidates for state and national office, which must be run by member newspapers, whether the individual editor agrees with the editorials or not. In the case of editorials on state, national, or international issues furnished by the Lindsay-Schaub home office,

---

[36] Benjamin Bagdikian, "The Myth of Newspaper Poverty," *Columbia Journalism Review* (March/April 1973), p. 24.

member newspapers have the option of not running these editorials, but they cannot run editorials taking a different position on the issues without first clearing them with the home office in Decatur, Illinois.[37] Other chains are much more tolerant of diversity in the editorials of member newspapers. In 1972, seven Knight newspapers endorsed Nixon, one endorsed McGovern, and two endorsed neither candidate. In what must be considered an acid test of one newspaper's commitment to diversity, the New York Times was reportedly prepared to countenance the endorsement by one of its Florida newspapers of George Wallace's candidacy for President of the United States.[38] Overall, chain ownership appears to have more of a homogenizing effect on the news outputs of member newspapers than on their editorials.[39]

Cross-Media Ownership and News Homogeneity

The combined effect of the two major wire services, the three major television networks, and newspaper chains is to standardize the

---

[37] "That Monopoly of Opinion," The Masthead (Fall 1974), pp. 21-23.

[38] Ibid., p. 27.

[39] The extent to which chain owernship influences the endorsements of Presidential candidates by member newspapers is unclear. According to Wackman et al., the overwhelming majority of chains are "homogeneous" in their endorsements of Presidential candidates. If homogeneous chains are defined as those in which 85% or more of the member newspapers making endorsements supported the same candidate, then over 75% of all chains were homogeneous in 1960, 1968, and 1972. See Daniel Wackman, Donald Gillmor, Cecilie Gaziano, and Everette Dennis, "Chain Newspaper Autonomy as Reflected in Presidential Campaign Endorsements," Journalism Quarterly (Autumn 1975), pp. 411-420. The problem with the Wackman study is that it provides no basis for comparison. The fact that 85% or more of the members of a particular chain endorsed the same candidate for President is not very significant if 85% of a comparable set of non-chain newspapers also endorsed the same candidate.

national and international news diet of millions of Americans. The late H. L. Mencken used to refer to such standardization as the "Fordization" of the news business.[40] While this is no small matter, most Americans do have access to numerous alternate sources of news on national and international issues, including magazines as diverse as the Rolling Stone, the New Republic, Newsweek, Fortune, the National Review, and the Plain Truth. In contrast, sources of local news are severely limited in most cities. To a lesser extent, this is also true of state news, since there are very few state magazines of interest to a general audience (the Texas Monthly is a notable exception) and since out-of-town newspapers are not always available on a home-delivery basis. For these reasons, the concentration of mass media ownership is an especially serious policy problem if it interferes with message pluralism in the flow of state and local news.

In addition to the joint ownership of two daily newspapers in the same city, there is a considerable amount of cross-media ownership in the same city. According to a Rand report, there are 292 radio stations owned by a daily newspaper in the same city.[41] If such cross-ownership results in news homogeneity, it could have serious consequences. Even more dangerous potentially is the joint ownership of a daily newspaper and a television station in the same city. As Roper

---

[40]H. L. Mencken, *A Gang of Pecksniffs*, ed. by Theo Lippman, Jr., (New Rochelle, N. Y.: Arlington House Publishers, 1975), p. 153.

[41]Walter Baer, Henry Geller, Joseph Grundfest, and Karen Possner, "Concentration of Mass Media Ownership: Assessing the State of Current Knowledge," <u>Rand Corporation Report</u> (Santa Monica, Calif.: September 1974), p. 63.

studies have shown, Americans consider newspapers and television stations their most important sources of news and information.[42] Because of the preeminence of newspapers and television stations as sources of state and local news, the joint ownership of a daily newspaper and a television station in the same city could be especially harmful, if it has a homogenizing effect on the state and local news outputs of the jointly owned media.

There are currently 72 television stations in 67 cities which are owned by the same company which owns a local daily (see Appendix A). In 14 of these cities, a single company owns the only daily and the only television station with a studio in the city.[43] At least one television station is owned by a local daily in 28 of the nation's top 50 television markets. Another way to measure the scope of cross-media ownership is to consider the average number of television households reached per day by television stations owned by a daily newspaper in the same city. From this vantage point, television stations owned by a daily newspaper in the same city reach an estimated 22,862,200 television households per day or 35.6% of all television households in the U.S. (see Appendix B).

Although little research has been done on the relationship between cross-media ownership and news content, Stempel did conduct a case study of cross-media ownership in Zanesville, Ohio, which indicated that cross-media ownership had a homogenizing effect on the

---

[42] According to 1972 Roper survey data, 46% of Americans cite television as their most important news source, 36% cite newspapers, 15% cite radio, and 4% cite magazines.

[43] In 15 cities, a single company owns the only daily and the only television station which has a studio in the city and which airs local newscasts.

news outputs of jointly owned media in Zanesville. Comparing jointly owned media in Zanesville with separately owned media in two cities of comparable size and education levels, Stempel found that the Zanesville radio station had the lowest proportion of "exclusive" stories and the Zanesville television station had the next lowest proportion, of all the mass media in the three cities.[44] While suggestive, the Stempel study suffers from the drawbacks of the case-study approach. What was true of Zanesville may not be true of other cities where cross-ownership exists.

In a considerably more extensive study, financed by the National Association of Broadcasters, Anderson conducted a content analysis of newspapers and television news scripts which he obtained from 29 cities where at least one daily newspaper owned a local television station. Within each city, Anderson compared jointly owned and separately owned media pairs by using several measures, including topic correspondence, story rating correspondence, and key word rating correspondence scores. In general, Anderson found no significant differences between jointly owned and separately owned media. One of the few significant findings to emerge indicated that television stations owned by a newspaper were less likely than other television stations to express attitudes toward key words similar to the attitudes expressed by the newspaper.[45]

---

[44] Stempel, op. cit., pp. 23-24.

[45] James Anderson, "Broadcast Stations and Newspapers: The Problem of Information Control: A Content Analysis of Local News Presentations," Broadcast Research Center Report (Athens, Ohio, 1971).

Despite the impressive scope of the Anderson study, the conclusions are suspect. The most notable problem with the study is that Anderson failed to obtain a sufficient number of overlapping stories (stories covered by both a newspaper and a television station) for analysis in each city. By requesting data for only three days, Anderson diminished the probability of capturing subtle differences between jointly owned and separately owned newspaper-television pairs. By requesting newspaper and television data for a Monday, a Wednesday, and a Friday rather than for contiguous days, Anderson made it impossible to code overlap which occurs on contiguous days rather than on the same day.[46] By coding only stories which appeared on the front page or the main local news page of a newspaper, Anderson further reduced the number of overlapping stories in his sample. In its analysis of the Anderson study, the Rand Corporation raised different objections, but reached the same conclusion--that Anderson's findings are not reliable.[47]

Thus, it is still unclear whether cross-media ownership has a homogenizing effect on the state and local news outputs of jointly owned newspapers and television stations. If indeed there are effects, three other questions need to be answered. First, what is the magnitude of the effect of cross-media ownership on news homogeneity? Second, through what intervening variables does cross-media ownership contribute to news homogeneity? Third, under what circumstances does cross-

---

[46] Approximately one-half of all newspaper-television overlap is on contiguous days (e.g., Monday-Tuesday) rather than on the same day (e.g., Monday-Monday).

[47] Baer et al., *op cit*., pp. 135-136.

media ownership contribute to news homogeneity? If certain effects can be attributed to cross-media ownership, it is important to understand how these effects occur. If cross-media ownership acts on news outputs through specific intervening variables, it is important to know what conditions increase the likelihood that these variables will be present.

When two news organizations independently decide that certain stories are worth covering or that certain issues are worth emphasizing, some citizens may benefit from such news homogeneity. Light media users, in particular, may be better informed about more important issues and may have a better set of priorities than if each news organization contrived to differ from other news organizations. Heavy media users, on the other hand, might actually benefit from a contrived diversity. Thus, the merits of news homogeneity resulting from independent journalistic decisions cannot be evaluated without considering the relative importance of the needs of light media users and heavy media users.

In contrast, any news homogeneity resulting from cross-media ownership is an artificial barrier to message pluralism. Such a barrier is especially dangerous if it interferes with diversity in the flow of state and local news and opinion in the mass media. Message pluralism can be undermined as effectively by the structure of the mass media market as by government censorship. If cross-media ownership contributes to pack journalism and interferes with message pluralism in the mass media, it is interfering with a prerequisite to successful self-government--namely, a public which is both well-informed and wise.

II

CROSS-MEDIA OWNERSHIP AND THE
POLICY-MAKING PROCESS

The Federal Communications Commission is required by law to serve "the public interest, convenience and necessity."[1] However, it is not clear that the public interest was served by the F.C.C.'s cross-media ownership rule, adopted January 28, 1975. Nor is it clear that the F.C.C.'s rule was formulated strictly on the basis of public interest considerations. There are at least three conceptual frameworks or models which might be used to explain the F.C.C.'s cross-ownership decision: a bounded rationality model, a pluralist politics model, and a symbolic politics model. Following a review of the steps which led to the F.C.C.'s decision, we will examine the decision from the vantage point of each of the three models.

Prelude to a Decision

Throughout television's early years, the F.C.C. awarded numerous television licenses to companies which owned a daily newspaper in the same city. Anxious to promote competition by increasing the number of television licensees, the F.C.C. had few, if any, qualms about granting a television license to a newspaper if the newspaper was the only applicant for the license.[2] Permitted to buy television stations, newspaper

---

[1] 47 U.S.C., Articles 307-309.

[2] Harvey Levin, <u>Broadcast Regulation and Joint Ownership of Media</u> (New York: New York University Press, 1960), p. 183.

owners rushed to do so--partly because they recognized a good investment and partly because they feared the impact of the new television medium on their older investments.

In the 1960's, however, trends toward mass media ownership concentration became apparent, the number of competing license applications increased, and the F.C.C. began to view newspaper owners applying for a television license with a critical eye. A study of the F.C.C.'s handling of 45 applications for 16 broadcasting licenses between 1967 and 1970 revealed that the F.C.C. had become reluctant to award new broadcasting licenses to newspaper owners.[3] Nevertheless, the most lucrative television licenses had already been allocated, and many of these were in the hands of companies which owned a daily newspaper in the same city. Thus, the crucial question was whether the F.C.C. would curb existing newspaper-television combinations, not prospective ones. If it chose to curb existing combinations, the F.C.C. could opt for either a rule-making approach (e.g., ordering the divestiture of newspaper-television combinations in certain kinds of cities) or a case-by-case approach (e.g., treating cross-ownership as a negative factor in license renewal proceedings).

In August 1968, the Justice Department sent a memo to the F.C.C. urging the abolition of all newspaper-broadcasting combinations in the same market. The Justice Department argued that such combinations lessened the number of news sources and viewpoints in a community, opened the door to unfair advertising practices, and generally restrained

---

[3] Roger Noll, Merton Peck, and John McGowan, Economic Aspects of Television Regulation (Washington, D.C.: Brookings Institution, 1973), p. 114.

competition.[4] Without indicating a preference for the case-by-case approach (as opposed to the rule-making approach suggested by the Justice Department), the F.C.C. resorted to a case-by-case approach in January 1969. For the first time in its history, the F.C.C. cited cross-media ownership as a negative factor in a license renewal decision. In refusing to renew the license of WHDH-TV, Boston, Massachusetts, the F.C.C. noted that WHDH was owned by the same company which owned the Boston Herald-Traveler. Thus, the F.C.C. was attempting to diversify media ownership in Boston.

However, the WHDH case involved more than cross-media ownership. First of all, the F.C.C. prefers that a television station's owners be involved in the actual management of the television station. The owners of WHDH-TV were not so involved, whereas Boston Broadcasters, Inc., which eventually obtained the license, pledged that six of its stockholders, owning 20 percent of the company's stock, would be working full-time at the television station. Second, the Herald-Traveler violated the law by shifting executive control of WHDH-TV in 1963 without the approval of the F.C.C. Third, WHDH-TV steadfastly refused to editorialize, in contrast to Boston Broadcasters, Inc., which promised to editorialize frequently. Furthermore, the WHDH decision was clouded by persistent allegations that Robert Choate, president of the company which owned WHDH, had twice tried to influence F.C.C. Chairman George McConnaughey on WHDH's behalf. While the issue of Choate's ex parte contacts was not cited by the F.C.C. in its decision, the ex parte contacts did result

---

[4] Christopher Sterling, "Newspaper Ownership of Broadcast Stations, 1920-68," <u>Journalism Quarterly</u> (Summer 1969), pp. 227-228.

in WHDH's appeal being denied by the courts.[5] Thus, the WHDH decision could not be construed as a clear precedent on cross-media ownership, and the F.C.C. stated as much in January 1970.[6]

Despite the ambiguity of the WHDH case, the WHDH ruling shocked the broadcasting industry. Fearful that the F.C.C. might try to "restructure" the broadcasting industry through the license renewal process, the National Association of Broadcasters and other interested parties appealed to Congress for relief. Members of Congress sympathized with critics of the WHDH decision, especially after it became clear that the Herald-Traveler was dying--presumably because it needed revenues generated by WHDH to survive. In response to these developments, Senator John Pastore (D.--R.I.), Chairman of the Communications Subcommittee of the Senate Commerce Committee, introduced S. 2004, which barred the F.C.C. from considering a competing application for a broadcasting license unless the incumbent broadcaster had failed to serve the public interest. If approved, S. 2004 would have given substantial protection to newspaper-owned broadcasting stations (as well as other broadcasting stations). In effect, the bill would have prohibited the F.C.C. from considering the cross-ownership factor during comparative license renewal hearings unless the incumbent licensee had failed to serve the public interest. Pastore held hearings on license renewal procedures

---

[5] For a full treatment of the WHDH case, see Sterling Quinlan, The Hundred Million Dollar Lunch (Chicago: J. Philip O'Hara, Inc., 1974); also see Jack Thomas, "Did Boston's 'Herald Traveler' Have to Fail?" Columbia Journalism Review (July/August 1972), pp. 41-44.

[6] Pam Eversole, "Concentration of Ownership in the Communications Industry," Journalism Quarterly (Summer 1971), p. 259.

in 1969, but the Communications Subcommittee did not report S. 2004 out of committee that year.[7]

In January 1970, before Congress reconvened, the F.C.C. adopted license renewal standards similar to those embodied in S. 2004. The F.C.C. said that it would renew an incumbent's license if the station "shows that its program service during the preceding license term has been substantially attuned to meeting the needs and interests of its area and that the operation of the station has not otherwise been characterized by serious deficiencies.[8] In short, the F.C.C. would not even consider the cross-ownership factor in comparative license renewal hearings if the incumbent's programming was "substantially attuned" to community needs and interests and not otherwise marred by serious deficiencies. The F.C.C.'s policy statement, which appeared to settle the license renewal controversy, satisfied Pastore, who concluded that it rendered S. 2004 superfluous. The policy statement also suggested that, the WHDH case notwithstanding, the F.C.C. did not look favorably on a case-by-case approach to cross-ownership.

Soon after rejecting a case-by-case approach to cross-ownership through comparative license renewal hearings, the F.C.C. proposed to adopt the cross-ownership rule suggested two years earlier by the Justice Department. Under this proposal, tentatively endorsed by the F.C.C. in April 1970, the divestiture of all newspaper-broadcasting combinations in the same market would be required within five years after the

---

[7]"Congress, F.C.C. Consider Newspaper Control of Local T.V.," *Congressional Quarterly* (March 16, 1974), p. 662.

[8]The Federal Communications Commission, "Policy Statement on Comparative Hearings Involving Regular Applicants," January 15, 1970.

promulgation of such a rule.[9] The F.C.C.'s proposal quickly provoked outcries from the National Association of Broadcasters and the American Newspaper Publishers Association, which proceeded to deluge the F.C.C. with comments in opposition to the proposed rule.[10]

In the meantime, the D.C. Court of Appeals overturned the F.C.C.'s policy statement on comparative license renewal hearings. In June 1971, the Court ruled that the F.C.C.'s policy statement was illegal, though not necessarily unconstitutional.[11] The Court did acknowledge that "superior" performance by an incumbent licensee "should be a plus of major significance in renewal proceedings."[12] However, the Court said that the F.C.C. could not, under existing law, disregard the cross-ownership factor during license renewal hearings. In the Court's language, "Diversification is a factor properly to be weighed and balanced with other important factors, including the renewal applicant's prior record, at a renewal hearing."[13]

---

[9] Stephen Barnett, "The F.C.C.'s Nonbattle Against Media Monopoly," Columbia Journalism Review (January/February 1973), p. 44.

[10] Approximately 200 parties filed comments in response to the proposed rule through August 1971, when the F.C.C. stopped receiving comments. The overwhelming majority of these parties owned newspapers or broadcasting stations or both.

[11] The D.C. Court of Appeals saw the F.C.C.'s policy statement as an attempt to do what Congress had chosen not to do, when it failed to pass the Pastore bill: "The Policy Statement administratively 'enacts' what the Pastore bill sought to do." See Citizens Communications Center vs. F.C.C., 447 F. 2d 1210 (1971).

[12] Citizens Communications Center vs. F.C.C., 447 F. 2d 1201 (1971).

[13] Citizens Communications Center vs. F.C.C., 447 F. 2d 1214 (1971).

Despite the Court's ruling in <u>Citizens Communications Center vs. F.C.C.</u>, the F.C.C. was able to renew the licenses of newspaper-owned broadcasting stations without considering the cross-ownership factor at all. In view of the fact that the F.C.C. had proposed to deal with cross-ownership through rule-making, the courts allowed the F.C.C. to defer ownership concentration issues raised in license renewal hearings to the cross-ownership rule-making docket--Docket 18110.[14] However, three years after proposing to adopt the cross-ownership rule suggested by the Justice Department, the F.C.C. had still not acted. The absence of an obvious solution, the bitterness of the dispute, and the lack of a consensus among the commissioners all contributed to the delay.

Finally, the Justice Department prodded the F.C.C. to resolve the cross-ownership matter through rule-making by reminding the F.C.C. that its alternative might be a time-consuming case-by-case approach. In November 1973, the Justice Department's Antitrust Division submitted an informal objection opposing the renewal of the newspaper-owned television license in Milwaukee, Wisconsin.[15] In January 1974, the Justice Department filed petitions to deny the renewal of television licenses owned by newspapers in Des Moines, Iowa and St. Louis, Missouri.[16] Later in 1974, Justice filed petitions to deny against television stations owned by newspapers in Minneapolis, Minnesota, Topeka,

---

[14] See National Citizens Committee for Broadcasting et al., <u>Petition for Review of the Federal Communications Commission's Second Report and Order in Docket 18110</u>, pp. 16-19.

[15] The F.C.C. defines a would-be petition to deny, submitted late, as an "informal objection." The F.C.C. tends to treat an informal objection as if it were a petition to deny.

[16] Susanna McBee, "Justice Department Move on Media Surprised White House," <u>The Washington Post</u> (January 21, 1974), p. 2.

Kansas, Salt Lake City, Utah, Fresno, California, and Spokane, Washington.[17] In its petitions, Justice contended that the jointly owned media in each of the targeted cities controlled an excessive amount of local advertising revenue and that such economic concentration posed a threat to competition.

The broadcasting industry and the Congress were also growing impatient--not so much with the F.C.C.'s failure to resolve the cross-ownership question through a rule as with the F.C.C.'s failure to adopt license renewal standards favorable to incumbent broadcasters and acceptable to the courts. On May 1, 1974, the House passed a bill revising the broadcast license renewal law. First, the bill renewed licenses of stations which have been "reasonably" responsive to community needs and interests, in the absence of a competing application for the license. Second, it renewed licenses of stations which have been "substantially" responsive to community needs and interests, in the presence of a competing application. Third, it prohibited the F.C.C. from considering such factors as cross-media ownership or integration of ownership and management at license renewal time. Fourth, it extended broadcast license terms from the current three years to five years.[18] Finally, it

---

[17] Walter Baer, Henry Geller, and Joseph Grundfest, "Newspaper-Television Station Cross-Ownership: Options for Federal Action," Rand Corporation Report (Santa Monica, California: September 1974), p. 6; "Justice Sights Seventh Target: KSL Stations," Broadcasting (September 9, 1974), pp. 30-32; "Petition-to-Deny Blitz Hits 25 in California; Justice Department Files Against McClatchy Stations," Broadcasting (November 4, 1974), p. 5; "U.W. Strikes Again," Broadcasting (January 6, 1975), pp. 7-10.

[18] The bill which eventually passed the House was even more favorable to incumbent licensees than the version reported by the House Committee on Interstate and Foreign Commerce, which only extended license terms to four years.

required the F.C.C. to conclude action in the cross-ownership rule-making docket (Docket 18110) within six months after the date of enactment.[19]

The F.C.C. Decides

While reluctant to adopt a cross-ownership rule, the F.C.C. was left with virtually no other option. Had the F.C.C. delayed any further, it would have run the risk of inviting additional Justice Department petitions, which can be time-consuming for the Commission's staff, especially when the petitions are designated for a hearing. Moreover, Congress seemed likely to insist on the expeditious resolution of the cross-ownership issue. Against this backdrop, the F.C.C. heard oral arguments on cross-media ownership July 24-26, 1974. The vast majority of witnesses consisted of broadcasters, newspaper publishers, and their attorneys, who opposed divestiture.

Opponents of divestiture raised different objections to the F.C.C.'s proposed rule, but most pointed to the lack of hard evidence that cross-ownership has harmful effects. Ernest Jennes, counsel to WTOP-TV and other Post-Newsweek stations, noted that diversity of ownership does not necessarily imply diversity of viewpoints. Furthermore, Jennes argued that a commitment to good journalism "is as likely to be found in newspaper-affiliated stations as in stations owned by other businesses."[20] Arthur Hansen, general counsel for the American

---

[19] Broadcast License Renewal Act, _Congressional Record--House_ (May 1, 1974), p. H 3430.

[20] Bob Kuttner, "F.C.C. Decision Urged," _The Washington Post_ (July 25, 1974), p. 4.

Newspaper Publishers Association, criticized the F.C.C.'s proposed rule on the grounds that it singled out newspaper owners as a class, as if they were "felons" or "aliens." The A.N.P.A.'s communications counsel, Aloysius McCabe, supplemented Hansen's testimony by warning that divestiture could result in reduced local ownership of broadcasting stations and in increased ownership by distant banks and insurance companies.[21] In response to the Justice Department's emphasis on the need for competition, Lee Loevinger, special counsel to the National Association of Broadcasters, observed that the F.C.C. is obligated to consider the public interest, of which competition is but one part.[22]

Although outnumbered, some critics of cross-ownership did testify during the oral arguments. Barry Grossman, Deputy Chief of the Justice Department's Antitrust Division, urged divestiture as a means of promoting competition. Stephen Barnett, a law professor at the University of California at Berkeley, cited examples of journalistic "abuses" involving the mishandling or suppression of specific stories by a newspaper-owned television station or a newspaper which owns a television station. Afraid that a case-by-case approach to such abuses might be unconstitutional, Barnett recommended divestiture, at least in cities served by only one newspaper and only one television station.[23]

While the F.C.C. was holding hearings on a cross-media ownership rule, the Senate Commerce Committee's Subcommittee on Communications

---

[21] "Old Arguments, New Impetus for Action on Crossownership," Broadcasting (July 29, 1974), pp. 16-17.

[22] Lee Loevinger, Oral Argument Before the F.C.C. in Docket 18110 (July 25, 1974), p. 264.

[23] Stephen Barnett, Oral Argument Before the F.C.C. in Docket 18110, pp. 296-316.

was holding hearings on license renewal legislation. On October 8, 1974, the Senate passed a license renewal bill increasing license terms from three to five years and granting incumbent broadcast licensees a "presumption" in favor of renewal if 1) they have followed F.C.C. community ascertainment procedures; 2) they have been "substantially" responsive to local needs; and 3) their operation has not been characterized by serious deficiencies.[24] Like the House bill, the Senate bill instructed the F.C.C. to complete its rule-making on cross-media ownership in the near future. In contrast to the House bill, the Senate bill did not prohibit the F.C.C. from considering cross-media ownership in license renewal proceedings. In fact, the committee report accompanying the bill provided that media concentration could be considered at license renewal time in unique cases" where the concentration is "compelling enough" to warrant attention.[25] Despite the fact that both the House and the Senate passed a license renewal bill, license renewal legislation was not enacted in 1974. A conference committee never met to iron out differences between the House and Senate versions of the license renewal bill, because Congressman Harley Staggers (D.--W.Va.), Chairman of the House Committee on Foreign and Interstate Commerce, refused to appoint House conferees. Staggers, who thought broadcasters had promised not to lobby for a five-year license term, was miffed when it

---

[24] "The Dream of Renewal Relief Gets Closer to Reality," Broadcasting (October 14, 1974), pp. 19-22.

[25] This was apparently a concession to Senator Phillip Hart, Chairman of the Commerce Committee's Antitrust Subcommittee, who had threatened to have the bill referred to his subcommittee if it flatly prohibited the consideration of cross-media ownership during license renewal proceedings. See "Renewal Relief: A Sudden Turn for the Worse," Broadcasting (August 26, 1974), pp. 16-17.

appeared that broadcasters had done precisely that.[26] Thus, one of the reasons for the F.C.C.'s decision to adopt a rule on cross-media ownership--namely, the expectation that Congress would require speedy action--eventually proved incorrect.

On January 28, 1975, the F.C.C. announced its decision on cross-media ownership. First, the F.C.C. ordered the divestiture within five years of newspaper-television combinations in seven of eight cities where the only daily newspaper owns the only television station placing a city-grade signal[27] over the city: Anniston, Alabama, Albany, Georgia, Mason City, Iowa, Meridian, Mississippi, Watertown, New York, Texarkana, Texas, and Bluefield, West Virginia.[28] Second, the F.C.C. ordered the divestiture within five years of newspaper-radio combinations in nine of ten cities where the only daily newspaper owns the only radio station placing a city-grade signal over the city in the daytime: Hope, Arkansas, Effingham, Illinois, Macomb, Illinois, Arkansas City, Kansas, Owosso, Michigan, Norfolk, Nebraska, Findlay, Ohio, DuBois, Pennsylvania, and Janesville, Wisconsin.[29] Third the F.C.C. allowed all other newspaper-

---

[26]"Renewal Relief Dies on Hill: What Chance of Reincarnation?" *Broadcasting* (December 16, 1974), pp. 19-20.

[27]The definition of a "city-grade signal" differs for television stations assigned to different channels. Television stations assigned to channels 2-6 place a city-grade signal over a city if their signal has a field strength of 74 dBu's (decibels above one microvolt per meter) in the city.

[28]The F.C.C. exempted the newspaper-television combination in Hickory, North Carolina, from its divestiture order on the grounds that the Hickory television station (a UHF independent) would be very difficult to sell.

[29]The F.C.C. exempted the newspaper-radio combination in Brookfield, Missouri, from its divestiture order in view of unusual circumstances there.

radio combinations in the same city to remain intact. Fourth, the F.C.C. banned all future acquisitions of newspaper-broadcasting combinations in the same city, as well as the transfer of such combinations from one owner to another. Finally, the F.C.C. said it would consider petitions for a waiver of its cross-media ownership rule in cases where 1) a broadcasting station or newspaper could not be sold for its full worth; 2) divestiture of one news medium would cause the collapse of the other news medium; or 3) the city is in fact served by other radio and television stations which cover the city's affairs.[30]

The F.C.C. reached its decision by a vote of 5-2, with Commissioners Benjamin Hooks and Glen Robinson dissenting. Only Robinson supported across-the-board divestiture. As a minimum, he argued, the F.C.C. should require divestiture in cities where a newspaper and a broadcasting station owned by the newspaper control 30% or more of their respective local circulations. In a statement accompanying its decision, the F.C.C. said it had decided that across-the-board divestiture would be unduly disruptive. On the other hand, the F.C.C. said, "It is unrealistic to expect true diversity from a commonly owned station-newspaper combination. The divergency of their viewpoints cannot be expected to be the same as if they were antagonistically run."[31] In

---

[30] The Federal Communications Commission, *Second Report and Order in Docket 18110* (January 28, 1975). For accounts of the F.C.C. decision, see "Paper-Broadcast New Combines Banned by the F.C.C.," *The Wall Street Journal* (January 29, 1975), p. 6; "F.C.C. At Last Defines Policy on Broadcast and Newspaper Crossownership," *Broadcasting* (February 3, 1975), pp. 23-24; "F.C.C. Bars Cross-Ownership, Breaks Up Media in 16 Cities," *Editor and Publisher* (February 1, 1975), pp. 9-26.

[31] The Federal Communications Commission, *Second Report and Order in Docket 18110*, p. 38.

ordering the abolition of newspaper-television and newspaper-radio monopolies, the F.C.C. adopted an approach suggested by Barnett, among others. However, the F.C.C.'s definition of a newspaper-broadcasting monopoly was different from others the F.C.C. might have chosen. Had the F.C.C. defined newspaper-television monopolies as cities where the only daily newspaper owns the only television station with a studio in the city, it would have required the divestiture of newspaper-television combinations in 14, rather than seven, cities.

Why did the F.C.C. act as it did? As Allison has suggested, explanations of policy decisions depend on the conceptual frameworks which underlie them: "Conceptual models not only fix the mesh of the nets that the analyst drags through the material in order to explain a particular action; they also direct him to cast his nets in select ponds, at certain depths, in order to catch the fish he is after."[32] A useful way to catch different fish is to employ more than one net.

Bounded Rationality Model

One framework which might be used to explain the F.C.C.'s decision on cross-media ownership is the bounded rationality model developed by March and Simon.[33] Because of limitations on the amount of available information and capacities to process information, decision-makers seldom choose the "best" policy alternative. However, decision-makers can and do "satisfice." As March and Simon have put it, "Most human decision-making, whether individual or organizational, is concerned with the

---

[32] Graham Allison, *Essence of Decision: Explaining the Cuban Missile Crisis* (Boston: Little, Brown & Company, 1971), p. 4.

[33] This model is in fact the basis of Allison's Organizational Process Model.

discovery and selection of satisfactory alternatives; only in exceptional cases is it concerned with the discovery and selection of optimal alternatives."[34]

In considering the cross-media ownership issue, the F.C.C. received conflicting evidence from social scientists about the actual effects of cross-ownership. Scholars using different methods to study the effects of cross-ownership on newspaper and television advertising rates reached different conclusions. Scholars using different methods to study the effects of cross-media ownership on the news outputs of jointly owned media also reached different conclusions. Case studies indicated that some broadcasting stations owned by newspapers were guilty of journalistic "abuses," but it was not clear that such stations were less responsible than stations not owned by newspapers. On the basis of an extensive review of the literature on the effects of cross-media ownership, the Rand Corporation concluded: "Most questions about the effects of media ownership concentration on media performance must be answered with the well-known Scotch verdict: 'Not proved.'"[35]

By postponing a decision, the F.C.C. might have been able to evaluate additional evidence on the effects of cross-media ownership. However, the costs of postponement were high, since the Justice Department threatened to file additional petitions to deny the licenses of newspaper-owned broadcasting stations until the F.C.C. dealt with cross-

---

[34] James March and Herbert Simon, *Organizations* (New York: John Wiley & Sons, Inc., 1958), pp. 140-141.

[35] Walter Baer, Henry Geller, Joseph Grundfest, and Karen Possner, "Concentration of Mass Media Ownership: Assessing the State of Current Knowledge," *Rand Corporation Report* (Santa Monica, California: September, 1974), p. ix.

ownership through rule-making. Furthermore, both Congress and the courts were growing impatient with the F.C.C.'s failure to resolve the cross-ownership matter through rule-making.[36] Pressured to act prematurely, the F.C.C.'s search for a satisfactory alternative was constrained by the amount of information available at the time. As Downs has noted, "Search is greatly affected by the time pressure associated with a given decision. The cost of delay--that is, procuring additional information--rises sharply with pressure to act quickly. Under such pressure, a rational decisionmaker will decide on the basis of less knowledge than he would if time pressure were lower."[37] Although delay might have yielded better estimates of the effects of cross-media ownership, it could not have yielded much information about the probable effects of divestiture on the communications market structure. In the final analysis, the effects of divestiture were very difficult to predict. Perhaps a divestiture order would have a depressing effect on the price of broadcasting stations owned by newspapers. Perhaps a divestiture order would result in the sale of broadcasting stations owned by local newspapers to distant banks and insurance companies. Perhaps a divestiture order would result in the collapse of still another

---

[36] Legislation passed by both the House and the Senate--though not enacted--stressed the need for prompt F.C.C. resolution of the cross-ownership controversy. The D.C. Court of Appeals, which upheld the F.C.C.'s right to renew the licenses of newspaper-owned broadcasting stations pending resolution of the cross-ownership matter, nevertheless encouraged the F.C.C. to "act expeditiously in this rulemaking" and reserved the right to overturn the Commission's deferral of cross-ownership considerations in license renewal cases if the F.C.C. continued to delay. See Columbus Broadcasting Coalition vs. F.C.C., 505 F. 2d 325 (1974).

[37] Anthony Downs, Inside Bureaucracy (Boston: Little, Brown & Company, 1967), p. 183.

newspaper. Whether these were realistic fears could not be known.

With limited information available, the F.C.C. resorted to satisficing. The F.C.C. rejected the option of across-the-board divestiture, apparently agreeing with Theodore Pierson, counsel for Lee Enterprises, who had termed such a step "radical surgery" for an "ailment" that had not been proven to exist.[38] The F.C.C. also rejected the option of doing nothing, because it was conceivable, if not probable, that cross-ownership interfered with diversity in the flow of news and opinion.

In choosing to prohibit future cross-media ownership combinations, the F.C.C. was able to prevent the spread of cross-ownership without tinkering with the existing market structure--an exercise fraught with uncertainty. In outlawing certain newspaper-television and newspaper-radio monopolies, the F.C.C. was able to focus on cities where effects of cross-ownership, if uniform across cities, would be most serious, due to the dearth of competing media. In providing for waivers, the F.C.C. was able to retain its flexibility for situations where divestiture could have a particularly disruptive effect. In short, the bounded rationality model suggests that the F.C.C. chose a satisfactory policy option, given the limited amount of information at its disposal.

Pluralist Politics Model

A second framework which might be used to explain the F.C.C.'s decision on cross-ownership is a pluralist politics model. According to this model, resources of influence are highly dispersed, and public

---

[38] "Old Arguments, New Impetus for Action on Crossownership," op. cit., p. 17.

policy emerges from the interaction of various political elites and interest groups.[39] In Lindblom's words, policy-making proceeds through a process of "partisan mutual adjustment."[40] According to this perspective, regulatory policy is not centrally coordinated by the body which has formal responsibility for the allocation of values in a given policy area. Rather, that body, which has its own partisans, is the focal point of intense political pressures by other partisans. Thus, public policy is the result of interaction among various decision-makers, including appointed officials, elected officials, and interest group leaders. As such, public policy is a patchwork of concessions, serving different purposes and satisfying different partisans.

Formal responsibility for broadcast regulation policy is in the hands of the F.C.C. Technically, the F.C.C. is free to adopt rules or guidelines in accordance with the criteria of "the public interest, convenience and necessity." But the F.C.C. must in fact tread softly. In its 38th Annual Report, the Commission describes itself as "an independent Government agency responsible directly to Congress."[41] Put less euphemistically, the F.C.C. surrenders its independence when it dares to defy the Congress. The F.C.C. was created by Congress in 1934 with

---

[39] For an application of the pluralist model which stresses the role of political elites, see Charles Lindblom, The Policy-Making Process (Englewood Cliffs, New Jersey: Prentice-Hall, Inc., 1968); for an application of the pluralist model which stresses the role of interest groups, see David Truman, The Governmental Process (New York: Alfred Knopf, 1962).

[40] Charles Lindblom, The Intelligence of Democracy (New York: The Free Press, 1965).

[41] Federal Communications Commission, 38th Annual Report (Washington, D.C.: 1972), p. xi.

the passage of the Communications Act. F.C.C. decisions are authoritative only because the F.C.C. has a mandate from Congress. Presidential nominees for F.C.C. commissioner must be approved by the Senate. The F.C.C.'s appropriations requests must be approved by both the House and the Senate. And the F.C.C. is regularly scrutinized by several House and Senate subcommittees and committees. Consequently, the F.C.C. must be wary of incurring congressional wrath.

Nor is Congress the only institution which the F.C.C. must take into account. The courts have demonstrated a willingness to challenge specific F.C.C. decisions on license renewals as well as the guidelines which undergird those decisions--for example, the guideline that "substantial" service should be sufficient to guarantee renewal of a license, which was later overturned by the courts. The F.C.C. must also reckon with the Antitrust Division of the Justice Department, which has the capacity to bog the F.C.C. down with expensive and time-consuming lawsuits. Similarly, the F.C.C. must consider the viewpoints of various citizens' groups, which can add to the Commission's backlog of license renewal cases by filing competing applications or petitions to deny licenses and which can also challenge F.C.C. rules in court. Finally, the F.C.C. must listen to broadcasters themselves. The Commission was first established at the request of the broadcasting industry, which quickly recognized the need for government regulation of the air waves. Because many F.C.C. employees have worked closely with the broadcasting industry, they tend to be sympathetic to appeals from broadcasters. Moreover, the broadcasters are popular on Capitol Hill, and Congress generally expects the F.C.C. to treat the broadcasting industry well. Thus, the F.C.C. is beleaguered on all sides and is severely circumscribed in its behavior.

Independent in name only, the F.C.C. could not ignore the recommendations and viewpoints of key groups. Out of deference to Congress, the F.C.C. avoided dealing with cross-ownership through the license renewal process--an approach which the House was on record as opposing. The F.C.C. also rejected the suggestion that it draw up "a laundry list of no-no's" for broadcasting stations owned by a local newspaper--an approach which the courts might construe as unconstitutional interference in the internal affairs of broadcasters.[42] To please the Justice Department and citizens' groups opposed to cross-ownership, the F.C.C. outlawed cross-ownership in 16 cities and banned the formation of new newspaper-broadcasting combinations. To satisfy the broadcasting industry and its supporters on Capitol Hill, the F.C.C. protected the overwhelming majority of broadcasting stations owned by newspapers and left open the possibility of waivers for the small number of corporations required to divest. Thus, the pluralist politics model suggests that the F.C.C. responded to intense political pressures by adopting a "grab-bag" rule including concessions to each interested group.

Symbolic Politics Model

A third framework which might be used to explain the F.C.C.'s decision on cross-ownership is the symbolic politics model developed by

---

[42] The laundry list suggestion was advanced by Frank Fletcher, counsel for WBEN, Inc., Buffalo, New York. See "Old Arguments, New Impetus for Action on Crossownership," op. cit., pp. 16-17.

Edelman. According to this model, regulatory policy typically involves tangible benefits for the regulated industry, symbolic benefits for the public. Well-organized, well-informed, and armed with specific objectives, the regulated industry insists on tangible rewards. In contrast, the public, which has only a vague understanding of what is at stake, seeks little more than reassurance that the regulated industry is being dealt with properly. In granting the industry's requests while placating the public with symbols, the regulatory agency is not consciously trying to deceive the public. Rather, the regulatory agency has absorbed the values of the regulated industry to such an extent that it cannot distinguish between the industry's interest and the public interest. In Edelman's words, "Administrative decision-makers on the regulatory commissions function in a setting in which they become in effect part of the management of the industry they are to regulate."[43]

Like other regulatory agencies, the F.C.C. has great sympathy for the industry it is supposed to regulate. Some F.C.C. employees are ex-broadcasters who remember all too well the financial and legal traumas which broadcasters experience.[44] Others expect to leave the F.C.C. eventually to accept jobs representing the broadcasting industry--a prospect which encourages friendly dealing with broadcasters.[45] Due to

---

[43] Murray Edelman, The Symbolic Uses of Politics (Urbana: University of Illinois Press, 1964), p. 66.

[44] The importance of this factor should not be exaggerated. Only one of the current commissioners--James Quello--is a former broadcaster. Nevertheless, a number of middle-level F.C.C. officials have had experience in the broadcasting industry.

[45] Two of the most articulate spokesmen for the broadcasting industry during the F.C.C.'s oral arguments concerning crossownership were ex-commissioners Lee Loevinger (representing the National Association of Broadcasters) and Rosel Hyde (representing KSL-TV, Salt Lake City, Utah, which is owned by the Deseret News).

the complexity of the broadcasting business, members of the F.C.C. need considerable information and advice, which broadcasters are in a unique position to provide. This results in frequent contacts between representatives of the F.C.C. and the broadcasting industry. Such contacts are facilitated by the fact that the National Association of Broadcasters' headquarters are located just a few blocks away from the F.C.C. Not surprisingly, then, the F.C.C. and the broadcasting industry develop close ties and understandings.

The F.C.C.'s own sympathy for the broadcasting industry is reinforced by the Commission's awareness of congressional support for the broadcasting industry. As a creature of Congress, the F.C.C. must be mindful of congressional sentiment in favor of broadcasters' demands. Should the F.C.C. anger the broadcasting industry, repercussions are soon felt on Capitol Hill, and the F.C.C. in turn must expect to bear the full brunt of congressional fury. There are several reasons for congressional sensitivity to demands by broadcasters. First, members of Congress depend on broadcasters for free air time, which assists them in getting re-elected. According to one estimate, 70% of U.S. Senators and 60% of members of the House regularly use free air time provided by broadcasting stations in their home state or district.[46] Second, the broadcasting industry makes noteworthy contributions to congressional campaigns. In 1974, for example, the National Association of Broadcasters spent $42,000 in support of 79 candidates for the House and Senate,

---

[46] Robert MacNeil, The People Machine: The Influence of Television on American Politics (New York: Harper & Row, 1968), p. 246.

mostly incumbents.[47] Third, it has been estimated that many members of Congress represent broadcasters through their law firms.[48] For such members of Congress, a vote against the broadcasting industry could result in the loss of a wealthy client. Finally, some members of Congress have a special incentive to fight for the prosperity of the broadcasting industry. In 1975, 21 members of Congress had direct or family interests in commercial radio or television stations.[49] As an agency responsible to the Congress, the F.C.C. must take into account congressional support for the broadcasting industry. In practice, the F.C.C. generally needs to fret only about the wishes of the broadcasting industry. If the F.C.C. satisfies the broadcasting industry, it is likely to satisfy Congress as well.

Stripped of rhetoric which reassured the public that the F.C.C. was troubled by the concentration of mass media ownership, the F.C.C.'s decision on cross-ownership was largely a victory for the broadcasting industry. The F.C.C. did pay lip-service to the concerns of those opposed to cross-ownership by agreeing that it was "unrealistic" to expect "true diversity" from jointly owned media. But the F.C.C.'s decision belied such rhetoric. The F.C.C. did prohibit cross-ownership in the same city in the future, but this did not particularly bother the National Association of Broadcasters, which represents incumbent licensees,

---

[47]"How N.A.B. Hands Out Political Tithes," <u>Broadcasting</u> (November 4, 1974), pp. 25-26.

[48]Bryce Rucker, <u>The First Freedom</u> (Carbondale, Illinois: Southern Illinois University Press, 1968), p. 224.

[49]"The Radio and Television Holdings on the Hill," <u>Broadcasting</u> (September 1, 1975), pp. 25-27.

not potential licensees. In fact, N.A.B. President Vincent Wasilewski had told Congress he wanted protection for incumbent licensees but was not opposed to the F.C.C.'s considering cross-media ownership as a relevant factor in initial license applications.[50] As for the F.C.C.'s restrictions on cross-ownership in 16 cities, the waiver provisions took the sting out of this "crackdown." By accumulating extensive written comments, hearing oral arguments, and taking years to adopt a rule on cross-ownership, the F.C.C. gave the appearance of agonizing over its decision. This served to keep the public from feeling threatened. In the end, however, the F.C.C.'s decision was largely favorable to the broadcasting industry. According to the symbolic politics model, this was a foregone conclusion.

Implications of Three Models

There are elements of truth in all three models. As the bounded rationality model suggests, the F.C.C. did not have enough information to know whether cross-media ownership poses a threat to the public interest. As the pluralist politics model suggests, the F.C.C. is not independent enough to consider the public interest alone. As the symbolic politics model suggests, the F.C.C. can neglect the public interest so long as the public is content with symbolic, rather than tangible, benefits. Together, the models contribute to an understanding of the F.C.C.'s decision. However, the three models are not equally plausible.

---

[50]Vincent Wasilewski, Testimony Before the Subcommittee on Communications and Power of the House Committee on Interstate and Foreign Commerce, <u>Broadcast License Renewal Hearings</u> (March 15, 1973), p. 162.

In portraying the F.C.C. as an organization of truth-seekers, the bounded rationality model ignores the political vulnerability of the F.C.C. Independent in name only, the F.C.C. must in fact serve several masters. Indeed, the F.C.C. acted on the basis of inadequate information because it was pressured to do so. Since the effects of cross-ownership were almost as moot in 1975 as they were in 1970, the bounded rationality model fails to explain why the F.C.C. reversed itself so dramatically between 1970 and 1975, in abandoning the proposed rule of across-the-board divestiture.

If the bounded rationality model is not entirely satisfactory, neither is the symbolic politics model. In focusing on the cozy relationship between the F.C.C. and the broadcasting industry, the symbolic politics model underemphasizes the political clout of the Justice Department and citizens' groups opposed to cross-ownership. As a result, the symbolic politics model does not adequately explain the concessions which the F.C.C. made to opponents of cross-ownership. Although the F.C.C. decision was largely a victory for broadcasters, it was not a clear-cut victory. In particular, broadcasters would have preferred that the F.C.C. leave all existing newspaper-television and newspaper-radio combinations intact.

In short, the bounded rationality model ignores the political milieu of the F.C.C., while the symbolic politics model dwells excessively on one group in the F.C.C.'s environment. In contrast, the pluralist politics model takes into account both the F.C.C.'s vulnerability to political pressures and the influence of groups with divergent aims (the National Association of Broadcasters and the National Citizens Committee for Broadcasting, for example). Of all three models, the pluralist politics model does the best job of capturing the realities of the F.C.C.'s decision-making process.[51]

If the pluralist politics model does in fact come closest to the truth, this has implications for the circumstances under which the F.C.C. might modify its decision on cross-media ownership. According to the bounded rationality model, the F.C.C. is open-minded. Should social scientists uncover new evidence on the effects of cross-ownership, the F.C.C. might be persuaded to revise its decision. However, the pluralist politics model suggests that the F.C.C. is unlikely to be convinced by new information alone. Unless additional pressure is brought to bear on behalf of the public interest, the F.C.C. will be guided primarily by the interests of the broadcasting industry.

There are at least two ways in which additional pressure could be brought to bear on behalf of the public interest. One would be for the courts, which are more effectively insulated from political pressures than the F.C.C., to remand the cross-ownership issue to the F.C.C. with instructions to give more weight to the public interest. Another way would be for the scope of conflict to be expanded--i.e., for media consumers to become more aware of the cross-ownership issue. Public

---

[51]To argue that the pluralist politics model serves useful descriptive purposes is not to endorse the model as an ideal. For a normative critique of the pluralist politics model, see Christian Bay, "Politics and Pseudopolitics," _American Political Science Review_ (March 1965), pp. 39-51.

[52]Paradoxically, it is the large group, not the small group, which encounters special organizational problems. The member of a large group has weaker incentives to participate in a collective effort than the member of a small group. This is because the large group's success is less contingent on one individual's participation and because the large group's benefits (if success is achieved) are more likely to be enjoyed by participants and non-participants alike. See Mancur Olson, _The Logic of Collective Action_ (New York: Schocken Books, 1968).

awareness does not always lead to effective political action.[52] However, broad public awareness of an issue increases the incentives of political leaders to take policy initiatives which further a resolution of the issue consistent with the public interest.[53]

Mass Media Coverage of the F.C.C.'s Decision

As Schattschneider has noted, "The outcome of every conflict is determined by the extent to which the audience becomes involved in it."[54] The more visible a conflict is, the more likely it is that members of the audience will be drawn into the fray. Thus, an expansion of the scope of conflict depends on publicity as surely as a narrowing of the scope of conflict depends on secrecy. If citizens do not know what cross-media ownership is, in which cities it exists, or what the F.C.C. has done about it, the scope of conflict cannot be expanded. Unless citizens know about the F.C.C.'s decision on cross-ownership, they cannot hold political leaders accountable for the decision. The public's knowledge of the F.C.C.'s decision was determined in large measure by the mass media's coverage of the decision at the time it was made.

On the evening of January 28, 1975, the day the F.C.C. announced its decision, the CBS Evening News with Walter Cronkite ran one sentence on the decision: "The Federal Communications Commission ruled today that newspaper owners may not purchase radio or television stations serving the same market as the newspapers and the F.C.C. ordered such

---

[53] See David Price, <u>Who Makes the Law?</u> (Cambridge, Massachusetts: Schenkman Publishing Company, 1972), pp. 59-60.

[54] E. E. Schattschneider, <u>The Semi-Sovereign People</u> (New York: Holt, Rinehart and Winston, 1960), p. 2.

existing combinations in 16 cities broken up by 1980."[55] CBS made no reference to the fact that the overwhleming majority of newspaper-broadcasting combinations in the same city were permitted to remain intact. On the same evening, neither the ABC Evening News nor the NBC Evening News ran a story on the F.C.C.'s decision. However, NBC did find the time to cover a story about efforts by Mickey Mouse, Donald Duck, Snow White and the Seven Dwarfs, and other Walt Disney characters at Disney World to organize their own union.[56]

On January 29, 1975, the day after the F.C.C.'s decision, the New York Times, which reaches many opinion leaders, ran a 10 paragraph story on the decision but consigned it to page 54.[57] The New York Daily News, which has the highest circulation of any newspaper in the U.S., made no mention of the F.C.C.'s decision on January 29. Table 1 contains the results of an examination of January 29 editions of 18 newspapers which own a local television station. As Table 1 indicates, three (17%) ran a story on the F.C.C.'s decision and mentioned their own broadcasting ties, seven (39%) ran a story without mentioning their own broadcasting ties, and eight (44%) did not cover the F.C.C.'s decision at all.[58] In general newspapers which ran a story portrayed the F.C.C.'s

---

[55]The author is grateful to James Pilkington, Administrator of the Vanderbilt University Television News Archive, who arranged for the author to see and transcribe this portion of the CBS Evening News Videotape for January 28, 1975.

[56]Vanderbilt Television News Archive, Television News Index and Abstracts, January 1975, p. 192.

[57]"Press Faces Curb on Broadcasting," The New York Times (January 29, 1975), p. 54.

[58]Some newspapers which did not cover the F.C.C.'s decision on January 29 may have done so at a later date.

Table 1. Next-Day Coverage of F.C.C. Decision on Cross-Media Ownership by 18 Newspapers Which Own a Local T.V. Station

Story Covered, Paper's Own Ties to T.V. Station Noted	Story Covered, Paper's Own Ties to T.V. Station Not Noted	Story Not Covered
Minneapolis Star (Minnesota)	San Francisco Chronicle (California)	Atlanta Constitution (Georgia)
Minneapolis Tribune (Minnesota)	Washington Post (District of Columbia)	Chicago Tribune (Illinois)
Milwaukee Journal (Wisconsin)	Des Moines Register (Iowa)	Louisville Courier-Journal (Kentucky)
	Detroit News (Michigan)	Baltimore Sun (Maryland)
	St. Louis Post-Dispatch (Missouri)	Boston Globe (Massachusetts)
	Greensboro Daily News (North Carolina)	New York Daily News (New York)
	Norfolk Virginian-Pilot (Virginia)	Columbus Dispatch (Ohio)
		Norfolk Ledger-Star (Virginia)

Note: The 18 newspapers examined were all those which own a local television station and which were available at the University of North Carolina's Wilson Library or Journalism School Library.

decision as tough and restrictive in their headlines. The headline in the Detroit News read: "F.C.C. Rule Limits Newspaper Ownership of T.V. and Radio."[59] The headline in the Washington Post read: "Bars Set on Media Owners."[60] Of the 18 newspapers examined, only one--the Minneapolis Star--ran a story with a headline emphasizing that the decision mainly preserved the status quo. The headline read: "Big Newspaper-Broadcast Ties Allowed to Continue."[61]

Why did the mass media give the F.C.C.'s decision such scant coverage? Newspapers which own a local television station may have downplayed or ignored the decision because they recognized that an expansion of the scope of conflict would not be in their best interest. Or perhaps such newspapers were squeamish about covering a story so "close to home" that it would be difficult to handle objectively. As for the networks, they may have been reluctant to deal with a decision as complex as the F.C.C.'s rule on cross-ownership. A more fundamental explanation is that journalists have serious reservations about government regulation of the mass media, which leads them to question the legitimacy of communications policy issues as matters of public debate.

Whether intentional or not, the mass media's treatment of the F.C.C.'s decision narrowed the scope of conflict. Many citizens in cities where cross-ownership exists could not find a word about the

---

[59] George Kentera, "F.C.C. Rule Limits Newspaper Ownership of T.V. and Radio," *The Detroit News* (January 29, 1975), p. 7.

[60] Carole Shifrin, "Bars Set on Media Owners," *The Washington Post* (January 29, 1975), p. D9.

[61] "Big Newspaper-Broadcast Ties Allowed to Continue," *The Minneapolis Star* (January 29, 1975), p. D9.

decision in their daily newspaper. Citizens who heard Walter Cronkite's fleeting reference to the decision or who read about the decision in their newspaper were probably reassured by a decision which was portrayed as a "crackdown" on the concentration of mass media ownership. Even the attentive public had a difficult time knowing about the F.C.C.'s decision, much less knowing whether that decision was in the public interest.

Aftermath of the F.C.C. Decision

Although the F.C.C.'s decision did not provoke a groundswell of public opposition, one citizens' group did move quickly to challenge the decision. Within an hour of the F.C.C.'s announcement, the National Citizens Committee for Broadcasting filed a notice of appeal with the U.S. Court of Appeals in Washington, D.C., contending that the F.C.C. had not gone far enough in restricting cross-ownership.[62] The newspaper industry--not completely satisfied with the rule--was not far behind. The American Newspaper Publishers Association petitioned the F.C.C. for partial reconsideration and clarification of the rule.[63] A number of parties affected by the divestiture order also petitioned the F.C.C. for reconsideration or sought a waiver of the order in their particular case.[64]

---

[62] "F.C.C. At Last Defines Policy on Broadcast and Newspaper Ownership," Broadcasting (February 3, 1975), pp. 23-24.

[63] "A.N.P.A. Takes a Stand," Broadcasting (March 17, 1975), p. 12.

[64] "F.C.C. Will Meet Resistance on Divestitures," Broadcasting (February 3, 1975), pp. 24-25.

In June 1975, the F.C.C. denied the petition for reconsideration submitted by the American Newspaper Publishers Association. In particular, the Commission held that its prospective ban on cross-ownership did not improperly single out newspaper owners and that its definition of newspaper-broadcasting monopolies was not overly technical or arbitrary. The F.C.C. also responded to objections raised by James Skewes and Southern Television Corporation, the Brockway Company, Gray Communications System, Inc., and Radio Stamford, Inc.[65]

In January 1976, the F.C.C. dealt with a request for a waiver of its rule prohibiting the transfer of a newspaper-broadcasting combination in the same city to a new owner. Joseph Allbritton, who had bought a controlling interest in the Washington Star, wanted to purchase the parent company's broadcasting companies as well, since the Star itself had lost $15 million over a four-year period. However, the parent company's broadcasting stations included WMAL-AM-FM-TV in Washington, D.C., which, according to the F.C.C.'s cross-ownership rule, could not be transferred to Allbritton. In his petition for a waiver, Allbritton argued that the survival of the Star depended on its being supported--at least temporarily--by revenue from the parent company's lucrative broadcasting stations in Washington, D.C.[66] Fearful that immediate divestiture might lead to the collapse of the Star, the F.C.C.

---

[65] The Federal Communications Commission, Memorandum Opinion and Order re Second Report and Order in Docket 18110 (June 5, 1975).

[66] "F.C.C.'s Dilemma: Should It Catch a Falling 'Star'?" Broadcasting (July 7, 1975), pp. 26-27; "New Deal for Allbritton on WMAL, 'Star' et al.," Broadcasting (August 11, 1975), pp. 22-23; and "Star Families and Allbritton Make New Deal," Broadcasting (September 8, 1975), pp. 30-32.

gave Allbritton three years to sell the Star's Washington broadcasting stations.[67]

In the meantime, lawyers for the F.C.C. and the National Citizens Committee for Broadcasting prepared to argue the merits of the F.C.C.'s cross-ownership rule before the D.C. Court of Appeals. As Commissioner Charlotte Reid had predicted when the F.C.C. handed down its cross-ownership rule, "I am certain that this will not be the last that we hear of this issue, either before the commission or in the courts."[68]

---

[67] The Federal Communications Commission, Memorandum Opinion and Order in Docket 20559 (January 27, 1976).

[68] Charlotte Reid, Statement Accompanying the Federal Communications Commission's Second Report and Order in Docket 18110.

III

METHODOLOGY

By comparing the news outputs of jointly owned and separately owned newspapers and television stations in a random sample of cities where cross-ownership exists, we might reach some conclusions about the effects of cross-media ownership. However, unless the sample were rather large, we would run the risk of ignoring important effects of cross-ownership in cities not included in the sample. By comparing the news outputs of jointly owned newspapers and television stations in all cities where cross-ownership exists, we could generalize about the effects of cross-ownership on news content.[1] However, such an approach would be costly and time-consuming. Moreover, it would not illuminate the processes by which cross-ownership influences news content.

In contrast, a three-stage research strategy permits the possibility of achieving statistically meaningful findings about both outputs and processes without undertaking a costly content analysis of news outputs in a large number of cities. The three stages consist of: 1--an analysis of the effects of cross-ownership on intermedia relations (through the questionnaire method): 2--an investigation of the

---

[1] The news outputs of jointly owned newspapers and television stations in "monopoly" cities could be compared with those of separately owned newspapers and television stations in similar cities where no cross-ownership exists.

dynamics of intermedia relations (through focused interviews); and 3--a study of the effects of intermedia relations on news outputs (through the technique of content analysis).

The distinctive feature of this approach is its focus on intervening variables. If cross-ownership has certain effects on the news outputs of jointly owned media, it is important to understand how these effects occur. If cross-ownership shapes news content through specific intervening variables, it is important to identify these variables and pinpoint the circumstances under which cross-ownership is associated with them.[2] Together, the three stages can yield generalizations about the effects of cross-ownership on both intermedia relations and news content.

Mailed Questionnaires

First of all, questionnaires were designed to determine whether any patterns of intermedia relations are more common among jointly owned media than among separately owned media. These questionnaires were sent to the managing editors of all daily newspapers and the news directors of all commercial television stations in all 67 cities where at least one newspaper owns a local television station. Each of the managing editors was asked about the size of his staff, whether any staff member has worked for a television station, whether any staff member monitors a local television newscast, whether the newspaper furnishes carbons of its stories to a television station, and which

---

[2] For policy purposes, it is important to know whether cross-ownership has greater effects in certain kinds of cities than in others.

television station most staff members prefer for state and local news reports. Each managing editor was also asked to estimate how often he interacts with television personnel, to rate the quality of television newscasts in the area, to express an opinion on whether newspaper and television reporters are members of one journalistic profession, and to comment on the role of the newspaper's owner in news decisions (for the text of the questionnaire sent to each managing editor, see Appendix C). Each television news director was asked comparable questions, as well as whether the television station broadcasts editorials (for the text of the questionnaire sent to each news director, see Appendix D).

To examine the effects of cross-ownership in the 14 cities with only one newspaper company and only one local television station, both of which are owned by the same company, a matched sample was drawn, consisting of 14 cities similar in several crucial respects but different in that they lacked cross-ownership.[3] The following criteria were used to match jointly owned and separately owned pairs in different cities: 1--there should be only one local newspaper company and only one local television station in both cities; 2--the cities should be in the same state or an adjacent state; 3--the cities should have populations as similar in size as possible; 4--the newspapers should have circulations as similar in size as possible; 5--the newspapers should be published

---

[3]If a "local" television station is defined as one which has a studio located in the city, then there are 14 cities served by only one newspaper and only one local television station, both of which are owned by the same company. However, if a local television station is defined as one which has a studio located in the city and which airs local newscasts, then there are 15 cities served by only one newspaper and only one local television station, both of which are owned by the same company.

at the same time of day; 6--the television stations should both be of the same frequency (i.e., both VHF or both UHF). As Table 2 indicates, the matched sample satisfied all of these criteria, although population sizes and newspaper circulation sizes could not be matched with precision. After the 14 matched cities were identified, questionnaires were sent to managing editors and news directors there.

The mailing of all questionnaires was delayed until after the F.C.C.'s cross-media ownership ruling of January 28, 1975, to avoid responses influenced by apprehension over an impending F.C.C. decision. To increase the response rate and the probability of obtaining candid responses, the confidentiality of individual questionnaire responses was guaranteed in a cover letter (for the text of the letter sent to each managing editor and news director, see Appendix E). Three weeks after the first mailing, a second mailing was sent to managing editors and news directors who had not returned their questionnaire. Of 349 managing editors and news directors contacted, 214 responded to the first or second mailing with a completed questionnaire, for a response rate of 61%. Some questionnaire responses were obtained from 95.1% (77/81) of the cities to which questionnaires were sent.[4]

The Effects of Cross-Media Ownership on Intermedia Relations

An analysis of the questionnaire data revealed that cross-ownership has two effects on intermedia relations which are statistically

---

[4] The four cities for which no questionnaire responses were obtained were Columbus, Mississippi, Las Vegas, Nevada, Texarkana, Texas, and Florence, Alabama.

Table 2. Characteristics of Newspaper-Television Monopolies and Matched Pairs

	Newspaper(s), Television Station	State	Population Size	Newspaper's Circulation Size	Newspaper's Publication Time	Television Station's Frequency
1.	Anniston Star* WHMA-TV*	Alabama	31,533	27,794	Evening	UHF
	Florence Times WOWL-TV	Alabama	34,031	28,558	Evening	UHF
2.	Albany Herald* WALB-TV*	Georgia	72,623	35,217	Evening	VHF
	Jackson Sun WBBJ-TV	Tennessee	39,996	31,675	Evening	VHF
3.	Rock Island Argus* WHBF-TV*	Illinois	50,166	26,381	Evening	VHF
	Moline Dispatch WQAD-TV	Illinois	46,237	37,107	Evening	VHF
4.	Mason City Globe-Gazette* KGLO-TV*	Iowa	30,379	24,764	Evening	VHF
	Ottumwa Courier KTVO-TV	Iowa	29,610	19,176	Evening	VHF
5.	Columbus Commercial Dispatch* WCBI-TV*	Mississippi	25,795	11,103	Evening	VHF

Table 2. Continued

	Newspaper(s), Television Station	State	Population Size	Newspaper's Circulation Size	Newspaper's Publication Time	Television Station's Frequency
	Greenwood Commonwealth WABG-TV	Mississippi	22,400	7,459	Evening	VHF
6.	Meridian Star* WTOK-TV*	Mississippi	45,083	24,272	Evening	VHF
	Hattiesburg American WDAM-TV	Mississippi	38,277	20,961	Evening	VHF
7.	Hastings Tribune* KHAS-TV*	Nebraska	23,580	18,425	Evening	VHF
	North Platte Telegraph KNOP-TV	Nebraska	19,447	16,010	Evening	VHF
8.	Watertown Times* WWNY-TV*	New York	30,787	41,008	Evening	VHF
	Altoona Mirror WTAJ-TV	Pennsylvania	63,115	35,968	Evening	VHF
9.	Greensboro Daily News* Greensboro Record* WFMY-TV*	North Carolina	144,076	78,685 35,740	Morning Evening	VHF

Table 2. Continued

Newspaper(s), Television Station	State	Population Size	Newspaper's Circulation Size	Newspaper's Publication Time	Television Station's Frequency
Winston-Salem Journal Twin City Sentinel WXII-TV	North Carolina	132,913	79,282 46,623	Morning Evening	VHF
10. Hickory Record* WHKY-TV*	North Carolina	20,569	27,263	Evening	UHF
Fredericksburg Free Lance-Star WHFV-TV	Virginia	14,450	22,401	Evening	UHF
11. Akron Beacon-Journal* WAKR-TV*	Ohio	275,425	173,224	Evening	UHF
Canton Repository WJAN-TV	Ohio	110,053	70,416	Evening	UHF
12. Temple Telegram* KCEN-TV*	Texas	33,431	23,254	Morning	VHF
Harlingen Valley Star KGBT-TV	Texas	33,503	19,342	Morning	VHF
13. Texarkana Gazette* Texarkana News* KTAL-TV*	Texas	52,179	29,395	Morning	VHF

62

Table 2. Continued

Newspaper(s), Television Station	State	Population Size	Newspaper's Circulation Size	Newspaper's Publication Time	Television Station's Frequency
Tyler Telegraph Tyler Courier-Times KLTV-TV	Texas	67,778	30,616	Morning	VHF
14. Bluefield Telegraph* WHIS-TV*	West Virginia	15,921	29,582	Morning	VHF
Harrisonburg News-Record WSVA-TV	Virginia	14,605	24,108	Morning	VHF

Key: * = Jointly owned media.

significant at an acceptable level ($p < .05$).

First, television stations owned by a local newspaper are more likely than comparable television stations (television stations in the same cities or in the matched cities which are not owned by a local newspaper) to receive carbon copies of newspaper stories on an exclusive basis (no other television station receives the newspaper's carbons). Moreover, the regression of carbon-sharing on cross-ownership is statistically significant at the .05 level, even after controlling for the number of television stations per city (see Table 3).

Second, television stations owned by a local newspaper are more likely than comparable television stations to have on their news staffs a reporter or editor who used to work for that newspaper. Since the mean staff size for newspaper-owned television stations is slightly higher than for other television stations, it might be argued that television stations owned by a newspaper are more likely to hire a newspaper reporter or editor simply because they have more staff openings available. However, the regression of cross-employment (from a newspaper to a television station) on cross-ownership is statistically significant at the .05 level, even after controlling for television staff size (see Table 4).

While there is some flow of employees from a television station to a newspaper, this is considerably less common, and cross-ownership has no statistically significant effect on this kind of cross-employment. Consequently, the cross-employment which needs to be examined is the flow of employees from a newspaper to a television station, rather

Table 3. Effects of Cross-Ownership on Carbon-Sharing, Controlling for the Number of T.V. Stations Per City[a]

Independent Variable	Standardized b[b]	F[c]
Number of T.V. stations/city	-.234	8.03[d]
Cross-media ownership	.160	3.74[e]

Note: Carbon-sharing is a dichotomous variable indicating whether or not a television station receives carbons from a newspaper in the same city on an exclusive basis.

[a] N = 140.

[b] A standardized b (or beta weight) measures the change in a dependent variable produced by a standardized change in an independent variable, with other independent variables held constant. A standardized b is obtained by multiplying an unstandardized b by the ratio of the standard deviation of the independent variable (not controlled) to the standard deviation of the dependent variable. See Hubert Blalock, Social Statistics (New York: McGraw-Hill Book Company, 1972), pp. 452-453.

[c] An F test for statistical significance proceeds by decomposing the portion of the total sum of squares that is unexplained by control variables in a regression equation into two parts: explained and unexplained. The F statistic is the ratio of the variance estimate of the explained part to the variance estimate of the unexplained part. See Blalock, op. cit., pp. 465-466.

[d] $p < .001$.

[e] $p < .05$.

Table 4. Effects of Cross-Ownership on Cross-Employment, Controlling for T.V. News Staff Size[a]

Independent Variable	Standardized b	F
T.V. news staff size	.183	3.56
Cross-media ownership	.172	3.12[b]

Note: Cross-employment is a dichotomous variable indicating whether or not at least one television news staff member has worked for a local newspaper which owns a local television station or for the only newspaper in town.

[a] N = 103.

[b] $p < .05$.

than vice versa. The questionnaire data also reveal that the newscasts of newspaper-owned television stations are more likely than the newscasts of comparable television stations to be monitored on an exclusive basis by a newspaper (no other station's newscasts are monitored by the newspaper). However, after controlling for television staff size, this relationship is not statistically significant at an acceptable level. In the interest of methodological rigor, it will not be asserted that cross-ownership has an effect on the monitoring of a television station's newscasts by a newspaper on an exclusive basis.

A Stratified Sample of 10 Cities

Thus, cross-media ownership has at least two effects on intermedia relations. As a result of cross-ownership, television stations owned by a newspaper are more likely to receive newspaper carbons on an exclusive basis. As a result of cross-ownership, television stations owned by a newspaper are more likely to hire a reporter or editor who has worked for that newspaper. While interesting, such effects are mere curiosities unless they in turn have some impact on the actual news outputs of newspapers and television stations.

To test the effects of the carbon-sharing (CS) and cross-employment (CE) variables, as defined above, we drew a stratified sample of 10 cities, in which some jointly owned newspaper-television pairs were characterized by neither CS nor CE, others by CS but not CE, others by CE but not CS, and still others by both CS and CE. As originally designed, the sample of 10 cities included at least three jointly owned newspaper-television pairs in each of the four cells. However, as a result of erroneous information supplied by news executives in their questionnaire responses, two of the three pairs thought to be characterized by both CS and CE actually belonged in a different cell.[5] While this produced a less symmetrical arrangement of jointly owned newspaper-television pairs than anticipated, it did not interfere with the ability to measure the separate effects of CS and CE or the direct effects of cross-ownership (those which could not be explained by CS or CE).

The cities in the sample, ranging in size from 45,288 to 7,867,760, were Fresno, California, Sacramento, California, Quincy, Illinois, Rock Island, Illinois, Portland, Maine, Dayton, Ohio, New York, New York, Rochester, New York, Dallas, Texas, and Norfolk, Virginia. Any sample drawn on the basis of questionnaire data must, of course, exclude from consideration cities for which no questionnaire data had been obtained. However, because the questionnaires concerned intermedia relations, it was often possible to establish that certain relationships did or did not exist between a newspaper and a television station, even if one of the two failed to respond. Indeed, several media were included in the sample despite the fact that they did not respond to the questionnaire.

Data-Gathering in 10 Cities

Once the sample of 10 cities was drawn, personally written letters were sent to the managing editor of each daily newspaper and the news director of each commercial television station in those

---

[5] The reliability of the questionnaire data was checked through personal interviews with news executives and reporters in each of the 10 cities.

cities. Each letter included a request for permission to interview the managing editor or news director and members of his staff, as well as a promise not to interfere with the normal flow of business. News directors were also asked for permission to make copies of television news scripts for a specified period.[6]

On the basis of an earlier pilot study in Greensboro, North Carolina, it was anticipated that newspapers and television news scripts for a one-week period would be sufficient for a content analysis if each television station aired at least one-half hour of state and local news Monday through Friday, since that would yield a minimum of 50 state and local television news stories (ten stories per day for five days) and an even greater number of state and local newspaper stories.[7] To err on the safe side, newspapers and news scripts were requested for a one-week period in the four cities where more than one television station aired one hour's worth (or more) of news in the early evening and for a two-week period in the remaining six cities where the television stations aired but one half-hour of news in the early evening. The early evening news scripts were requested, since these include more state and local stories than the late evening news scripts, which typically include several national and international stories.[8]

---

[6] Television stations are not required by the F.C.C. to make their news scripts available for public inspection or duplication.

[7] The pilot study, which included a content analysis of WFMY-TV's news scripts for seven days, revealed that WFMY airs approximately 10 state and local news stories per early evening newscast. Subsequent analyses in other cities indicated that most television stations air more than 10 state and local news stories per early evening newscast.

[8] In three cases where the early and late evening news scripts were not kept in separate files (KHQA-TV, WGEM-TV, and WROC-TV), both the early and late evening news scripts were used.

To hold constant one possible source of variation among cities, the data requested were for a time period when the relevant State Legislature was in session.[9]

By choice, data were not obtained for three of New York City's six commercial television stations, on the grounds that three television stations, along with the city's three newspapers, were sufficient for a comparison of jointly owned and separately owned New York media, provided that WPIX-TV, which is owned by the New York Daily News, remained in the sample.[10] Of necessity, a Dallas, Texas, television station, KDFW-TV, was excluded from the analysis, since the station's news director refused to make news scripts available for inspection.[11] A vice-president of WPIX-TV also refused to permit access to his station's scripts, but it was possible to obtain tape-recordings of the newscasts from another source.[12] Ultimately, arrangements were made to obtain data from 25 television stations and 19 daily newspapers (see Table 5).

The field work, which was conducted entirely by the principal investigator, involved spending approximately one week in each of the

---

[9] In Norfolk, Virginia, it was impossible to obtain newspapers for a time period when the State Legislature was in session. Instead, newspapers and news scripts were obtained for a time period shortly after the Legislature adjourned.

[10] The three excluded television stations were WOR, WCBS, and WNBC. WOR was eliminated because it did not air an evening newscast; WCBS and WNBC were eliminated because their news directors indicated a reluctance to cooperate.

[11] Since that time, KDFW's President and General Manager, John McCrory, has agreed to provide interested parties with audio recordings of the station's evening newscasts in return for a nominal fee.

[12] Tape-recordings of the WPIX newscasts were purchased from Radio TV Reports, 41 E. 42nd Street, New York, New York.

Table 5. News Media in the Sample

City	City Size	Newspaper	T.V. Station
Fresno, California	165,972	Bee*	KFSN KJEO KMJ*
Sacramento, California	254,413	Bee* Union	KCRA KOVR* KXTV
Quincy, Illinois	45,288	Herald-Whig*	KHQA WGEM*
Rock Island, Illinois	50,166	Argus*	WHBF*
Moline, Illinois	46,237	Dispatch	WQAD
Portland, Maine	65,116	Express* Press-Herald*	WCSH WGAN*
Dayton, Ohio	243,601	Daily News* Journal-Herald*	WHIO* WLWD
New York, New York	7,867,760	Daily News* Post Times	WABC WNEW WPIX*
Rochester, New York	296,233	Democrat & Chronicle* Times-Union*	WHEC* WOKR WROC
Dallas, Texas	844,401	Morning News* Times-Herald	KXAS WFAA*
Norfolk, Virginia	307,951	Ledger-Star* Virginian-Pilot*	WAVY WTAR* WVEC

Key: * = Jointly owned media.

10 cities, to conduct interviews, procure newspapers, and duplicate news scripts.[13] To obtain data as rich in detail as possible, a stubborn effort was made to interview the managing editor or news director and at least five reporters at each of the 44 news organizations in the sample.[14] Whenever possible, other persons were also interviewed, including city editors, state editors, news editors, assignment editors, general managers, and even librarians.[15] No pledge of confidentiality was offered during these interviews, but requests that all or part of an interview be used on a "not for attribution" or "off the record" basis were respected in full when made at the time of an interview.

Checking the Reliability of Questionnaire Data

In addition to generating new data, interviews with reporters in the 10 cities provided an opportunity to check the reliability of questionnaire information supplied by managing editors and news directors. As mentioned earlier, each managing editor or news director was asked in the questionnaire to estimate the frequency of his contacts with members of other news organizations. Answers to these questions

---

[13] Most television news directors were helpful in arranging for the duplication of news scripts. One news director even volunteered to help with the stapling himself.

[14] In Rochester, New York, stubbornness gave way to cowardice when a blizzard threatened to leave the principal investigator stranded at one of the local television stations.

[15] The most effective strategy involved interviewing reporters first, their superiors second. Many news executives avoid volunteering information which could prove embarrassing to their news organization. In contrast, reporters are more glib. As a result, information supplied by reporters was often useful in drawing news executives out on subjects they might otherwise have avoided.

proved poor surrogates for staff behavior.[16] On the other hand, each managing editor or news director was also asked several questions as to whether a particular relationship existed between his news organization and another news organization (e.g., the sharing of carbons). Answers to these questions proved highly reliable.

Of 15 managing editors whose questionnaire responses could be checked through interviews with reporters and others, only two provided inaccurate information about the sharing of carbons with a television station. Of 17 news directors whose questionnaire responses could be checked through interviews with reporters and others, only one provided inaccurate information about the newspaper experience of his reporters. In two of the three cases, the person who furnished erroneous information was new on the job. In the third case, the person furnished information which had been true until recently but which was no longer true. In general, questionnaire responses about the sharing of carbons and cross-employment were highly reliable.

In addition to providing an opportunity to check the reliability of questionnaire data, interviews permitted an inquiry into the possibility that one or more important variables had been overlooked. In Portland, Maine, New York, New York, Norfolk, Virginia, and Dallas, Texas, reporters cited the location of a newspaper and a television station within the same complex of buildings as a factor

---

[16]The simple r between television news directors' professional interaction with newspaper personnel (as determined by questionnaire responses) and television reporters' information exchanges with newspaper personnel (as determined by personal interviews with television reporters) was -.074. In all probability, the interaction categories used in the questionnaire (never, rarely, occasionally, and regularly) were too vague to be meaningful.

which influences intermedia relations (and hence a factor which might have a homogenizing effect on news outputs). A subsequent data analysis confirmed that there is a positive relationship between the location of a newspaper and television station within the same complex of buildings and interaction between news staffs (simple r = .362).

An examination of newspaper and television addresses disclosed that newspaper-owned television stations are more likely than other television stations to be located within the same complex of buildings as a newspaper. Furthermore, the regression of news organization location on cross-ownership is statistically significant at the .001 level, even after controlling for city size (see Table 6). Consequently, a

Table 6. Effects of Cross-Ownership on News Organization Location, Controlling for City Size[a]

Independent Variable	Standardized b	F
City size	.108	2.18
Cross-Media ownership	.200	7.50[b]

Note: News organization location is a dichotomous variable indicating whether or not a television station is located within the same complex of buildings as a newspaper.

[a] N = 183.
[b] p < .001.

news organization location variable was included as a possible intervening variable between cross-ownership and news homogeneity. Like the carbon-sharing and cross-employment variables, this variable was treated as a dichotomy--either a newspaper and a television station are located within the same complex of buildings or they are not.

Coding the Data

Six persons were hired to code the stories in the data base. When examining newspapers, coders were instructed to analyze all state or local news stories on general news pages, except for stories under three paragraphs in length. When examining news scripts, coders were instructed to analyze all state or local news stories. For each of 9,335 stories, coders noted what topics or issues were involved (no more than three per story), where the story was positioned (on a newspaper's front page, third in a television newscast, etc.), and what levels of interest were involved (local, state, local and state, local and national, state and national, or local, state, and national). For each television story, coders also noted whether film was used and whether the story appeared in a particular newspaper in the same city on the same day, the previous day, or the following day.[17] Inter-coder reliability for the determination of story overlap between a television station and a newspaper was .916, using the rigorous pair-wise comparison method.[18] The coding of story overlap in this fashion provided a means of measuring news homogeneity, defined here as the extent to which two news

---

[17] Coders occasionally encountered story overlap on non-contiguous days, but did not code such overlap. For this reason, and because newspaper stories smaller than three paragraphs in length, newspaper stories on specialty pages, and newspaper photos accompanied only by a cutline were excluded from the analysis, all overlap figures slightly understate the extent to which newspapers and television stations cover the same stories.

[18] The pair-wise comparison method involves computing a percentage agreement score for each possible pair of coders. Thus, if there are six coders, 15 percentage agreement scores are computed. The scores are then averaged for an overall inter-coder reliability score. This method is discussed in Richard Budd, Robert Thorp, and Lewis Donohew, <u>Content Analysis of Communications</u> (New York: The Macmillan Company, 1967), p. 68.

organizations cover the same stories. Story overlap was operationally defined as the proportion of a television station's state and local news stories which also appeared in a particular newspaper on either the same day, the previous day, or the following day.

There are basically two ways to examine the effects (if any) of cross-ownership on story overlap. One is to compare the news outputs of jointly owned and separately owned newspaper-television pairs within the same city. The other is to compare the news outputs of jointly owned and separately owned newspaper-television pairs across different cities. The first method has the advantage of permitting an analysis of data in a relatively raw form, since it requires fewer controls than comparisons across cities. The second method, on the other hand, has the advantage of providing a more sophisticated measurement of the overall effects of cross-ownership, as well as the effects of carbon-sharing, cross-employment, and the location of a newspaper and a television station within the same complex of buildings. Because both approaches have advantages, both have been employed.

Controls for Story Overlap Comparisons Within Cities

Whenever a specific issue of a newspaper was not available, missing data controls were designed on the basis of whether the missing newspaper, if available, would involve a comparison with a television newscast for the same day, a previous day, or a following day. By calculating separately the average number of overlapping stories per day for each newspaper-television pair for each of the three time sequences (same day, previous day, following day), and by adding the appropriate figure to the number of overlapping stories, it was possible to apply missing data controls tailored to the actual behavior of a specific newspaper-television pair.[19]

Provided that comparisons between jointly owned and separately owned media involve the same newspaper, it is not necessary to control for the number of stories in that newspaper. However, it is essential to control for differences in the number of television stories per newscast. In some cities, the average number of stories per newscast varies considerably from one television station to another. In making comparisons between newspaper-television pairs, it is not enough to divide the total number of overlapping stories by the total number of television stories. In many cases, such raw story overlap scores decline as the "slice" of a newscast analyzed gets larger.

For example, the number of stories covered by both the Rock Island Argus and WHBF-TV divided by the number of stories covered by WHBF-TV is .80 if one considers the first three stories per newscast, .60 if one considers the first ten stories per newscast, and .49 if one considers the entire newscast (see Figure 1). A television station's "lead" stories are usually important enough to be covered by the local newspaper as well, whereas stories positioned later in the newscast are often less likely to be covered by the newspaper. As a result, there tends to be more overlap percentage-wise for a television station which covers fewer stories than a competing television station.

To control for this effect, the average number of stories per newscast has been calculated for each television station. Where that

---

[19] A missing newspaper was defined as one which could not be obtained, whether because all copies had been sold out or because the newspaper did not exist (some newspapers do not publish on Sundays).

FIGURE 1. RELATIONSHIP BETWEEN SLICE OF NEWSCAST ANALYZED AND RAW STORY OVERLAP SCORE: ROCK ISLAND ARGUS AND WHBF-TV

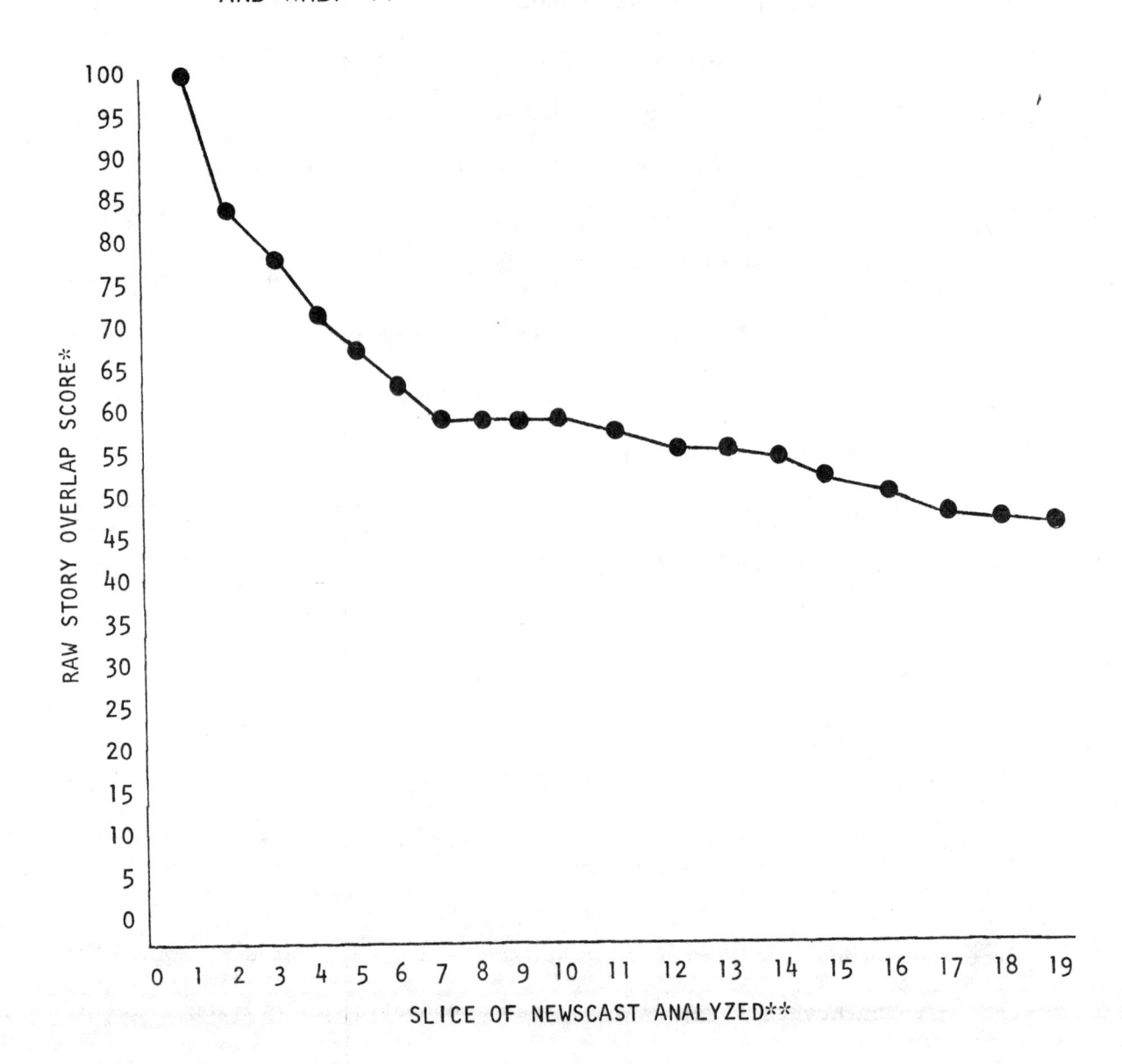

*Number of Overlapping Stories divided by number of T.V. Stories.
**First Story, First Two Stories, First Three Stories, etc.

average differs for television stations in the same city, the lowest average has been selected as the appropriate "slice" of a newscast to be examined in that city. Thus, in Fresno, where one station averages 15 stories per newscast, another averages 15 stories per newscast, and a third averages 24 stories per newscast, the first 15 stories per newscast have been analyzed.

A control which proved necessary in three cases is one which takes into account the location of a television station's studio(s). For example, both WGEM-TV and KHQA-TV have their headquarters in Quincy, Illinois. However, KHQA's primary obligation, under F.C.C. rules, is to its city of license, which happens to be Hannibal, Missouri, just across the river from Quincy. In keeping with this obligation, KHQA maintains a small studio in Hannibal and covers more Hannibal stories than WGEM (8.5% of KHQA's state and local news stories are Hannibal stories, as opposed to 4.5% of WGEM's). It is very unusual for the Quincy Herald-Whig to cover Hannibal stories, since the Hannibal Courier-Post dominates circulation in Hannibal, and Quincy readers are mainly interested in Quincy news. As a result, a fair assessment of the effects of cross-media ownership in Quincy should exclude Hannibal stories when comparing story overlap between the Herald-Whig and WGEM with story overlap between the Herald-Whig and KHQA.[20]

The Norfolk and Sacramento markets are similar to the Quincy market in this respect. One of the television stations in the Norfolk

---

[20] It might be thought that Missouri state government stories should also be excluded, since KHQA-TV might be expected to cover more of such stories than WGEM-TV. This expectation, however, was not confirmed. Indeed, WGEM covered more Missouri state government stories than KHQA.

market, WVEC-TV, is licensed to Hampton and has a studio in Hampton, where two reporters are based. Although WVEC and WTAR both have offices in Norfolk and Hampton, WVEC tends to cover more Hampton and Newport News (peninsula) stories than other stations in the market. This is worth noting because peninsula stories are less likely than other stories to be covered by the Norfolk newspapers, which generally leave that task to the peninsula newspapers. Consequently, it is important to exclude peninsula stories when making comparisons within Norfolk.

In the Sacramento market, KOVR-TV has studios in both Sacramento and Stockton (KOVR's city of license), in contrast to KCRA-TV and KXTV-TV, which have studios in Sacramento alone. KOVR covers more Stockton stories than the other stations, while the Sacramento Bee gives Stockton news short shrift, since most of its readers live in Sacramento. Therefore, it is important to exclude Stockton stories when making comparisons within Sacramento.

Because controls for studio location increase the story overlap scores of the separately owned media more than those of the jointly owned media in two of the three cities (Quincy and Norfolk), they have the practical effect of imposing a harsher, but fairer, test on the hypothesis that cross-media ownership has a homogenizing effect on news content.

Through a difference of proportions test, story overlap between a jointly owned newspaper-television pair can be compared with story overlap between the same newspaper and another television station in the same city.[21] By subtracting one overlap score from the other, we can measure the difference between pairs. Such comparisons within cities permit an investigation of the effects of unique relationships between news organizations which cannot be examined in a multiple regression equation. Furthermore, comparisons involving jointly owned pairs characterized by CS (carbon-sharing), CE (cross-employment), or CB (location within the same complex of buildings) permit a preliminary examination of the effects of these three variables.

Controls for Story Overlap Comparisons Across Cities

While instructive, comparisons within cities do not permit generalizations about the magnitude of the effects of certain variables or the overall explanatory power of these variables. Only through comparisons across cities can the effects of cross-ownership and other variables be adequately quantified. By analyzing all 48 newspaper-television pairs within the same city included in the sample, we can assess the effects of particular independent variables on differences in story overlap. Through multiple regression analysis, the effects of cross-ownership and related variables can be measured and compared with the effects of other variables. Through path analysis, the direct, indirect, and total effects of cross-ownership can be separated.[22] For

---

[21] For a discussion of the difference of proportions test, see Hubert Blalock, Social Statistics (New York: McGraw-Hill, Inc., 1972), pp. 228-232.

[22] For a discussion of path analysis techniques, see Kenneth Land, "Principles of Path Analysis," in Sociological Methodology 1969 (San Francisco: Jossey-Bass, Inc., 1969), ed. by Edgar Borgatta et al., pp. 3-37; also see Donald Stokes, "Compound Paths: An Expository Note," The American Journal of Political Science (February 1974), pp. 191-214.

these techniques to be applicable, however, overlap scores must be made comparable across cities, through the use of slightly different controls than those appropriate for comparisons within cities.

As in comparisons within cities, it is necessary to control for differences in the number of television stories per newscast. When comparisons are made across cities, the same "slice" of a newscast should be examined in all 10 cities. Since one of the 25 television stations in the sample covers an average of 10 stories per newscast, and no television station in the sample has a lower average than that, the first ten stories per newscast should be analyzed in all 10 cities. As a result, missing data controls should be based on the first 10 stories per newscast, when comparisons across cities are made. Controls for studio location, when necessary, should also be based on the first 10 stories per newscast.

In addition to these minor modifications, it is necessary to control for differences among newspapers in the average number of state and local news stories covered per day, since there is a modest positive relationship between the number of newspaper stories and story overlap. Because newspaper stories are positioned in a more complex manner than television stories, controls for the number of newspaper stories cannot be devised as simply as controls for the number of television stories. An attempt to identify the "first" 25 stories in a newspaper, for example, would be tendentious at best. Consequently, a different approach has been devised to control for the number of newspaper stories.

By treating the average number of state and local news stories per day per newspaper as the independent variable and the average overlap score of television stations in that city per newspaper as the dependent variable, we derived a linear equation: $Y = .297 + .0044X$ (see Figure 2). The equation expresses the relationship between the number of newspaper stories per day and the overlap score (the number of overlapping stories divided by the number of television stories, corrected for missing data, studio location, and differences in the number of stories per television newscast). By subtracting the average number of newspaper stories per day for a particular newspaper from the average number of newspaper stories per day for all newspapers in the sample (30.6), multiplying that by the slope of the line (.0044), and adding the result to the overlap score, it is possible to control for the number of newspaper stories per day.

Thus, an overlap score suitable for comparisons across cities is:

$$\frac{N_o}{N_t} + .0044 (30.6 - \bar{N}_n) = \frac{\text{number of overlapping stories}}{\text{number of television stories}}$$
$$+ .0044 (30.6 - \text{number of newspaper stories/day})$$

Before considering the relationship between cross-media ownership and story overlap, we need to control for any independent variables which affect both cross-media ownership and story overlap. One such variable is city size. Because there is cross-media ownership in every city in the sample, and there are more newspaper-television pairs in the larger cities, more of the newspaper-television pairs in the smaller cities are jointly owned than in the larger ones. A control for city size is needed, since city size has some direct effects on story overlap. In a very small city, the total pool of news events is

FIGURE 2. RELATIONSHIP BETWEEN AVERAGE NUMBER OF STORIES PER DAY PER NEWSPAPER AND AVERAGE STORY OVERLAP SCORE PER NEWSPAPER

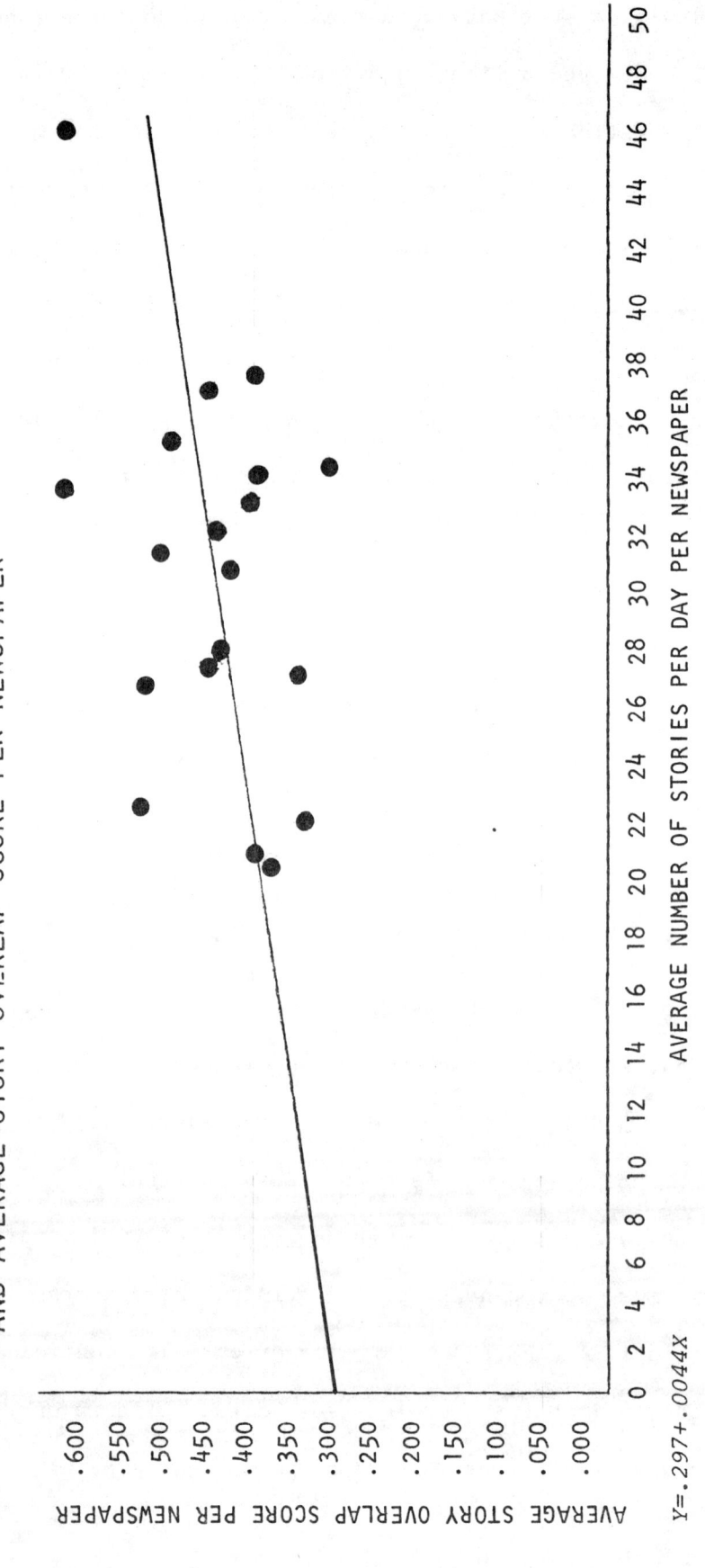

$Y = .297 + .0044X$

NOTE: The story overlap score for each newspaper-television pair has been determined by dividing the number of overlapping stories by the number of television stories, with controls for missing newspapers, studio location, and differences in the number of television stories per newscast. The average story overlap score per newspaper has been determined by adding the story overlap scores of all newspaper-television pairs in the same city involving that newspaper and by dividing that figure by the number of television stations in the city.

smaller than in much larger cities, where there is no dearth of potential news stories. Consequently, news organizations in small cities are more likely to cover the same stories than news organizations in larger ones. Thus, as Table 7 indicates, there is an inverse relation-

Table 7. Simple Correlations of Four City Size Variables With Story Overlap[a]

Variable	Simple r[b]
City size	−.174
Log of city size	−.192
T.V. market size	−.184
Log of T.V. market size	−.239

[a] $N = 48$.

[b] Simple r is the Pearson's product-moment correction coefficient, which measures the extent to which variation in one variable is related to variation in another. See Hubert Blalock, *Social Statistics* (New York: McGraw-Hill Book Company, 1972), p. 379.

ship between city size and story overlap (simple $r = -.174$). The correlation between television market size and story overlap is slightly stronger (simple $r = -.184$). Even stronger is the correlation between the log of television market size, which reduces extreme variations in the independent variable, and story overlap (simple $r = -.239$). To place as harsh a test as possible on the hypothesis that cross-media ownership has a homogenizing effect on news content, the most powerful of these three variables (the log of television market size) has been used as a control variable. An effort to locate additional variables which might affect both cross-media ownership and story overlap proved fruitless.[23]

Effects of Cross-Media Ownership on Similarity of Issue Emphasis

Although story overlap and similar issue emphasis are both types of news homogeneity, they are discrete concepts. It is possible that cross-ownership has a homogenizing effect on which stories are covered without affecting issue emphasis or that cross-ownership has a homogenizing effect on issue emphasis without affecting which stories are covered. One way to operationalize similarity of issue emphasis is to consider the extent to which a newspaper and a television station emphasize ten top issues in the same way. This might be referred to as issue ranking similarity.

To measure issue ranking similarity, the top ten issues for all 9,335 coded stories were identified (see Table 8). Ten issues were singled out for two reasons. First, Blalock has suggested that N should be equal to or greater than ten, if a normal distribution is to be assumed when computing rank-order correlations.[24] Second, the principal investigator discovered in previous research that the agenda-setting power of the mass media may be weak if the issues which comprise the agenda are too numerous or too specific.[25] Thus,

---

[23] The inclusion of controls for newspaper circulation share and television news audience share has a negligible effect on the relationship between cross-ownership and story overlap.

[24] Blalock, op. cit., p. 417.

[25] See William T. Gormley, Jr., "Newspaper Agendas and Political Elites," Journalism Quarterly (Summer 1975), pp. 304-308.

Table 8. Top Ten Issues for News Media in the Sample[a]

Issue	Number of Stories Per Issue
1. Law and Order	1,800
2. Elementary and Secondary Education	636
3. Transportation	561
4. Health	516
5. Government Spending	328
6. Higher Education	296
7. Recession, Unemployment	289
8. Environment	269
9. Utilities	263
10. Taxes	248

[a] N = 9,335.

the inclusion of ten issues in a news medium's agenda was consistent with Blalock's recommendation as well as the principal investigator's research findings.

Once the top ten issues were identified, a news medium's agenda was determined by ranking the issues on the basis of the relative number of stories the news medium devoted to each issue. The Spearman's r_s correlation was used to measure the similarity between newspaper and television agendas.[26] To permit the inclusion of story overlap as an intervening variable between cross-ownership and issue

---

[26] See Blalock, op. cit., pp. 416-418.

ranking similarity, the same stories used to examine the effects of cross-ownership on story overlap were also used to examine the effects of cross-ownership on issue ranking similarity. In short, issue ranking similarity scores, like story overlap scores, contained controls for missing newspapers, studio location, and differences in the number of television stories per newscast.

Because effects of cross-ownership on issue ranking similarity might be confounded by differences in city size between jointly owned and separately owned newspaper-television pairs, the relationship between four different city size variables and issue ranking similarity was tested (see Table 9). The variable with the strongest correlation

Table 9. Simple Correlations of Four City Size Variables With Issue Ranking Similarity[a]

Variable	Simple r
City size	.241
Log of city size	.161
T.V. market size	.229
Log of T.V. market size	.155

[a] $N = 48$.

with issue ranking similarity--city size--was used as a control variable. By regressing issue ranking similarity on city size and cross-ownership, we measured the effects of cross-ownership on issue ranking similarity.

Another way to operationalize similarity of issue emphasis is to consider the extent to which a newspaper and a television station agree on what the top ten issues are. This might be referred to as agenda composition similarity. The same stories used to examine the effects of cross-ownership on story overlap were also used to examine the effects of cross-ownership on agenda composition similarity. To measure agenda composition similarity, each newspaper's top ten issues were compared with the top ten issues of each television station in the same city. If an issue was among a news organization's top ten issues, it received a value of 1; if not, it received a value of 0. By multiplying newspaper and television values for each issue and by adding the products, an agenda composition similarity score was obtained for each newspaper-television pair. Thus, if two news organizations emphasized the same top ten issues, they were given an agenda composition similarity score of 10, regardless of how they ranked the top ten issues. If two news organizations agreed on nine of the top ten issues, they were given an agenda composition similarity score of 9, regardless of how they ranked the top ten issues.[27] The city size variable with the strongest correlation with agenda composition similarity--the log of city size--was used as a control variable (see Table 10). By regressing agenda composition similarity on the log of

---

[27] Where ties made it impossible to identify a news organization's top ten issues, values were based on probabilities. Let us say that a television station's top seven issues could be identified, but four issues were tied after that. Each of these four issues would be given a value indicating that its probability of being in the top ten was 3/4 or .75. If one of these issues was also in the newspaper's top ten, it contributed .75 to the pair's agenda composition similarity score (.75 X 1) rather than 1 (1 X 1).

Table 10. Simple Correlations of Four City Size Variables With Agenda Composition Similarity[a]

Variable	Simple r
City size	-.464
Log of city size	-.577
T.V. market size	-.468
Log of T.V. market size	-.539

[a] $N = 48$.

city size and cross-ownership, the effects of cross-ownership on agenda composition similarity were measured.

IV

THE SPECTRUM FROM COMPETITION
TO COOPERATION

If all newspaper and television reporters were unstintingly cooperative, cross-ownership could not have much of an effect on intermedia relations. Conversely, if all newspaper and television reporters were incorrigibly competitive, cross-ownership could not have much of an effect on intermedia relations. For cross-ownership to make a difference, reporters must be rather open-minded about the relative merits of cooperation and competition. To understand how it is possible for cross-ownership to have effects on intermedia relations, we need to consider the mixed incentives which account for reportorial behavior.

Newspaper and television reporters alike are reluctant to part with hard-earned, important information which no one else has--information which might yield an "exclusive" story or an exclusive "angle" to a story other reporters are pursuing. "If it's something I've been working hard on," a Dayton newspaper reporter explains, "I keep my mouth closed." A Dallas television reporter expresses a similar view: "If it's a major story--an initiative story--I wouldn't share it with the rest of the media." When a reporter working on an "enterprise" story does confide in another reporter, he is apt to stipulate that he be permitted to break the story first.[1] Reporters do not begrudge their colleagues the right to an "exclusive" when a story has eyebrow-raising potential. As one journalist puts it, reporters do not expect other reporters to "share the keys to the kingdom."

While loath to divulge information obtained through blood, sweat, and tears, most reporters have no qualms about exchanging routine background information with other reporters. Such information might include the spelling of a person's name, the phone number of an already identified news source, the meaning of an obscure legal term, the name of the hospital where an accident victim has been taken, etc. If a reporter arrives at the scene of an accident later than another reporter, he can usually count on some help. "At a catastrophe," a Norfolk newspaper reporter explains, "I'm scrambling around trying to find out who did what to whom. They (television reporters) will sometimes point out people to me when they beat me to the scene of an accident." Similarly, if a television reporter arrives late for a press conference, he can usually get a newspaper reporter to fill him in on what he has missed. Late or not, a reporter may rely on other reporters for help if he is confused. "Take the Criminal Courts Building," a New York television reporter mentions as an example. "I'm lost because I don't work the building, except on rare occasions. I'll walk in and say, 'What the hell's going on?' They (newspaper reporters) will tell me a verdict is about to be handed down." Such assistance gives a reporter a chance to get his bearings. A modicum of assistance is widely

---

[1] An enterprise story is one which requires some digging and which is usually conducted at the reporter's own initiative.

regarded as a courtesy reporters have a right to expect.[2]

In their dealings with one another, most newspaper and television reporters do their best to avoid extreme behavior. They do not let other reporters in on important secrets, but they do provide routine background information, when asked. Beyond these two norms, though, there are few constants in intermedia relations. Most reporters can identify a threshold in the spectrum from competition to cooperation beyond which they will not be pushed. However, that threshold varies from reporter to reporter and from news organization to news organization.

Relations between newspaper and television reporters run the gamut from the chummy to the chilly. Some newspaper and television reporters swap a considerable amount of information, while others exchange little more than the time of day. A New York television reporter says she shares information with newspaper reporters "every time I'm out on a breaking story." In contrast, another reporter for the same station rarely communicates with newspaper reporters. "I don't really like to discuss a story with other reporters that much," she says.

Some newspaper and television reporters go out of their way to help one another, while others go out of their way not to help. A Rochester television reporter recalls the time he showed up late for an evening meeting, only to find that the building he needed to enter

---

[2] Such assistance may be regarded as a social exchange, even though the reciprocal nature of the relationship is not made explicit. In Blau's words, social exchange "involves the principle that one person does another a favor, and while there is a general expectation of some future return, its exact nature is definitely not stipulated in advance." See Peter Blau, Exchange and Power in Social Life (New York: John Wiley & Sons, Inc., 1964), p. 93.

was locked. Fortunately for him, he caught the attention of a newspaper reporter on the fifth floor who came downstairs, opened a ground floor window, and helped him crawl into the building. But newspaper reporters are not always so obliging. In fact, some newspaper reporters purposely save their best questions at a press conference until after the television lights are out and the television people have begun to depart. They do this so that their story will have an angle which the television story will not.

Some newspaper and television reporters "tip" one another as if they were comrades in arms. A Norfolk newspaper reporter, for example, telephoned a local television reporter on a Saturday night to tell her that a prominent Watergate figure was in town and was available for an interview that evening. Other reporters find such cooperation unthinkable. In the words of a Rochester newspaper reporter, "I'll stab the television people in the back whenever I get the chance."

The Professional Vacuum

If journalism were a profession, relationships between newspaper and television reporters might be more uniform. But journalism is not a profession in the sense that law and medicine are professions. There are no entrance requirements for admission to the practice of journalism, with the result that persons undergo very different socialization experiences prior to becoming journalists. There are no disciplinary mechanisms whereby persons can be prohibited from practicing journalism because they have violated widely accepted norms or procedures.

There are codes of ethics which journalistic organizations have adopted, but these codes are different for print and electronic journalists. Furthermore, none of the codes attempts to prescribe relationships between newspaper and television reporters. The Canons of Journalism, adopted by the American Society of Newspaper Editors, deal with freedom of the press, accuracy, truthfulness, decency, and other subjects, but do not deal with intermedia relations at all. Neither does the Television Code of the National Association of Broadcasters. Thus, the journalistic "profession" is officially silent on the subject of intermedia relations.

Non-Interventionist News Executives

Newspaper managing editors and television news directors, who have immediate responsibility for their respective news departments, might be expected to instruct their reporters on how to deal with members of other news organizations--either through a memo, a recitation of do's and don't's, or an informal chat. However, very few news executives tell their reporters how much sharing of information is permissible.

Ralph Langer, managing editor of the Dayton Journal Herald, says his newspaper has no "policy" on intermedia relations. Instead, he counts on his reporters to use common sense. "Anybody in a competitive town like this who goes around helping other reporters is crazy," Langer says. The news director of KMJ-TV in Fresno, Al Buch, has not discussed norms of intermedia relations with his reporters. Neither has Marty Haag, news director of WFAA-TV in Dallas, who feels that a lecture on intermedia relations would be superfluous: "Generally, people know these things without setting them down."

More to the point, a sermon on intermedia relations might fall on deaf ears, since news executives cannot effectively monitor the behavior of their reporters in the field. Paul Thompson, news director of KCRA-TV in Sacramento, does not try to lay down rules about sharing information, because he thinks there is little he can do about it. "I don't see any way you can prevent sharing," Thompson says. "It happens everywhere."

There is some evidence to support Thompson's belief that a policy on intermedia relations cannot be enforced--at least not a policy designed to restrict cooperation between reporters. Ray Miller, news director of KPRC-TV in Houston, wrote an instruction booklet for his reporters, which included the following guidelines: "You will have or will form personal friendships with other people working for newspapers and radio and television stations. Friendships are fine. But we do not depend upon other radio, television or newspaper reporters for help and we do not in the course of normal news coverage help them because in any such tradeouts, we are sure to come out on the short end, giving more than we get." These instructions notwithstanding, a former KPRC reporter says that Miller's advice was "generally ignored" by KPRC reporters. "We cooperated anyway," the ex-reporter recalls.

The Views of News Executives

Even if news executives agreed that newspaper and television reporters should gather news independently, they could not impose that orthodoxy on reporters. Still, insofar as reporters value the judgment of their superiors, the views of news executives are important. Another reason for differences in relations between newspaper and television reporters is that news executives disagree about the extent to which newspapers and television stations are competing media.

Some television news directors are struck by similarities in the news dissemination functions of newspapers and television stations. In the words of one news director, "We both strive to do the same job with different tools." Using plainer language, another news director argues that newspapers and television stations "are in direct competition with one another." Still another news director expresses the operational equivalent of this view: "If we have information we have developed, we're not going to tell the newspapers. It would be like Macy's telling Gimbel's."

While many television news directors feel this way, others prefer the notion that newspapers and television stations serve "complementary" functions in reporting the news. As one news director puts it, "Newspapers cannot match our immediacy, nor bring to their reporting the special dimension that film, videotape and sound can offer. But television cannot report as comprehensively and with as much detail as can newspapers." Another news director echoes this refrain: "Hard as it is for (the) pencil press to swallow, television has them beat hands down on time; hard as it is for us to swallow, print has us edged on length." Impressed by fundamental differences in the very nature of newspapers and television stations, many television news directors regard fierce competition as unnecessary. The sharing of information between newspaper and television news staffs is compatible with this view.

Like their broadcasting counterparts, newspaper managing editors disagree about the extent to which newspapers and television stations are competing media. Some stress that both are in the business of keeping the public informed. Others note that newspapers and television stations have different strengths. Still others get positively apoplectic at the very suggestion that newspaper and television reporters are journalists in the same sense of that word. These managing editors regard television news outfits as too inept to be worthy of serious consideration.

A substantial minority of newspaper managing editors view television news staffers with thinly disguised or even blatant contempt. These news executives think of television news staffers as "show-biz" personalities masquerading as journalists. As one managing editor puts it, "The airmen are entertainers and the legmen are an unlettered, unruly mob." While television news directors generally refer to newspaper reporters with respect, newspaper managing editors occasionally are downright venomous in their evaluations of television reporters. One managing editor suggests that television reporters are "like dogs in heat--they cluster where the fastest action takes place." Another managing editor describes television reporters as "almost a fly-by-night group" who "lend themselves to sensationalism or drivel."

At times, it is difficult to discern whether a particular managing editor is upset with the caliber of television personnel, the constraints of newscast formats, or the television medium itself. The most common criticism of television news reports--that they are "superficial"--could be attributed to reporters who don't know how to dig for details, producers who insist that stories be no longer than one or two minutes, or a medium which necessitates a "headline service" approach to the news.

Despite all their faults, local television newscasts have improved considerably in recent years. Television stations have hired more reporters and better educated reporters. Stations in large and medium-sized cities have acquired mini-cameras which permit the live transmission of reports from remote locales. Dozens of stations have expanded their early evening newscasts from one-half hour to one hour or more, making possible stories richer in details.

Still, managing editors have some cause to snicker. In Dayton, where the television newscasts are probably better than average, the anchorman at the CBS affiliate gives the impression that he has modeled himself after Walter Cronkite. The pursed lips, bobbing head, arched eyebrows, and familiar inflections all suggest that the anchorman is a chip off the old Cronkite block. At Dayton's NBC affiliate, the first half-hour of an hour-long early evening newscast sometimes appears to be a dress rehearsal for the second half-hour, with reporters lounging about in their shirt-sleeves sipping bottles of pop and giving sneak previews of stories they will report in a few minutes. On April 23, 1975, the NBC affiliate's lead story announced that that day was the birthday of William Shakespeare and Shirley Temple Black.

Not surprisingly, many Americans, including managing editors, have a sense of deja vu when they see anchorman Ted Baxter on the Mary Tyler Moore Show. In fact, Allan Burns, the co-creator of the show, has received numerous phone calls from people wanting to know if the Ted Baxter character was based on the anchorman in their city.[3] In a speech before an audience of broadcasters, CBS reporter Charles Kuralt--hardly a malcontent--referred to local television news as "the continuing disgrace of this profession." Having watched local television newscasts

---

[3] Interview with Allan Burns (Los Angeles: June 6, 1975).

in dozens of cities across the nation, Kuralt reached a sad conclusion: "The plain truth is that in a society which depends for its life on an informed citizenry, and in which most citizens receive most of their information from television, millions are getting that life-giving information from a man, or a woman, whose colleagues wouldn't trust to accurately report on his or her afternoon round of golf."[4]

A substantial number of newspaper managing editors would say amen to that. Furthermore, many of them are so vehement on the subject that their reporters probably know where they stand. To the extent that reporters absorb the views of their superiors, reporters' behavior may be shaped by cues from above.

If a news executive regards newspapers and television stations as "complementary" media, his reporters may feel free to cooperate with other reporters who perform a different societal function. If a news executive considers newspapers and television stations to be in direct competition, his reporters may be more wary of cooperating with "rivals." If a managing editor perceives television reporters as buffoons, his reporters may treat television reporters as pariahs. Thus, reporters may be influenced by subtle pressures when their superiors voice opinions about the functions of other news media or the caliber of other newsmen.

Overall, though, newspaper and television reporters have a considerable amount of leeway in their dealings with one another. Reporters are not hemmed in by a professional code of ethics, since no such code deals with intermedia relations. Nor can reporters be prevented

---

[4] Charles Kuralt, "All Those Pretty TV News Anchormen," *The Quill* (October 1975), p. 9.

by their superiors from cooperating with other reporters. Indeed, most news executives do not even try to monitor the behavior of their reporters in the field. For these reasons, the individual reporter tends to be highly autonomous. In most instances, the reporter is free to decide for himself the balance between competition and cooperation which he wishes to strike.

The Urge to Compete

There are several reasons why newspaper and television reporters compete with one another, the most basic of which is that reporters find competition challenging and exhilarating. Few things satisfy a reporter more than knowing that he "scooped" the opposition.[5] "I'm a very competitive journalist," a New York television reporter explains. "I like to come home with a piece so I can say I've beaten the crap out of the other guys." A Norfolk television reporter goes even further: "I live and breathe for scoops." Bouts with alcoholism, ulcers, and ruined marriages attest to the fact that many reporters pay a high price for the thrill of the chase for news.

The worst excesses of extreme competition between newspaper and television reporters appear to have faded from the scene. Veteran New York television reporter Gabe Pressman can remember fistfights between newspaper and television reporters years ago but none in recent years. Also, there are few reporters today who would try to bamboozle other

---

[5]The desire to be the first to make a discovery is not unique to journalists. In scientific research, similar sentiments give the quest for knowledge a special urgency. To cite a celebrated example, Watson and Crick were plainly anxious to "scoop" other researchers who hoped to discover the structure of DNA. See James Watson, <u>The Double Helix</u> (New York: Mentor Books, 1969).

reporters the way that Hildy Johnson and Walter Burns did in the play, The Front Page.[6] Still, the urge to compete is strong, and reporters take great delight in bragging about scoops, exclusives, or angles no other reporter had.

The quest for scoops is not merely a matter of pride. For better or worse, a reporter's career is enhanced with every scoop he obtains--provided, of course, that he has gotten his facts straight. Speed is not the only criterion by which reporters are judged, but it is a convenient yardstick which many news executives use for want of a better one. As Sigal has noted, "The difficulty of agreeing to standards for judging the quality of a reporter's stories means that editors and publishers and consequently reporters themselves tend to fall back on an older index of reporting skill: who gets stories first."[7]

At times, reporters wonder if perhaps the quest for scoops is a silly fetish, especially when there is no question that certain information will be released soon. Tom Wicker has expressed this feeling of futility that "all we're going to do is let people who don't much care find out a little earlier about a fact they're going to learn anyway."[8] Reporters sometimes feel this way. When stalking big game, however, reporters take the quest for scoops seriously indeed. Even Woodward and Bernstein, whose Watergate exclusives in the Washington Post had

---

[6] Ace reporter Hildy Johnson and his managing editor, Walter Burns, hid an escaped convict in a pressroom desk and did their best to lead other reporters astray in a desperate effort to obtain an "exclusive" interview with the convict.

[7] Leon Sigal, Reporters and Officials: The Organization and Politics of Newsmaking (Lexington, Massachusetts: D. C. Heath & Company, 1973), p. 72.

[8] Tom Wicker, Facing the Lions (New York: The Viking Press, 1973), p. 17.

already established their reputation, felt bitterly disappointed on October 4, 1972 when the Los Angeles Times came up with a Watergate exclusive of its own. Anxious to beat the Times again as quickly as possible, Woodward and Bernstein rushed another exclusive into print two days later. The story subsequently proved to be incorrect.[9] With stories less significant than Watergate, reporters may be less trigger-happy, but the impulse to scoop the opposition can be overpowering.

If some reporters compete in search of scoops, others compete as a matter of principle. The notion that the public interest is served by diversity and that competition begets diversity is not far from the minds of many reporters. "I feel very funny about sharing information," a Dallas newspaper reporter explains. "Sharing detracts from an individual point of view." The publication of Timothy Crouse's *The Boys on the Bus*, which attacks "pack journalism," seems to have heightened reporters' awareness of the dangers of "group-think." The more alert reporters are to these dangers, the more competitive they tend to be.

Another factor which discourages cooperation in the field is that reporters cannot be sure their favors will be reciprocated. Beat reporters, in particular, tend to feel this way. Since they are knowledgeable and experienced, they are often being sought out by general assignment reporters who are not familiar with the ways of the beat. Eventually, this may grate on beat reporters, who come to regard general assignment reporters from other news organizations as parasites. One veteran courthouse reporter puts it this way: "There are some people who are on a constant fishing expedition and want me to do their

---

[9] Carl Bernstein and Bob Woodward, *All the President's Men* (New York: Simon and Schuster, 1974), pp. 108-111.

work for them." The lines of cleavage between beat reporters and general assignment reporters are frequently lines between newspaper and television reporters.[10] Thus, the resentment which the beat reporter feels toward the general assignment reporter is apt to be that of a newspaper reporter toward a television reporter.

Although few newspaper reporters will admit it, the reluctance of newspaper reporters to cooperate with television reporters must be attributed in part to a latent fear of the television medium's strength in the marketplace. Between 1948 and 1970, the percentage of mass media advertising dollars allotted to newspapers declined substantially, while the percentage allotted to television increased dramatically.[11] Since 1963, more Americans have said they get most of their news from television rather than newspapers. Furthermore, the gap has widened in recent years.[12] As added proof of this, the percentage of adults who said they watched television yesterday increased from 81% to 85% between 1970 and 1975, while the percentage who said they read a newspaper yesterday declined from 77% to 73%.[13]

No matter how bravely newspaper reporters view these developments, the figures indicate that television's success has been--and may

---

[10] Because newspapers have larger news staffs than television stations, they are considerably more likely to operate on a beat system.

[11] Edwin Emery, The Press and America: An Interpretative History of the Mass Media (Englewood Cliffs, New Jersey: Prentice-Hall, Inc., 1972), p. 619.

[12] The Roper Organization, "Trends in Public Attitudes Toward Television and Other Mass Media: 1959-1974" (New York: Television Information Office, 1975), pp. 2-3.

[13] "Television: The More Medium," Broadcasting (September 15, 1975), pp. 53-54.

continue to be--partially at the expense of newspapers. Although there are several possible explanations for the negative attitudes which many newspaper reporters have toward television reporters, one possibility is that their fears occasionally bubble to the surface and take the form of anger and contempt.

Whatever the origins of these feelings, many newspaper reporters are as snide as some managing editors in their assessments of television reporters. A Dayton reporter minces no words: "I hate obnoxious bastards in television." A Portland (Maine) reporter is more charitable, mentioning one television reporter he respects. As for the rest? "The rest," he says, "are a bunch of baboons." A frequent complaint of newspaper reporters is that television people turn press conferences into circuses, as noisy cameramen lumber in with their equipment, wasting precious time while everyone else waits impatiently to begin. Newspaper reporters also lament what they see as a tendency for television reporters to ask too many questions at press conferences. A Dayton newspaper reporter remembers the time he berated a television "pretty boy" who "wouldn't shut up." With some pride, the newspaper reporter recalls telling the television reporter, "You're the biggest horse's ass I've met all day."

In addition to griping about press conference behavior, newspaper reporters argue that television newscasts distort the truth by condensing complicated news stories into headlines. Newspaper reporters also criticize what they perceive as sensationalism and sexism in television newscasts. A Rochester newspaper reporter sums up these complaints: "Television people cover anything that bleeds, burns, or has boobs." If all reporters indulge in too much ambulance-chasing, television reporters seem to do so with a special vengeance. If television reporters are no more lecherous than newspaper reporters, nevertheless they have cameras with zoom lenses which zero in on buxom blondes with some regularity. There may be as much sexism in newspapers as television, but televised sexism is less subtle.

In general, newspaper reporters cooperate more if they respect television reporters than if they regard them with disdain. The sentiments of fear, contempt, and pity do not always produce identical effects. Newspaper reporters who pity television reporters may be more inclined to help than newspaper reporters who regard television reporters as equal competitors. Overall, though, animosities between newspaper and television reporters spur competition by depleting the reservoir of good will which is so essential to cooperation.

The Urge to Cooperate

While most newspaper and television reporters have an urge to compete with one another, they also recognize that cooperation has its advantages. One factor which encourages cooperation is the difficulty of deciding what is newsworthy and what is not. Newsworthiness is such an abstract concept that reporters find themselves using other reporters as sounding boards in an effort to corroborate their own news judgment.[14] As a New York television reporter explains, "Colleagues can give you an instant frame of reference." Without feedback from colleagues, reporters

---

[14] As Dunn puts it, "News is imitative because individual reporters need to have their news sense validated. The lack of concrete news definitions leaves the reporter insecure in his independent decision as to what is news . . . He seeks assurance from other reporters that his judgment is correct." See Delmer Dunn, Public Officials and the Press (Reading, Massachusetts: Addison-Wesley Publishing Company, 1969), p. 30.

might be duped more easily by public officials who do their best to exaggerate the importance of some of their endeavors and minimize the importance of others in the hope of obtaining favorable publicity and avoiding bad publicity. To escape brainwashing of this kind, reporters depend on other reporters to offer more detached observations on the newsworthiness of events and developments.

Another motive for close cooperation is the fear of missing a story. If reporters delight in beating the opposition to a story, so do they also worry about being beaten. The reporter who is (figuratively) caught napping can expect to incur the wrath of his superiors. Even if news executives resist the temptation to administer a severe tongue-lashing, their discomfiture is often evident. "My entire day can start well or bad, depending on what I see in the Journal Herald," a Dayton television news director explains. "If we missed a story, I get uptight." The news director's misery is bound to be felt by the reporter who missed the story. If the reporter misses too many stories, he may find himself given unenviable assignments. If the reporter repeatedly misses stories, he may find himself unemployed.

To avoid the embarrassment of missing a story, many reporters work closely together and trade tips. As a low-risk strategy, this approach has considerable appeal to reporters. In the argot of the racetrack, a reporter "wins" with an exclusive story, "places" with an exclusive angle to a story others have, "shows" with basically the same story that others have, and "loses" when he misses a story altogether. Many reporters find it is better to place and show consistently than to win occasionally and lose often.

Even reporters who have a gambling instinct share some information with other reporters, out of a commitment to accuracy. When a reporter suspects that another reporter has been misinformed, he may contact that reporter before he goes public with his erroneous information. "If you know a reporter has some false information, you call him up to wave him off the story," a Norfolk newspaper reporter explains. Whether a reporter suspects that another reporter has been misinformed or not, he may share information to reduce the probability that others will provide inaccurate information to the public. "I'll be cooperative with the tube people," a Dallas newspaper reporter comments. "I hate to see them peddling bullshit to the public." When a story is very complicated, reporters from different news organizations may share information in an effort to get the facts straight. For example, several New York newspaper and television reporters working on nursing home stories held an informal meeting recently to confirm facts they had gathered and enhance their understanding of nursing home problems.

In this same spirit, veteran reporters sometimes come to the aid of reporters who are wet behind the ears, to keep them from botching a story and misleading the public. Other motives may be present as well. Old-timers may empathize with cub reporters, as they remember their own bewilderment when they first learned the ropes. Also, some reporters may enjoy the feeling of superiority which comes from playing the "inside dopester" role. These reporters may relish the opportunity to provide information to other reporters, whether they are neophytes or not.[15]

---

[15] As paradoxical as it may seem, the absence of reciprocity can be rewarding. As Blau has noted, "A person who gives others valuable gifts or renders them important services makes a claim for superior status by obligating them to himself . . . If they fail to reciprocate with benefits that are at least as important to him as his are to them, they

Because newspapers and television stations have different capacities and strengths, they cannot handle all stories equally well. For this reason, newspaper and television reporters tip one another when they doubt that their own news medium can do a particular story justice. From time to time, a television reporter will alert a newspaper reporter to a story too complicated for him to handle. "With statistical stories we'll run across, I have taken the story and given it to a newspaper reporter," a Dallas television reporter notes. This trading also works the other way around, when a newspaper reporter stumbles across a feature or human interest story likely to be dull in print, moving on television.

Obviously, reporters have little to lose if they simply share information about stories they have no intention of covering themselves. Some newspaper reporters feel they have little to lose in sharing information about stories they do intend to cover. These reporters make the familiar argument that television news is too superficial to be any sort of threat. As the old joke goes, if Moses handed down the Ten Commandments, television's lead would be, "Moses today came down from the mountain with the Ten Commandments, the two most important of which were . . ."[16] While newspaper reporters who regard television reporters with contempt may share very little information with them, those who regard newspapers and television stations as performing complementary functions may share a great deal of information indeed. In the words of a Sacramento newspaper reporter, "You can go all the way with

---

validate his claim to superior status." See Blau, op. cit., p. 108.

[16] David Halberstam, "CBS: The Power and the Profits, Part II," The Atlantic Monthly (February 1976), p. 62.

television people in exchanging information, because there's only so much that television can do."

Newspaper reporters are positive that they are in competition with other newspapers, but they are not always sure about television. As a result, some newspaper reporters have a double standard: they exchange some information with television reporters but exchange nothing with reporters for other newspapers. A Norfolk Virginian Pilot reporter, for example, shares some information with television reporters but not with reporters for the Norfolk Ledger-Star, which is located in the same building. "We are really secretive with the newspaper people downstairs," the reporter observes. Similarly, a Dayton Journal-Herald reporter admits to an occasional exchange of information with television reporters but expresses horror at the idea of cooperating with the Dayton Daily News, located in the same building. "I wouldn't give information to the Daily News over my dead body!" she exclaims.

Under certain circumstances, a reporter's desire to get a particular story publicized may supersede his loyalty to his own news organization. When a reporter's own news organization refuses to run a delicate or embarrassing story, the reporter may "leak" the story to another news organization. The Dallas Morning News, for example, has "killed" a number of stories which Dallas Morning News reporters have promptly leaked to the local public television station. The newspaper's city editor, Bob Miller, denounces such behavior as "immature." Defending the leaks, a Dallas Morning News reporter asserts, "My commitment is to journalism, not to a specific organization."

Even when a reporter's own news organization agrees to run a story, the reporter may tip another news organization in advance in the hope that it will cover the story as well. Reporters do this if they believe a story is so important that it deserves maximum exposure or if they like the idea of maximum exposure in general. Newspaper reporters who tip television reporters in this fashion argue that people want to know more about a story which appears in their morning newspaper if they heard about the story on television the night before. Thus, some newspaper reporters go out of their way to tip television reporters the day before a story is published, to encourage the television people to air the story that evening. These newspaper reporters contend that the television story serves as a "teaser" for their own story the next day.

Of all the reasons why newspaper and television reporters cooperate, perhaps the most important is that they run into each other in the line of duty. The more they encounter one another, the greater the need to reach some sort of modus vivendi, whether they like one another or not. For the sake of pleasant working conditions, reporters feel obliged to be at least civil towards one another.[17] At this stage, reporters exchange basic background information and cover for one another, when necessary. During protracted courtroom proceedings, for example, a television reporter may cover for a newspaper reporter who has to make a phone call, visit the lavatory, etc. As newspaper and television reporters interact on this level, they come to realize that some of the stereotypes are wrong--that all newspaper reporters are not whiskey-breathed busybodies and that all television reporters are not empty-

---

[17]Barnard refers to this incentive as the desire for a "condition of communion" or "the feeling of personal comfort in social relations that is sometimes called solidarity, social integration, the gregarious instinct, or social security." See Chester Barnard, <u>The Functions of the Executive</u> (Cambridge, Massachusetts: Harvard University, 1968), p. 148.

headed prima donnas.

After discarding these stereotypes, newspaper and television reporters discover that they enjoy conversing with one another. After all, they have much in common. Together, they can poke fun at thieving politicians, long-winded Rotarians, and spendthrift bureaucrats. If they have time after a press conference or a city council meeting, they may continue their banter at a restaurant or a bar--perhaps at the Dutch Kitchen in Norfolk or David's Bar in Sacramento. In addition to swapping anecdotes, they may casually discuss the stories on which they are working. They may even trade a tip or two.

Before long, these casual ties develop into friendships--bonds which may become more important than the desire for scoops or loyalty to a particular news organization. Once this threshold has been crossed, newspaper and television reporters find it very difficult to keep secrets from one another. As a Dallas newspaper reporter puts it, "It's hard not to tell a friend."

Effects of Cross-Ownership on Intermedia Relations

There are good reasons for newspaper and television reporters to compete, but there are also good reasons for them to cooperate. If the urge to compete were far stronger than the urge to cooperate, cross-ownership might have a negligible impact on intermedia relations. However, the relative merits of competition and cooperation are so debatable that the choice is a difficult one for most reporters. In such a fluid situation, cross-ownership increases cooperation more easily than if all reporters were stubbornly competitive.

The increased cooperation which cross-ownership promotes may or may not be accompanied by changes in the attitudes of reporters. Newspaper and television reporters who work for the same company occasionally remark that they are "members of the same corporate family." Since the company's financial health depends on the success of both the newspaper and the television station, they argue, cooperation benefits the company and ultimately benefits information donors as well as information recipients. This attitude encourages cooperation, although it is not a prerequisite to it.

Cross-ownership also increases cooperation by increasing interaction between newspaper and television reporters. The more reporters interact, the more they cooperate. They do not need to like one another. They do not even need to respect one another. Frequently, of course, increased interaction reduces feelings of contempt and fear and paves the way for friendships. When this happens, reporters cooperate to an even greater extent. However, cross-ownership need not change reporters' attitudes to increase cooperation.

The Sharing of Carbons

Cooperation does not depend on reporters' attitudes when cooperation is required as a matter of corporate policy. This is because cooperation can be mandated--through a policy requiring carbon-sharing, for example. Overall, 9.4% of newspaper-owned television stations receive newspaper carbons on an exclusive basis, as opposed to 1.1% of television stations not owned by a newspaper (see Table 11). In at least five cities, a newspaper-owned television station receives carbons of some newspaper stories while other stations in these cities do not. Three

Table 11. Crosstabulation of Cross-Ownership by Carbon-Sharing[a]

	T.V. station owned by newspaper	T.V. station not owned by newspaper
Receives carbons on an exclusive basis	5 (9.4%)	1 (1.1%)
Does not receive carbons on an exclusive basis	48 (90.6%)	86 (98.9%)
	53 (100.0%)	87 (100.0%)

[a] N = 140.

of the five cities are Portland, Maine, Rock Island, Illinois, and Quincy, Illinois.[18]

In Portland, where the Express, Press-Herald, and WGAN-TV are owned by the same company, the Express and Press-Herald make carbons of "almost all" their stories available to WGAN-TV before the stories are published. The carbons are placed in bins on the desks of the city editors of the Express and Press-Herald, which share a newsroom. Once or twice a day, someone from WGAN, which is located in the same building as the two newspapers, picks up the carbons. The carbons are not always picked up during the morning or afternoon. However, WGAN's anchorman, Ross Hammons, is a creature of habit. Every night at around 9 p.m., he picks up carbons for possible use on WGAN's 11 p.m. newscast.

The managing editor of the Press-Herald, John Murphy, does not recall when the practice began, but he thinks it has gone on for over

---

[18] The identity of the other two cities cannot be divulged, due to a promise of confidentiality.

two decades. Murphy justifies the sharing of carbons on the grounds that people are more likely to read a newspaper story if they have heard about it on television: "If there's a good story, television makes people want to know more about it." The city editor of the Express, Byron Israelson, feels the same way. "Television whets the appetite of a person interested in news," Israelson says. "Television is an aperitif."

Express and Press Herald reporters do not share the enthusiasm of their editors for the carbon-sharing arrangement. A number of reporters get very upset when a story they have worked hard on is aired by WGAN radio or television before their newspaper is published. Although Express and Press Herald reporters are theoretically required to place carbons of all their stories in a bin for WGAN, they sometimes refuse to put carbons of important stories in the WGAN bin. "Frankly, if we don't want a story in, we won't put it in the damn box," one reporter explains. Another reporter estimates that he withholds an average of 20 carbons per year from the WGAN bin. "If I cover something by my own initiative, I don't see any reason why I should do all that work and let them (the WGAN people) have it," the reporter says.

In Rock Island, Illinois, where the Argus and WHBF-TV are owned by the same company, the Argus and WHBF have a carbon-sharing arrangement. Argus reporters do not complain much about the arrangement, though, because they are not required to supply WHBF with carbons of "exclusives" or "features." In contrast to Portland, the picking up of carbons is highly systematic in Rock Island. Also, the carbon-sharing is less one-sided in Rock Island, since WHBF furnishes some carbons daily to the Argus.[19]

Every day at approximately 7:30 a.m., the chief photographer for the Argus visits WHBF, just a few blocks away, to pick up carbons of WHBF radio's early morning stories, some of which are rewrites of stories aired on WHBF-TV the night before. Twice during the morning--at around 9 a.m. and 11 a.m.--a WHBF custodian stops by the Argus to pick up carbons which have accumulated. Shortly after 12:30 p.m., which is the copy deadline for the Argus' first edition, an Argus receptionist collects carbons from a bin and delivers them to WHBF. Since the first edition of the Argus "hits the streets" at 1:30 p.m., carbons delivered after 12:30 p.m., do not arrive much earlier than the first edition itself. However, carbons furnished by the Argus in the morning do provide WHBF with valuable lead time. According to WHBF-TV assistant news director, Max Molleston, "Carbons are helpful in leads--very much so."

Although WHBF probably benefits more from the carbon-sharing arrangement than the Argus does, the Argus finds that some WHBF carbons are useful, especially carbons of stories concerning Davenport, Iowa, which is just across the river from Rock Island. Since the Argus feels obligated to cover some Davenport news but shrinks from hiring another reporter to cover Davenport, it relies on WHBF, which has a Davenport reporter, to keep it supplied with Davenport news. At least one Argus reporter has questioned the policy of sharing carbons, but his editors have not been very responsive. "They shrug their shoulders and say 'that's the policy,'" the reporter says.

In a number of cities where newspaper-owned television stations

---

[19] WGAN furnishes carbons to the Express and Press-Herald only upon request.

used to receive newspaper carbons, the practice has been eliminated in recent years. In Fresno, California, where the Bee owns KMJ-TV, the Bee stopped furnishing carbons to KMJ late in 1974. Although opinions differ on why the practice was ended, two explanations seem most plausible. First, the Bee and KMJ were apprehensive that the sharing of carbons might weaken their parent corporation's defense against a petition to deny filed by the Justice Department late in 1974.[20] Second, the Bee, which had been located directly across the street from KMJ, was on the verge of moving to a new location over a mile away, which would have rendered carbon-sharing more complicated than before.

In Rochester, New York, where the Democrat & Chronicle, the Times-Union, and WHEC-TV are all owned by the Gannett Company, the two newspapers stopped furnishing carbons to WHEC in 1968 or 1969. According to Howard Hosmer, then news director of WHEC, the practice ended when the newspapers--with the apparent blessing of the Gannett Company--told WHEC the carbons would no longer be supplied unless WHEC paid the taxicab costs of having them delivered. WHEC balked at this idea and the practice stopped. Old hands at the two newspapers say the monetary demand was made in an effort to end a practice which had become a source of irritation to newspaper reporters who disliked hearing their stories on the air before seeing them in print.

In Quincy, Illinois, where the Herald-Whig owns WGEM-TV, there is an institutionalized flow of information between the Herald-Whig and WGEM, but carbons play a very minor role in this exchange. Although the Herald-Whig once supplied WGEM with a substantial number of carbons,

---

[20] For information about the Justice Department's petition, see Lanny Larson, "U.S. Attempts to Sever Bee, Three KMJ Stations," The Fresno Bee (November 2, 1974).

the flow of carbons has been reduced to a trickle. Every day at approximately 4:30 p.m., WGEM's news director, Charles Griffith, walks a few blocks to the Herald-Whig to pick up those carbons and press releases which are set aside for WGEM. Today, the carbons are meager. Every month, the Herald-Whig's associate editor, Donald Kesler, writes a story about Quincy's Park Board (of which he is a member) and places a carbon of the story in a bin designated for WGEM. However, the bin usually contains nothing but press releases and photographs. While only the vestiges of the carbon-sharing practice remain, ties between the Herald-Whig and WGEM are very strong indeed. These ties are facilitated by a telephone "tie-line" connecting the Herald-Whig and WGEM,[21] which seems to belie the parent company's official policy of maintaining "separate and independent" operations.[22]

Every morning, Harold Gilbert, the Herald-Whig's state editor, telephones WGEM's "morning man," Bob Turek. By the time Gilbert calls, Turek has already telephoned sheriff's offices and radio stations in outlying areas to inquire about accidents and crimes. Turek or another reporter passes this information along to the Herald-Whig--an arrangement which one reporter refers to as "profit-sharing" since it reduces the long-distance phone bills of the Herald-Whig and, ultimately, the parent company. Later in the day, a WGEM reporter or the anchorman may call up the Herald-Whig. "I'll call them up and ask what's going on," one reporter explains. In the evening, the Herald-Whig state desk

---

[21] To contact someone at WGEM, a Herald-Whig staffer merely dials 8 and a two-digit extension number.

[22] Oral Argument of Thomas A. Oakley, Quincy Broadcasting Company and Quincy Newspapers, Inc., before the Federal Communications Commission re Docket 18110 (July 26, 1974).

calls WGEM again to see if anything has happened which the Herald-Whig missed.

Thus, there is an institutionalized flow of information over the telephone between the news staffs of the Herald-Whig and WGEM. This flow of information is not in keeping with official corporate policy. However, Herald-Whig and WGEM news staffers apparently doubt that management genuinely opposes cooperation between the two news staffs, whatever management may tell the F.C.C. The symbolic "tie-line" connecting the newspaper and television station and the continued exchange of some carbons suggest that management's official commitment to "separate and highly competitive news staffs" is intended to stave off F.C.C. intervention, not to curb the actual flow of information between the two news organizations.

Hiring Patterns

In addition to relatively overt effects on the flow of information, cross-ownership increases cooperation between newspaper and television news staffs by influencing hiring patterns of newspaper-owned television stations. Newspaper-owned television stations are more likely than comparable television stations to hire a reporter or editor who has worked for the newspaper which owns the television station. As Table 12 indicates, 27.9% of television stations owned by a newspaper have hired a reporter or editor who worked for the newspaper, whereas only 11.7% of comparable television stations have hired a reporter or editor who worked for a local newspaper which owns a local television station or for the only newspaper in town. In at least 12 cities, a reporter or editor for a newspaper-owned television station used to

Table 12. Crosstabulation of Cross-Ownership by Cross-Employment[a]

	T.V. station owned by newspaper	T.V. station not owned by newspaper
News staffer(s) worked for local newspaper which owns local T.V. station or for only newspaper in town	12 (27.9%)	7 (11.7%)
No news staffer(s) worked for local newspaper which owns local T.V. station or for only newspaper in town	31 (72.1%)	53 (88.3%)
	43 (100.0%)	60 (100.0%)

[a] N = 103.

work for the newspaper which owns the television station. Among these cities are Rochester, New York, Norfolk, Virginia, Dallas, Texas, and Fresno, California.[23]

The high number of job transfers from a newspaper to a television station owned by the same company appears to be largely attributable to corporate practices permitting the retention of benefits when a person transfers from one branch of the company to another. While newspaper reporters may have an easier time getting hired at television stations owned by the same company, the more important factor seems to be that television stations have an easier time recruiting newspaper reporters if they work for the same company.

---

[23] The identity of the other eight cities cannot be divulged, due to a promise of confidentiality.

According to persons who have switched from print journalism to broadcast journalism while staying within the same company, their transition was sweetened by the cross-ownership factor. Most "switchers" were able to retain their pension benefits and medical benefits. Some were also able to retain vacation benefits and seniority privileges. In very large cities, such monetary inducements may matter very little, because the salaries of television news staffers tend to be extremely high in the nation's largest cities. In most cities, however, the salaries of television news staffers are low enough that newspaper reporters and editors have to think twice before changing jobs, especially if they have years of experience.

Howard Hosmer, now retired, made the transition from print journalism to broadcast journalism after 27 years with the Rochester Times-Union. Hosmer, who left the Times-Union to become news director of WHEC-TV, which is owned by the same company, says he would never have accepted the television job had it meant throwing his years of service down the drain. Hosmer, who was trying to raise four children and make mortgage payments on a large house when he left the newspaper, believes that someone in such circumstances "would be crazy" to "change horses" otherwise. "You have to think of the eternal verities of existence," Hosmer says. "Where will I be when I'm 70?"

By increasing cross-employment, cross-ownership increases cooperation between newspaper and television news staffs. There are several reasons for this. First of all, most of those who leave a newspaper for a television station in the same city maintain their friendships with newspaper people to some extent. Mike Hartman, who worked for the Fresno Bee for six years before joining KMJ-TV, says he has "a lot of close friends at the Bee." Mike Power, who worked for the Rochester Democrat & Chronicle for two years before joining WHEC-TV, has friends at the Democrat & Chronicle as well as at the Rochester Times-Union. Since the two newspapers have adjacent newsrooms, Power got to know some reporters for both newspapers well. These friendships encourage the sharing of information.

Cross-employment also promotes cooperation, because newspaper reporters have greater respect for television reporters with newspaper experience than for those lacking such experience. Even newspaper reporters who regard most television reporters with disdain often single out television reporters with newspaper experience for special praise. A Fresno Bee reporter refers to KMJ reporter Hartman as "the most knowledgeable television reporter around." A Rochester Times-Union reporter speaks highly of WHEC reporter Power while dismissing other television reporters as ignorant. "Most of the others don't know what's going on," he says. These attitudes encourage contacts between newspaper reporters and the ex-newspaper reporters they respect.

In fact, it may be that "once a newspaper reporter, always a newspaper reporter." Trained as a print journalist, a person who switches to broadcast journalism is likely to retain the instincts he developed earlier. He may still define newsworthiness the same way, rely on the same sources, and work the same beat when he can. As a result, he tends to interact more with newspaper reporters, because he looks for news where they also look for it.

News Organization Location

Another factor which promotes cooperation between news staffs is the location of a newspaper and a television station within the same building or complex of buildings. Overall, 8.3% of newspaper-owned television stations are located within the same complex of buildings as a newspaper, in contrast to 0.9% of television stations not owned by a newspaper (see Table 13). In four cities--Cedar Rapids, Iowa,

Table 13. Crosstabulation of Cross-Ownership by News Organization Location[a]

	T.V. station owned by newspaper	T.V. station not owned by newspaper
Located within same complex of buildings as a newspaper	6 (8.3%)	1 (0.9%)
Not located within same complex of buildings as a newspaper	66 (91.7%)	110 (99.1%)
	72 (100.0%)	111 (100.0%)

[a] $N = 183$.

Paducah, Kentucky, Portland, Maine, and New York, New York--a jointly owned newspaper and television station are located within the same building. In two other cities--Dallas, Texas, and Norfolk, Virginia--a jointly owned newspaper and television station are located within the same complex of buildings. Whether management intended it or not, the location of a newspaper and a television station within the same building or complex of buildings increases interaction between news staffs. Interaction, in turn, begets cooperation.

Of course, there is only so much cooperation which can take place between reporters riding the same elevator or using the same revolving doors. Consequently, the building factor is important not so much because it increases chance encounters as because it makes planned encounters less of a bother. In Portland, Maine, where WGAN and the city's two newspapers are only an elevator ride away, WGAN's news director, Mike Craig, sometimes visits the Express and Press Herald newsroom to chat with reporters there about city affairs. On other occasions, WGAN reporter Dave Silverbrand stops by the newsroom to ask one of the city hall reporters a few questions about the city budget or other matters. Now and then, Silverbrand gets a tip this way. "They (the newspaper people) will say there's a story coming up which they think I should cover," Silverbrand says.

Chance and planned encounters are both increased when newspaper and television reporters share not only the same roof but the same cafeteria as well, as they do in Portland. While use of the cafeteria varies from person to person (and from waistline to waistline), Max Wiesenthal, telegraph editor of the Portland Express, eats lunch daily with WGAN people at the cafeteria. In Dallas, Texas, where the Dallas Morning News and WFAA-TV are separated only by a parking lot, WFAA employees have access to the newspaper's cafeteria, since the Dallas Morning News and WFAA are owned by the same company. The cafeteria's location facilitates contacts between WFAA-TV news director Marty Haag and two old friends at the Dallas Morning News, where Haag once worked. In Fresno, KMJ reporters often dined at the Bee's cafeteria, when it was located across the street. Although the Bee's cafeteria is now over a mile away from KMJ, some KMJ reporters still eat there occasionally. The Bee cafeteria provides good, cheap food (with three grinning, dancing bees emblazoned on each napkin), and Bee reporters sometimes provide a tip.

If hunger prompts some television reporters to visit a newspaper, the thirst for knowledge motivates others. With longer histories and more detailed stories than television stations, newspaper libraries or "morgues" contain valuable reference material. While most librarians at newspapers which own a local television station say their files are available for use by all reporters, they also say that reporters from the newspaper-owned television station use the files more often than other television reporters do. In Dallas, the Morning News has an excellent library, which WFAA reporters use regularly. According to head librarian Frances Barger, "WFAA people use our facilities daily--at least." In contrast, Barger says, other television reporters rarely use the facilities. The difference may be due to the fact that WFAA is only a hop, a skip, and a jump away from the Morning News, whereas other television stations are more distant. In Norfolk, a similar situation exists. The Virginian-Pilot and the Ledger-Star, which own WTAR-TV, have a library used more often by WTAR reporters than by other television reporters. Here, too, the main factor seems to be that WTAR is located within the same complex of buildings as the two newspapers, in contrast to the other television stations, which are further away. Another factor, however, may be that WTAR reporters find the library's welcome mat more visible than other television reporters do. Head librarian Bess Whitworth says that WTAR reporters are free to walk in and use the library's facilities, while other television reporters have to get permission first.

Equipped with better libraries than television stations, newspapers also have a more impressive collection of photographs. The New

York Daily News, which owns WPIX-TV, may well have a better collection of photographs than any newspaper in the world. Until April 1975, WPIX, which is located in the same building as the Daily News, paid the Daily News a nominal fee of $25 per week in return for access to the newspaper's photograph collection. No other New York television station had such an arrangement with the Daily News. Informed of this, Michael O'Neill, then executive editor of the Daily News, instructed an aide to see to it that WPIX pays "as much as anybody else" for Daily News photographs. In other cities, television stations owned by a newspaper have access to the newspaper's photographs free of charge. Theoretically, so do other television stations, but they rarely request photographs from a newspaper which owns another television station. In general, television stations owned by a newspaper are more likely to borrow newspaper photographs if the two news organizations are located within the same building or complex of buildings.

The sharing of photographs, use of the same library, and use of the same cafeteria are all more likely when a newspaper and a television station are close at hand. There is nothing sinister about these practices themselves. Nor is there anything diabolical about a corporate decision to house a newspaper and a television station in the same building or complex of buildings. However, such a corporate decision does bring newspaper and television news staffs closer together in ways that are difficult to control. Furthermore, the symbolism of sharing the same roof or the same parking lot serves to remind newspaper and television reporters that they work for the same company and that one news organization's gain is not necessarily the other news organization's loss. Not surprisingly, then, the location of a newspaper and a television station within the same building or complex of buildings results in increased cooperation between newspaper and television news staffs.

Conclusion

The joint ownership of a newspaper and a television station in the same city increases cooperation between newspaper and television news staffs. It does so through at least three mechanisms--the sharing of carbons, cross-employment, and news organization location. The sharing of carbons, as a matter of corporate policy, is an institutionalized form of cooperation. Moreover, the practice of sharing carbons may be interpreted by reporters as a signal that the parent company encourages fraternization between newspaper and television reporters. A television station's decision to hire a local newspaper reporter or editor who works for the same company may not be designed to encourage cooperation between newspaper and television news staffs, but it has this effect. A corporate decision to locate a newspaper and television station within the same building or complex of buildings may not be designed to encourage cooperation between newspaper and television news staffs, but it also has this effect.

Cooperation between newspaper and television reporters is not easily criticized. Viewed at close range, it appears innocent enough. Those who seek help are often motivated by humility, curiosity, or a commitment to the public interest. Those who give help are often motivated by compassion, friendliness, or a commitment to the public interest. Undoubtedly, some cooperation is in the public interest. When one reporter helps another to get his facts straight, the public is being well served. When one reporter alerts another to a story he cannot pursue himself or to a story his news organization has suppressed, the public is being well served.

Nevertheless, cooperation, like so many other things, is a vice if carried too far. When reporters cover the same stories not because they are worth covering but because reporters have tipped one another in advance (whether through carbons or word of mouth), the public is not being well served. When reporters define newsworthiness the same way merely because they have forged a consensus among themselves, the public is not being well served. Through specific acts of cooperation, reporters may help one another to earn a living and may create a pleasant working environment for one another. However, these same acts of cooperation may have a homogenizing effect on the news which the public receives. It is for this reason that cooperation between newspaper and television reporters can be so dangerous in a democratic society which depends on public exposure to diverse information, priorities, and opinions.

V

EFFECTS OF CROSS-MEDIA OWNERSHIP ON STORY OVERLAP

Effects of cross-media ownership on intermedia relations variables have policy significance only if the intermedia relations variables in turn have effects on news content. Newspaper-owned television stations are indeed more likely than comparable television stations to receive newspaper carbons on an exclusive basis. Also, newspaper-owned television stations are more likely than comparable television stations to have hired a person who worked for the newspaper which owns the television station or for the only newspaper in town. Finally, newspaper-owned television stations are more likely than comparable television stations to be located within the same complex of buildings as a newspaper. While these effects are suggestive, they do not in themselves prove that cross-ownership increases story overlap.[1]

Although carbon-sharing, cross-employment, and location within the same complex of buildings all increase cooperation between news staffs, they are not the only factors which determine the level of cooperation between news staffs. Furthermore, cooperation is not the only determinant of story overlap, and other factors may have more powerful countervailing effects. As the Rand Corporation put it,

---

[1] Story overlap has been defined as the proportion of a television station's state and local news stories also appearing in a particular newspaper on either the same day, the previous day, or the following day.

"Measuring the impact of media ownership may be like measuring the strength of a ripple amidst much larger waves."[2] Another possibility is that cross-ownership influences story overlap but through variables which have not been identified. If so, effects of cross-ownership can be measured but cannot be satisfactorily explained. For these reasons, it is important to test whether cross-ownership has effects on story overlap through the three related variables which have been identified--carbon-sharing, cross-employment (from a newspaper to a television station), and location within the same complex of buildings.

One way to measure the effects of a cross-ownership-related variable (such as carbon-sharing) is to compare jointly owned media characterized by that variable with separately owned media in the same city which are not characterized by that variable, for all jointly owned media which are characterized by that variable. Although this approach does not permit sophisticated quantitative estimates of the effects of each cross-ownership-related variable (controlling for other cross-ownership-related variables) or of the overall effects of cross-ownership, it can be a useful adjunct to comparisons across cities. First of all, comparisons within cities allow the use of data in a relatively raw form to test whether each cross-ownership-related variable has effects on story overlap. Provided that comparisons between jointly owned and separately owned newspaper-television pairs involve the same newspaper, no control for the number of newspaper stories is required. Also, the "slice" of a newscast analyzed can often be larger

---

[2] Walter Baer, Henry Geller, Joseph Grundfest, and Karen Possner, "Concentration of Mass Media Ownership: Assessing the State of Current Knowledge," <u>Rand Corporation Report</u> (Santa Monica, California: September 1974), p. 143.

when comparisons are made within cities than when comparisons are made across cities.[3] Second, comparisons within cities, when aggregated, capture the range of differences in story overlap between jointly owned and separately owned newspaper-television pairs in the same city. Perhaps cross-ownership makes a big difference in some cities, no difference in others. If so, comparisons within cities can place measures of the overall effects of cross-ownership in perspective. Finally, comparisons within cities permit an investigation of the effects of uncommon relationships between news organizations--specifically, relationships which are unique among the 48 newspaper-television pairs in the sample. For example, extensive telephone communication between jointly owned media in Quincy, Illinois cannot be examined in the context of a multiple regression equation, because it is a characteristic of only one newspaper-television pair in the sample. However, a rough estimate of the effects of extensive telephone communication can be obtained by making comparisons within Quincy itself. Thus, while comparisons within cities lack the quantitative sophistication of comparisons across cities, they can serve several important purposes.

Within-City Story Overlap Comparisons
Involving Jointly Owned Media
Which Share Carbons

In all three cities in the sample where a jointly owned newspaper and television station share carbons, story overlap between the

---

[3] Since story overlap scores tend to decline as the slice of a newsnewscast analyzed gets larger, only the first ten stories per newscast (the lowest common denominator) can be analyzed when comparisons are made across cities, to control for this effect. However, when comparisons are made within a city, the number of stories per newscast included in the analysis need be no lower than the average number of stories per newscast of the television station with the lowest average in that city.

jointly owned media is higher than story overlap between separately owned media within the same city (see Table 14). In Portland, Maine,

Table 14. Story Overlap Comparisons Involving Jointly Owned Media Which Share Carbons

City	Overlap Score, Jointly Owned Media	Overlap Score, Separately Owned Media	Overlap Score of Jointly Owned Media Minus Overlap Score of Separately Owned Media
Portland, Maine	WGAN-TV Express .420	WCSH-TV Express .238	+.182[a]
	WGAN-TV Press-Herald .533	WCSH-TV Press-Herald .452	+.081
Quincy, Illinois	WGEM-TV Herald-Whig .537	KHQA-TV Herald-Whig .434	+.103[b]
Rock Island-Moline, Illinois	WHBF-TV Argus .605	WQAD-TV Argus .538	+.067

Note: The overlap scores have been left in as raw a form as possible and do not include controls for the average number of state and local news stories per newspaper (these are unnecessary when comparisons involve the same newspaper). The number of stories per newscast analyzed in each city is the average number of stories per newscast of the television station with the lowest average number of stories per newscast in that city.

[a] $p < .002$.

[b] $p < .02$.

overlap between the jointly owned Express and WGAN-TV (.420) exceeds overlap between the separately owned Express and WCSH-TV (.238) by .182.[4] Overlap between the Press-Herald and WGAN-TV (jointly owned) exceeds overlap between the Press-Herald and WCSH-TV (separately owned) by .081. The fact that WGAN (the newspaper-owned station) has access to Express and Press-Herald carbons, while WCSH does not, helps to explain why Portland's jointly owned media have more homogenous news outputs than the city's separately owned media. Also, WGAN and the two newspapers are located within the same building, which facilitates interaction between the news staffs of the two newspapers and WGAN.

As Table 14 indicates, the gap between WGAN-Express overlap and WCSH-Express overlap (.420 - .238 = .182) is greater than the gap between WGAN-Press-Herald overlap and WCSH-Press-Herald overlap (.533 - .452 = .081). This may be due in part to the fact that the Express is published in the afternoon, while the Press-Herald is published in the morning. Because the Express is an afternoon newspaper, Express carbons are available considerably earlier in the day than Press-Herald carbons. In fact, all Express copy must be submitted by 11:35 a.m., whereas Press-Herald copy is due much later. Although WGAN people pick up Press-Herald carbons more regularly than Express carbons, Express carbons are more likely to be picked up early enough to be incorporated into WGAN's early evening newscast, and it is this newscast which is included in the data base. Thus, while there is more overlap between WGAN's 6 p.m. newscast and the Press-Herald, such overlap may be less

---

[4] In other words, 42.0% of WGAN's state and local news stories also appeared in the Express on the same day, the previous day, or the following day. In contrast, only 23.8% of WCSH's state and local news stories also appeared in the Express on the same day, the previous day, or the following day.

influenced by the carbon-sharing arrangement than overlap between WGAN's 6 p.m. newscast and the Express. Another possibility is that the cross-employment variable is having an effect. The wire editor for the Express, Max Wiesentahl, used to work for WGAN, and he chats regularly with WGAN reporters over lunch. As a result, Wiesenthal and WGAN reporters exchange more information than would otherwise be the case. In contrast, no Press-Herald reporter or editor has worked for WGAN. Indeed, one Press-Herald reporter worked for WCSH for three years, and he occasionally huddles with his former boss at WCSH to discuss their common hobby--collecting rare books. Even if they do not trade tips, it is possible that they pay closer attention to one another's news outputs because they have worked together--a factor which could increase story overlap between the two news organizations. Thus, the cross-employment variable may widen the gap between WGAN-Express overlap and WCSH-Express overlap, while reducing the gap between WGAN-Press-Herald overlap and WCSH-Press-Herald overlap.

In Quincy, Illinois, overlap between WGEM-TV and the Herald-Whig (jointly owned) exceeds overlap between KHQA-TV and the Herald-Whig (separately owned) by .103.[5] Although the vestiges of a carbon-sharing arrangement remain (the Herald-Whig still furnishes a very small number of carbons to WGEM), this factor probably has a minimal impact on story overlap between WGEM and the Herald-Whig. The more important factor

---

[5]Although KHQA-TV operates primarily out of a Quincy studio, KHQA is licensed to Hannibal, Missouri, just across the river from Quincy. Whereas WGEM only has a Quincy studio, KHQA has a studio in Hannibal as well. To control for KHQA's Hannibal studio, we have excluded Hannibal stories from the analysis in computing story overlap scores involving KHQA, WGEM, and the Herald-Whig.

appears to be the extensive telephone contacts which take place between members of the WGEM and Herald-Whig news staffs. These frequent telephone contacts often take the form of a fishing expedition. A WGEM reporter says he calls up the Herald-Whig and asks, "What's going on?" Another WGEM reporter says the Herald-Whig's state editor calls up WGEM and asks, "You got anything?" The cumulative effect of these daily phone calls is to increase the extent to which WGEM and the Herald-Whig cover the same stories.

In the Quad Cities, overlap between WHBF-TV and the Argus (jointly owned) exceeds overlap between WGAD-TV and the Argus (separately owned) by .067.[6] The carbon-sharing arrangement in Rock Island is highly systematic, and WHBF receives Argus carbons on at least three separate occasions during the day. The arrangement is also reciprocal, inasmuch as WHBF radio furnishes some rewrites of WHBF television

---

[6] The Quad Cities include Rock Island, Illinois, Moline, Illinois, Davenport, Iowa, and Bettendorf, Iowa. In Rock Island, there is one daily newspaper (the Argus) and one commercial television station (WHBF-TV). In adjacent Moline, there is one daily (the Dispatch) and one commercial television station (WQAD-TV). It was originally anticipated that overlap between the Rock Island Argus and WHBF would be compared with overlap between the Moline Dispatch and WQAD. Since WQAD is licensed to Moline, it was expected that WQAD would cover more Moline stories than WHBF and that these stories would be less likely than other WQAD stories to be covered by the Argus. As expected, WQAD covers more Moline stories than WHBF. Surprisingly, however, WQAD's Moline stories are more likely to be covered by the Argus than other stories covered by WQAD. Also, overlap between WQAD and the Argus is substantially higher than overlap between WQAD and the Dispatch. This phenomenon is made possible by a highly unorthodox arrangement between the separately owned Argus and Dispatch. The Moline Dispatch furnishes Moline carbons to the Rock Island Argus (in return for Rock Island carbons), thereby enabling the Argus to cover Moline stories without sending a reporter to Moline. Due to this arrangement, the use of WQAD-Argus overlap (rather than WQAD-Dispatch overlap) as a control for WHBF-Argus overlap actually has the effect of posing a harsher test on the hypothesis that cross-ownership has a homogenizing effect on the news outputs of Rock Island's jointly owned media.

stories to the Argus every day. Another factor which helps to explain the high story overlap between WHBF and the Argus is that a member of WHBF's staff used to work for the Argus.[7] The gap between WHBF-Argus overlap and WQAD-Argus overlap might be even greater, were it not for the fact that WQAD's assistant news director, Dick Griffin, is the son-in-law of Argus political reporter, John Michaletti. These bonds of kinship strengthen ties between the two separately owned news organizations (at least between Griffin and Michaletti) and may be partially responsible for the relatively high story overlap between WQAD and the Argus.

Within-City Story Overlap Comparisons Involving Jointly Owned Media Characterized by Cross-Employment (From the Newspaper to the Television Station)

There are five cities in the sample where a reporter or editor for a newspaper-owned television station used to work for the newspaper which owns the television station. In four of the five cities, story overlap between the jointly owned media characterized by cross-employment (from the newspaper to the television station) exceeds story overlap between separately owned media within the same city (see Table 15). The Rock Island case has already been discussed. In Fresno, California, overlap between the Bee and KMJ-TV (jointly owned) exceeds overlap between the Bee and KJEO-TV (separately owned) by .141; overlap between the Bee and KMJ exceeds overlap between the Bee and KFSN-TV (separately owned) by .060. In the case of the Bee and KMJ, cross-employment is reciprocal: KMJ reporter Mike Hartman used to work for the Bee, and Bee reporter Lanny Larson used to work for KMJ. Hartman, who worked

---

[7]Since the time period for which data were obtained, that person has assumed other responsibilities at WHBF.

Table 15. Story Overlap Comparisons Involving Jointly Owned Media Characterized by Cross-Employment (From the Newspaper to the Television Station)

City	Overlap Score, Jointly Owned Media	Overlap Score, Separately Owned Media	Overlap Score of Jointly Owned Media Minus Overlap Score of Separately Owned Media
Fresno, California	KMJ-TV Bee .438	KJEO-TV Bee .297	+.141[a]
	KMJ-TV Bee .438	KFSN-TV Bee .378	+.060
Dallas, Texas	WFAA-TV Morning News .558	KXAS-TV Morning News .487	+.071
Rock Island-Moline, Illinois	WHBF-TV Argus .605	WQAD-TV Argus .538	+.067
Rochester, New York	WHEC-TV Democrat & Chronicle .441	WROC-TV Democrat & Chronicle .350	+.091
	WHEC-TV Democrat & Chronicle .441	WOKR-TV Democrat & Chronicle .414	+.027

Table 15. Continued

City	Overlap Score, Jointly Owned Media	Overlap Score, Separately Owned Media	Overlap Score of Jointly Owned Media Minus Overlap Score of Separately Owned Media
Norfolk, Virginia	WTAR-TV Virginian-Pilot .469	WVEC-TV Virginian-Pilot .462	+.007
	WTAR-TV Virginian-Pilot .469	WAVY-TV Virginian-Pilot .532	-.063

Note: The overlap scores have been left in as raw a form as possible and do not include controls for the average number of state and local news stories per newspaper (these are unnecessary when comparisons involve the same newspaper). The number of stories per newscast analyzed in each city is the average number of stories per newscast of the television station with the lowest average number of stories per newscast in that city.

[a] $p < .01$.

six years for the Bee, has maintained his friendships there. "I have a lot of close friends at the Bee," he says. "I get together with various people for drinks. The conversation is always a lot about news." These informal contacts contribute to story overlap, as reporters trade tips and reach a consensus about what is newsworthy and what is not. Obviously, however, the cross-employment factor does not explain why the gap between KMJ-Bee overlap and KJEO-Bee overlap (.438 - .297 = .141) is greater than the gap between KMJ-Bee overlap and KFSN-Bee overlap (.438 - .378 = .060). One possible reason for this difference is that most Bee reporters rate KJEO's newscasts as "poor," while they have a more favorable view of KMJ and KFSN. Lacking respect for KJEO's news staff, Bee reporters are unlikely to watch KJEO's newscasts often enough to glean story ideas from KJEO; they are also unlikely to associate much with KJEO reporters whom they encounter on assignment. Thus, the low regard which Bee reporters have for KJEO's newscasts helps to account for the low story overlap between KJEO and the Bee.

In Dallas, Texas, overlap between WFAA-TV and the Morning News (jointly owned) exceeds overlap between KXAS-TV and the Morning News (separately owned) by .071.[8] Several factors may be responsible for this difference. First of all, WFAA-TV news director Marty Haag used to work for the Morning News. Although Haag left the newspaper over 15 years ago, he still has friends there, including city editor Bob Miller and assistant city editor Bob Compton. Haag occasionally gets together with Miller and Compton for coffee, to renew old ties. More importantly, Miller monitors WFAA's early evening newscast every night. "I watch WFAA only," Miller says. This preference for WFAA may be due in large measure to the respect Miller has for Haag--respect which, in turn, may be due to the fact that the two men worked together. Whatever the origins of the sentiment, the city editor of the Morning News watches WFAA's newscasts to the exclusion of other newscasts in the market. Insofar as Miller gleans story ideas

---

[8] Although KXAS-TV has a studio in Dallas, KXAS also has a studio in nearby Fort Worth (its city of license), and KXAS is slightly more likely than WFAA to run Fort Worth stories. However, KXAS's Fort Worth stories are no less likely than its other stories to overlap with the Morning News. Consequently, it is not necessary to exclude Fort Worth stories from consideration, when comparing WFAA-Morning News overlap with KXAS-Morning News overlap.

from WFAA's newscasts, overlap between WFAA and the Morning News is increased. A final factor in Dallas is that WFAA and the Morning News are located within the same complex of buildings (separated only by a parking lot). This facilitates interaction between the two news staffs, which is likely to increase story overlap.

In Rochester, New York, overlap between WHEC-TV and the Democrat & Chronicle (jointly owned) exceeds overlap between WROC-TV and the Democrat & Chronicle (separately owned) by .091; overlap between WHEC and the Democrat & Chronicle exceeds overlap between WOKR-TV and the Democrat & Chronicle (separately owned) by .027. Here, as in Fresno and Dallas, cross-employment appears to contribute to story overlap. WHEC reporter Mike Power, who used to work for the Democrat & Chronicle, is widely known and respected by Democrat & Chronicle reporters. Power confirms that he runs into Rochester newspaper reporters--some of whom are old friends--"at a saloon or while covering a story." Although Power says he does not divulge information he has "dug loose" through hard work, he readily exchanges "background information" with newspaper reporters. Such cooperation may increase the extent to which WHEC and the Democrat & Chronicle cover the same stories.

Cross-employment, of course, does not explain why the gap between WHEC-Democrat & Chronicle overlap and WROC-Democrat & Chronicle overlap (.441 - .350 = .091) is greater than the gap between WHEC-Democrat & Chronicle overlap and WOKR-Democrat & Chronicle overlap (.441 - .414 = .027). This difference may be due to the animosity which some WROC news staffers perceived as existing between Rochester's two newspapers (owned by the Gannett Company) and WROC (in competition with the Gannett station, WHEC) during the time period under investigation. WROC's newscasts, which had led the pack in previous years, slipped badly in the ratings during 1974 and fell behind both WHEC and WOKR. Some WROC news staffers pinned the blame for this slump on attacks by Gannett Company entertainment writers, including Tom Green, then television critic for the Democrat & Chronicle. Denying charges that he was out to get WROC, Green attributed WROC's misfortunes to drastic changes in format and ill-advised choices of personnel. However, WROC's assistant news director, Tom Ryan, expressed suspicion at the Gannett newspapers' motives for "singling out" WROC for criticism. "It's a very subtle way of increasing viewership for their television station," Ryan argued. In retaliation for what was perceived as excessive criticism, WROC ran an editorial early in April 1975 which criticized the Gannett Company and its two Rochester newspapers. One WROC reporter summed up the situation this way: "We're at war with the Gannett Company." In such an atmosphere, it is not surprising that story overlap between WROC and the Democrat & Chronicle was lower than story overlap between WHEC and the Democrat & Chronicle.

In Virginia's Tidewater area, where cross-employment also exists, the results of story overlap comparisons are mixed. Although overlap between WTAR-TV and the Virginian-Pilot (jointly owned) exceeds overlap between WVEC-TV and the Virginian-Pilot (separately owned) by .007, overlap between WTAR and the Virginian-Pilot is actually lower than overlap between WAVY-TV and the Virginian-Pilot (separately owned). As Table 15 indicates, overlap between the separately owned WAVY and the Virginian-Pilot exceeds overlap between the jointly owned WTAR and the

Virginian-Pilot by .063.[9] These figures are surprising, since three WTAR news staffers (the news director, the assignment editor, and a reporter) used to work for the Virginian-Pilot. Also, WTAR and the Virginian-Pilot are located within the same complex of buildings. Furthermore, the Virginian-Pilot's city editor and metropolitan editor monitor WTAR's early evening newscast every night. All these factors are likely to increase story overlap, but the fact remains that overlap between WAVY and the Virginian-Pilot is higher than overlap between the Virginian-Pilot and the television station it owns. The most probable explanation for this is that WAVY covers an inordinately high number of "stale" news stories--i.e., stories which have already been covered by one or both of the Norfolk newspapers.[10]

The Norfolk situation illustrates one of the weaknesses of within-city comparisons. Effects of cross-ownership and related variables in a particular city may look smaller or larger than they actually are if story overlap between separately owned media is abnormally high or low. In Fresno, story overlap between separately owned media is very low. In Norfolk, on the other hand, story overlap between separately

---

[9] There are three commercial television stations in Virginia's Tidewater area: WTAR (licensed to Norfolk), WAVY (licensed to Portsmouth), and WVEC (licensed to Hampton). Since WAVY is no more likely than WTAR to run Portsmouth stories, it is not necessary to exclude Portsmouth stories from the analysis. However, WVEC is more likely than WTAR to run Hampton and Newport News (peninsula) stories, and WVEC's peninsula stories are less likely than its other stories to be covered by Norfolk's newspapers. Consequently, it is necessary to exclude peninsula stories but not Portsmouth stories from the analysis, when comparisons are made involving WTAR, WAVY, and WVEC.

[10] If stale news is defined as the percentage of a television station's news stories which have already been covered by one or more local newspapers, then WAVY covers more stale news than any other television station in the sample.

owned media is very high. Consequently, within-city comparisons may make the effects of cross-employment in Fresno look greater than they actually are, while failing to capture the effects of cross-employment and news organization location in Norfolk.

Within-City Story Overlap Comparisons Involving Jointly Owned Media Located Within the Same Complex of Buildings

There are four cities in the sample where a jointly owned newspaper and television station are located within the same building or complex of buildings. In two of the four cities (Portland, Maine and Dallas, Texas), story overlap between the jointly owned media is greater than story overlap between the separately owned media. In the other two cities (Norfolk, Virginia and New York, New York), the results are mixed (see Table 16). The situations in Portland, Dallas, and Norfolk

Table 16. Story Overlap Comparisons Involving Jointly Owned Media Located Within the Same Complex of Buildings

City	Overlap Score, Jointly Owned Media	Overlap Score, Separately Owned Media	Overlap Score of Jointly Owned Media Minus Overlap Score of Separately Owned Media
Portland, Maine	WGAN-TV Express .420	WCSH-TV Express .238	+.182[a]
	WGAN-TV Press-Herald .533	WCSH-TV Press-Herald .452	+.081

Table 16. Continued

City	Overlap Score, Jointly Owned Media	Overlap Score, Separately Owned Media	Overlap Score of Jointly Owned Media Minus Overlap Score of Separately Owned Media
Dallas, Texas	WFAA-TV Morning News .558	KXAS-TV Morning News .487	+.071
New York, New York	WPIX-TV Daily News .406	WNEW-TV Daily News .318	+.088
	WPIX-TV Daily News .406	WABC-TV Daily News .429	−.023
Norfolk, Virginia	WTAR-TV Ledger-Star .615	WVEC-TV Ledger-Star .522	+.093
Norfolk, Virginia	WTAR-TV Ledger-Star .615	WAVY-TV Ledger-Star .662	−.047
	WTAR-TV Virginian-Pilot .469	WVEC-TV Virginian-Pilot .462	+.007
	WTAR-TV Virginian-Pilot .469	WAVY-TV Virginian-Pilot .532	−.063

Note: The overlap scores have been left in as raw a form as possible and do not include controls for the average number of state and local news stories per newspaper (these are unnecessary when comparisons involve the same newspaper). The number of stories per newscast

Table 16. Continued

analyzed in each city is the average number of stories per newscast of the television station with the lowest average number of stories per newscast in that city.

[a] $p < .002$.

have already been mentioned. In Portland, where WGAN and the city's two newspapers are located within the same building, newspaper and television reporters use the same cafeteria and the same library. Also, WGAN news staffers drop by the newspapers' newsroom from time to time, to pick up carbons, trade tips, or exchange background information. In Dallas, WFAA and the Morning News are separated only by a parking lot. Here, too, newspaper and television reporters run into one another in the cafeteria, library, or parking lot which they use in common. The cumulative effect of such contacts in Dallas, as in Portland, is to increase story overlap between the jointly owned media.

In the Norfolk area, the results of within-city story overlap comparisons are mixed, despite clear evidence that there is more cooperation between Norfolk's two newspapers and the television station they own than between the newspapers and other television stations in the market. Overlap between WTAR-TV and the Ledger-Star (jointly owned) exceeds overlap between WVEC-TV and the Ledger-Star (separately owned) by .093, but overlap between WAVY-TV and the Ledger-Star (separately owned) exceeds overlap between WTAR and the Ledger-Star by .047. As has been mentioned, overlap between WTAR and the Virginian-Pilot (jointly owned) exceeds overlap between WVEC and the Virginian-Pilot (separately owned) by .007, but overlap between WAVY and the Virginian-

Pilot (separately owned) exceeds overlap between WTAR and the Virginian-Pilot (jointly owned) by .063. Located within the same complex of buildings, the two Norfolk newspapers and the television station they own are within easy walking distance of one another. This facilitates contacts of all sorts, including chance encounters at such nearby restaurants as Angelo's and the Dutch Kitchen. Nevertheless, while the location of jointly owned media within the same complex of buildings may have a homogenizing effect in Norfolk, within-city story overlap comparisons do not capture that effect.

In New York, New York, where the Daily News and WPIX-TV are located within the same building, results of within-city comparisons are also mixed. Overlap between the Daily News and WPIX-TV (jointly owned) exceeds overlap between the Daily News and WNEW-TV (separately owned) by .088, but overlap between the Daily News and WABC-TV (separately owned) exceeds overlap between the Daily News and WPIX by .023. These ambiguous figures coincide with ambiguous evidence concerning the level of cooperation which exists between the news staffs of the Daily News and WPIX. WPIX reporter Frank Casey, for example, says he has more contacts with Daily News reporters than with reporters for the New York Times or the New York Post--a phenomenon which Casey attributes to the fact that WPIX and the Daily News are housed in the same building. On the other hand, Casey can recall at least one instance where Daily News reporters refused to provide information he requested. Nick Loiacono, who "works the desk" for WPIX in the evening, says he telephones the Daily News more often than the Times or the Post when he needs help. However, the Daily News does not always cooperate. In fact, according to Loiacono, the Daily News "has a higher percentage of grouches" than the Times or the Post. Daily News night city editor Richard Blood may or may not be a grouch, but he does believe that WPIX should get its own stories. "We're beating the bushes," Blood argues. "Why should we let television have our story?"

An incident which occurred early in 1975 illustrates the paradoxical nature of the relationship between WPIX and the Daily News. At approximately 9 p.m. one night, a WPIX employee strolled into the newsroom of the Daily News and started asking questions about a New Jersey murder case. Daily News rewriteman Harry Stathos, who was working on the story, agreed to provide some details, in view of the corporate ties binding the Daily News and WPIX. "I was trying to be cooperative, because they (WPIX) are in the same family," Stathos explains. However, Stathos grew offended when he got the impression that the WPIX employee thought he had "a God-given right to our copy." As soon as city editor Blood saw what was happening, he unceremoniously ordered the WPIX employee out of the newsroom. According to Blood, the WPIX employee seemed miffed and threw his pencil across the room. "He left the room in an awful huff," Blood recalls. This incident illustrates the paradoxical nature of the relationship between WPIX and the Daily News. Since they work within the same building and are owned by the same company, employees of WPIX and the Daily News have more contacts than would otherwise be the case. However, cooperation between the two news organizations is circumscribed by the reluctance of many Daily News reporters and editors to provide WPIX with information which, in their opinion, WPIX should obtain on its own. The mixed results of story overlap comparisons within New York may reflect this paradox.

147

Within-City Story Overlap Comparisons Involving Jointly Owned Media Lacking Particular Ties

There are three cities in the sample where a jointly owned newspaper and television station do not share carbons, are not characterized by cross-employment (from a newspaper to a television station), and are not located within the same complex of buildings. In one of the three cities (Rochester, New York), the results are mixed, but the jointly owned pair's overlap score (.426) is higher than the average overlap score of the separately owned pairs (.382). In the other two cities (Sacramento, California and Dayton, Ohio), story overlap is higher for separately owned media than for jointly owned media (see Table 17). In

Table 17. Story Overlap Comparisons Involving Jointly Owned Media Lacking Particular Ties

City	Overlap Score, Jointly Owned Media	Overlap Score, Separately Owned Media	Overlap Score of Jointly Owned Media Minus Overlap Score of Separately Owned Media
Rochester, New York	WHEC-TV Times-Union .426	WROC-TV Times-Union .313	+.113[a]
	WHEC-TV Times-Union .426	WOKR-TV Times-Union .451	−.025
Dayton, Ohio	WHIO-TV Journal-Herlad .415	WLWD-TV Journal-Herald .445	−.030

Table 17. Continued

City	Overlap Score, Jointly Owned Media	Overlap Score, Separately Owned Media	Overlap Score of Jointly Owned Media Minus Overlap Score of Separately Owned Media
	WHIO-TV Daily News .353	WLWD-TV Daily News .452	-.099
Sacramento, California	KOVR-TV Bee .333	KXTV-TV Bee .375	-.042
	KOVR-TV Bee .333	KCRA-TV Bee .462	-.129[b]

Note: The overlap scores have been left in as raw a form as possible and do not include controls for the average number of state and local news stories per newspaper (these are unnecessary when comparisons involve the same newspaper). The number of stories per newscast analyzed in each city is the average number of stories per newscast of the television station with the lowest average number of stories per newscast in that city.

[a] $p < .01$.

[b] If direction is predicted in accordance with the hypothesis that cross-ownership has homogenizing effects, then this difference is not statistically significant at an acceptable level. However, if direction is predicted in the opposite direction of our hypothesis, then $p < .06$.

Rochester, overlap between WHEC-TV and the Times-Union (jointly owned) exceeds overlap between WROC-TV and the Times-Union (separately owned) by .113, while overlap between WOKR-TV and the Times-Union (separately owned) exceeds overlap between WHEC and the Times-Union by .025. The relatively low overlap between WROC and the Times-Union may reflect the viewpoint in vogue at WROC--namely, that WROC is locked in mortal combat with the Gannett Company's Rochester television station and two Rochester newspapers. Guided by this perception, WROC may glean fewer story ideas from the Times-Union than might otherwise be the case.

In Sacramento, where KOVR-TV is owned by the Bee, cross-ownership does not appear to have a homogenizing effect on the news outputs of KOVR and the Bee. Indeed, the news outputs of Sacramento's separately owned media are more homogenous than those of the city's jointly owned media. Overlap between KXTV-TV and the Bee (separately owned) exceeds overlap between KOVR and the Bee (jointly owned) by .042. Overlap between KCRA-TV and the Bee (separately owned) exceeds overlap between KOVR and the Bee by the even more substantial margin of .129.[11] It is not particularly surprising that overlap between KOVR and the Bee is no higher than overlap between KCRA and the Bee or between KXTV and the Bee. KOVR and the Bee do not share carbons, they are several miles apart, and no KOVR news staffer has worked for the Bee. The Bee's night city editor used to work for KOVR, but he did so in 1966, and for only one year. Turnover at KOVR has been so high that no member of KOVR's current news staff was also at KOVR in 1966. As a result, the night city editor's ties with KOVR have long since been snapped. These factors suggest that effects of cross-ownership should be negligible in Sacramento. However, they do not explain why overlap between KOVR and

---

[11]Although KOVR operates primarily out of a Sacramento studio, KOVR also has a studio in nearby Stockton (its city of license). KOVR covers more Stockton stories than either KCRA or KXTV, and KOVR's Stockton stories are considerably less likely than its other stories to be covered by the Bee. Consequently, it is necessary to exclude Stockton stories from the analysis, when comparisons are made involving KOVR, KCRA, and KXTV.

the Bee is so low or why overlap between KCRA and the Bee is so high.

One reason for the low overlap between KOVR and the Bee may be the poor quality which Bee reporters attribute to KOVR's newscasts. One Bee reporter calls KOVR's newscasts "absolutely abysmal." Another says KOVR's newscasts are "sometimes God-awful." Whatever the merits of these opinions, they make it unlikely that Bee reporters will watch KOVR often enough to get story ideas from KOVR's newscasts. In contrast, KCRA, which has the largest news staff of any television station in northern California, commands the respect of many Sacramento print reporters; to a lesser extent, this is also true of KXTV. When newspaper reporters respect a particular television station's news staff, this encourages them to watch that station more often and to cooperate more readily with the station's reporters.

In Dayton, as in Sacramento, relations between the jointly owned media are not close. Indeed, employees of the Journal-Herald, the Daily News, and WHIO-TV (all jointly owned) appear to have bent over backwards to avoid being accused of collusion. According to WHIO-TV reporter Bob Sweeney, there is "less cooperation than usual" between WHIO and Dayton's newspapers since there is "sort of a feeling of maintaining a distance because of group ownership." As evidence of that, overlap between WLWD and the Journal-Herald (separately owned) exceeds overlap between WHIO and the Journal-Herald (jointly owned) by .030. When Journal-Herald editor Charles Alexander resigned on March 24, 1975, WLWD-TV (not owned by the newspapers) actually broke the story before WHIO-TV (owned by the newspapers)--a symbol of the absence of special ties between WHIO and the Journal-Herald.

If there are no special ties between WHIO and the Journal-Herald, there are in fact special ties between WLWD and the Daily News, despite the corporate connection between WHIO and the Daily News. Since late 1974 or early 1975, the Daily News has sent a consumer reporter and an entertainment writer over to WLWD to do filmed reports twice a week, free of charge. The Daily News also collaborated with WLWD in producing "The Squeeze," an unusual newspaper-television project which examined the impact of inflation in Dayton. On the morning of April 13, 1975, the Daily News ran a special supplement in its Sunday newspaper, including detailed figures on the finances of three different Dayton families. That evening, WLWD-TV aired an hour-long program on the same three families and their attempts to cope with inflation. The inflation project promoted interaction between the Daily News and WLWD. Moreover, Daily News managing editor Arnold Rosenfeld and WLWD-TV news director Ed Hart expect to do something similar again.[12] Together with WLWD's routinized

---

[12] Reactions to the inflation project were mixed. Most enthusiastic were Rosenfeld (who conceived the idea of a newspaper-television venture) and Hart (who suggested that the venture focus on inflation). While reserving judgment on whether the newspaper and television efforts meshed, Rosenfeld found both efforts worthwhile. "Both projects were very good," Rosenfeld asserted. "Whether they mesh is unclear." Hart felt that the two projects "enhanced" one another and said he was "ecstatic" that the televised special on inflation commanded a sizeable audience (behind "Cher," ahead of "The Six Million Dollar Man" in the ratings). Others were less ecstatic, for different reasons. Daily News television editor Tom Hopkins found the television special superficial. Daily News art director Don Vanderbeek, who provided art graphics for both the Daily News and WLWD, complained that WLWD's decision-makers seemed to prefer cliches to creative ideas. According to Vanderbeek, WLWD people kept coming up with "hackneyed ideas" and he had to fight "battle after battle" to make any headway with them. Daily News reporter Ron Roat, who worked long and hard on the inflation project, was embittered by the experience. Although Roat had the impression that WLWD had pledged to work in tandem with the Daily News in interviewing members of the three families, he says he wound up doing the lion's share of the interviews by himself. "I was a one-man show for a couple months," Roat recalls. "I would never do it again."

"borrowing" of the two Daily News employees, contacts fostered by "The Squeeze" help account for the fact that overlap between the Daily News and WLWD exceeds overlap between the Daily News and WHIO by .099.

Lessons of Within-City Comparisons

In all three cities where the jointly owned media share carbons, there is greater story overlap between the jointly owned media than between the separately owned media. In four of the five cities where a news staffer for a newspaper-owned television station has worked for a newspaper which owns the television station, there is greater story overlap between the jointly owned media than between the separately owned media. In the fifth city, the results are mixed. In two of the four cities where a jointly owned newspaper and television station are located within the same complex of buildings, there is greater story overlap between the jointly owned media than between the separately owned media. In the other two cities, the results are mixed. In contrast are three cities where jointly owned media do not share carbons, are not characterized by cross-employment (from a newspaper to a television station), and are not located within the same complex of buildings. In two of three cities, there is less story overlap between the jointly owned media than between the separately owned media. In the third city, the results are mixed.

In cities where story overlap between separately owned media is abnormally high or low, within-city comparisons can be misleading. Nevertheless, within-city comparisons serve several important purposes. First, they suggest that cross-ownership increases story overlap by encouraging carbon-sharing, cross-employment (from a newspaper to a television station), and the location of a newspaper and a television station within the same complex of buildings. Second, they suggest that cross-ownership increases story overlap in at least one city (Quincy, Illinois) by encouraging daily exchanges of information over the telephone between newspaper and television reporters who work for the same company. Third, they suggest that cross-ownership has a substantial effect on story overlap between jointly owned media in some cities (such as Portland, Maine and Quincy, Illinois) but no effect in others (such as Dayton, Ohio and Sacramento, California).

Despite the utility of within-city comparisons, story overlap comparisons across cities offer several analytical opportunities which within-city comparisons do not. First, they permit generalizations about the overall effects of cross-ownership on story overlap. Second, they allow the separation of direct and indirect effects of cross-ownership on story overlap.[13] Third, they make possible an examination of the effects of different combinations of cross-ownership-related variables. Fourth, they permit a comparison of the overall explanatory power of cross-ownership-related variables with that of non-cross-ownership-related variables which might be expected to influence story overlap.

Overall Effects of Cross-Ownership on Story Overlap

Through a multiple regression analysis involving all 48 newspaper-television pairs within the same city included in the sample, the

---

[13] Direct effects are those which are not transmitted through other variables in the model. Indirect effects are those transmitted through the sharing of carbons, cross-employment (from a newspaper to a television station), or location within the same complex of buildings.

overall effects of cross-ownership on story overlap can be measured. Such a procedure requires a control for the log of television market size, since it is a variable which influences both the incidence of cross-ownership and the level of story overlap. As Table 18 indicates,

Table 18. Effects of Cross-Media Ownership on Story Overlap, Controlling for the Log of T.V. Market Size (Unweighted Sample)[a]

Variable	Standardized b	Unstandardized b[b]	F
Log of T.V. market size (LT)	-.159	-.012	1.31
Cross-media ownership (CM)	+.357	+.068	6.65[c]

Note: Story overlap (SO) = .568 - .012 LT + .068 CM, where 0 indicates the absence of cross-ownership and 1 indicates the presence of cross-ownership.

[a] $N = 48$.

[b] An unstandardized b measures the change in a dependent variable produced by a change of one unit in an independent variable, with other independent variables held constant.

[c] $p < .01$.

the standardized b for the regression of story overlap on cross-ownership, after controlling for the log of television market size, is .357.[14] Using unstandardized b's, we can estimate that if SO = story overlap, LT = the log of television market size, and CM = cross-media ownership, then SO = .568 - .012 LT + .068 CM, where 0 indicates the absence of cross-ownership and 1 indicates the presence of cross-

---

[14] $p < .01$.

ownership. Substituting the mean value of the log of television market size in the sample (13.34) for LT, we can further estimate that, in a market of average size, SO = .408 + .068 CM. In other words, the average overlap score for separately owned newspaper-television pairs in a market of average size is .408, while the average overlap score for jointly owned newspaper-television pairs in a market of average size is .408 + .068 (1) or .476.[15] In more concrete terms, this means that cross-media ownership increases story overlap by 16.7% over what it would otherwise be (.068/.408 = 16.7%).

One objection to the approach which has been employed might be that the regression equation designed to measure the effects of cross-ownership lacks a sufficient number of control variables. A Rand Corporation report, for example, has suggested that studies of the effects of cross-ownership need to control not only for market size but for television audience shares, newspaper circulation shares, and the number of competitors in the market as well.[16] Controls for television audience shares (in this case, news audience shares) and newspaper circulation shares can be applied, in accordance with the Rand Corporation's suggestion.[17] However, as a comparison of Table 18 and

---

[15] Put another way, an average of 40.8% of the stories of television stations not owned by a newspaper are covered by a newspaper in the same city with which the television station is being compared. In contrast, an average of 47.6% of the stories of newspaper-owned television stations are covered by a newspaper within the same city which owns the television station and with which the television station is being compared.

[16] Walter Baer et al., "Concentration of Mass Media Ownership: Assessing the State of Current Knowledge," <u>Rand Corporation Report</u> (Santa Monica, California: September 1974), p. 143.

[17] The television news audience share variable has been operationalized as an ordinal scale with integral values ranging from 0 to 5, since the sample includes no markets with more than six commercial

Table 19. Effects of Cross-Media Ownership on Story Overlap, Controlling for the Log of T.V. Market Size, T.V. News Audience Share and Newspaper Circulation Share (Unweighted Sample)[a]

Variable	Standardized b	Unstandardized b	F
Log of T.V. market size	−.146	−.011	0.82
T.V. news audience share	+.032	+.003	0.04
Newspaper circulation share	+.007	+.001	0.00
Cross-media ownership	+.353	+.067	6.01[b]

[a] N = 48.

[b] $p < .001$.

Table 19 indicates, the standardized b for cross-ownership does not change much when controls for television news audience shares and newspaper circulation shares are added to the control for the log of television market size. Without these two controls, the standardized b for cross-ownership is .357; with them, it is .353. The inclusion of controls for the number of newspapers and the number of television stations (with newscasts) in the market actually increases the standardized b for cross-ownership. However, controls for the number of competitors in the market seem ill-advised, because of high multicollinearity between the log of television market size, on the one hand, and variables

---

television stations airing newscasts. If a television station's early evening newscast had higher ratings than the newscast of any other television station in the market, it received a value of 5; if its newscast ranked second, it received a value of 4, etc. In the cases of WPIX-TV and WNEW-TV, which have no early evening newscasts, ratings for 10 p.m. newscasts were used. The newspaper circulation share variable has been operationalized as an ordinal scale with integral values ranging from 3 to 5, since the sample includes no markets with more than three dailies in the same city.

measuring the number of competitors in the market, on the other hand.[18]
Thus, only one of the controls suggested by the Rand Corporation--a
control for market size--is warranted.

Another objection to the findings which have been reported
might be that the sample of 48 newspaper-television pairs cannot be
used to draw inferences about the larger population. As mentioned
earlier, jointly owned media which share carbons were purposely over-
sampled to ensure that the effects of this practice could be measured.
To correct for this, the weight of jointly owned media which share carbons can be reduced, to bring the sample into line with the universe
of newspaper-television pairs in cities where cross-media ownership
exists. When this is done (see Table 20), the standardized b for cross-

Table 20. Effects of Cross-Media Ownership on Story Overlap, Controlling for the Log of T.V. Market Size (Weighted Sample)[a]

Variable	Standardized b	Unstandardized b	F
Log of T.V. market size (LT)	-.137	-.010	0.95
Cross-media ownership (CM)	+.314	+.058	4.99[b]

Note: Story overlap (SO) = .544 - .010 LT + .058 CM, where 0 indicates the absence of cross-ownership and 1 indicates the presence of cross-ownership.

[a] N = 48.
[b] $p < .05$.

---

[18] The simple r between the log of television market size and the number of daily newspapers in a city is .877. The simple r between the log of television market size and the number of television stations with newscasts in the market is .942. We have used the log of television market size as a control variable because it is more strongly related to story overlap than either the number of daily newspapers in a city or the

ownership declines from .357 to .314.[19] In short, the effects of cross-ownership on story overlap are slightly stronger in the unweighted sample than in the weighted sample, but not by much.[20] Because of the methodological risks involved in weighting a small sample, and because the effects of cross-ownership are only slightly stronger in the unweighted sample than in the weighted sample, the use of an unweighted sample for data analysis purposes seems preferable to the use of a weighted sample.

Direct vs. Indirect Effects of Cross-Ownership on Story Overlap

We have identified three intervening variables through which cross-ownership appears to influence story overlap--carbon-sharing, cross-employment (from a newspaper to a television station), and location within the same complex of buildings. Effects of cross-ownership on story overlap which are transmitted through these three intervening variables may be referred to as indirect effects, as opposed to direct effects, or those not accounted for by the three variables. Through path analysis, the direct and indirect effects of cross-ownership on

---

number of television stations with newscasts in the market.

[19] $p < .05$.

[20] The gap between the unweighted sample and the larger population is probably even smaller than the gap between the unweighted sample and the weighted sample. In correcting for the oversampling of jointly owned media which share carbons, it was necessary to assign a weight factor of .339 to jointly owned media which share carbons and a weight factor of 1.265 to jointly owned media which do not share carbons. Inevitably, such a procedure corrected not only for the sharing of carbons (as intended) but also (unfortunately) for other characteristics of the jointly owned media which share carbons. In particular, this procedure reduced the weight of jointly owned media in very small cities--cities such as Quincy, Illinois, where carbon-sharing is not the only cause of high story overlap between the jointly owned media.

story overlap can be measured and compared. As a vehicle for path analysis, a six-variable causal model has been constructed (see Figure 3). The model includes one exogenous variable: the log of television market size (LT). The model also includes five endogenous variables: cross-media ownership (CM), cross-employment (CE), location within the same complex of buildings (CB), carbon-sharing (CS), and story overlap (SO).

The six-variable model assumes that LT influences each of the other variables in the model and that CM influences each of the other variables, with the exception of LT.[21] The model also assumes that the three intervening variables (CE, CB, and CS) do not influence one another, with the exception that CB influences CS. The latter assumption is based on the fact that the location of a newspaper and television station within the same complex of buildings facilitates a carbon-sharing arrangement, by making it easier for carbons to be picked up. The assumption is also based on the observation that the simple r between CB and CS is substantially higher than that between CB and CE or between CS and CE. Like other causal models, the six-variable model makes three additional assumptions: first, that the model is recursive (there are no feedback loops); second, that the residual terms are uncorrelated with the predetermined variables in their structural equations; and third, that the residual terms are uncorrelated

---

[21] The log of television market size "influences" cross-media ownership in the sense that the percentage of jointly owned newspaper-television pairs located in small cities (where the log of T.V. market size is also small) is larger than the percentage of separately owned pairs located in small cities.

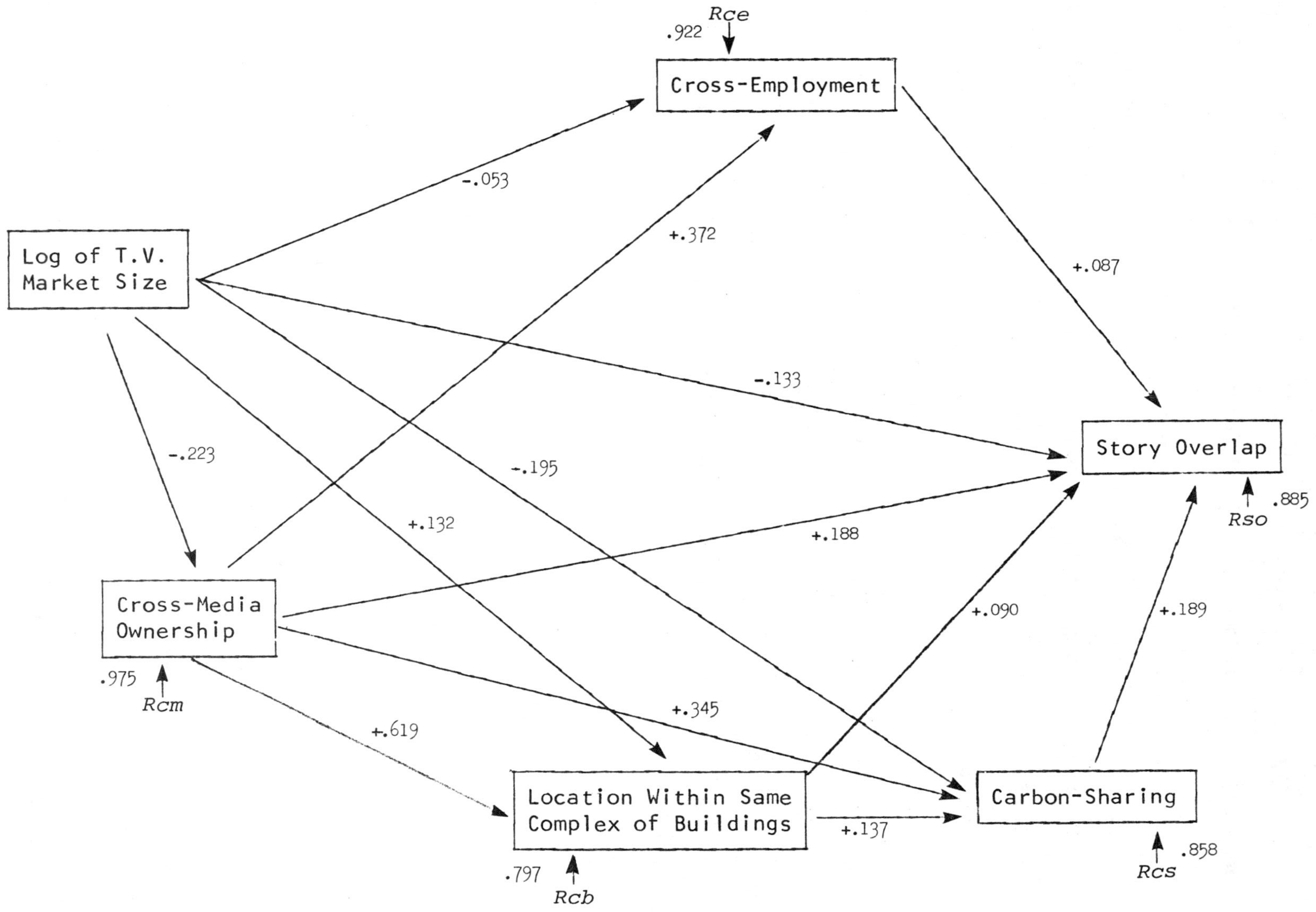

FIGURE 3. CAUSAL MODEL: EFFECTS OF CROSS-OWNERSHIP-RELATED VARIABLES ON STORY OVERLAP

with one another.[22]

As Figure 3 indicates, cross-ownership does have direct effects on story overlap--i.e., effects which cannot be accounted for by the three intervening variables in the model (CE, CB, and CS). The direct effects of cross-ownership are represented by a standardized b of .188, which is the path between CM and SO. The fact that the path between CM and SO has not disappeared suggests that it would be a mistake to infer from within-city comparisons that cross-ownership only influences story overlap through CE, CB, and CS. In Dayton, Ohio and Sacramento, California, where the jointly owned media are not characterized by CE, CB, or CS, cross-ownership does not increase story overlap. However, the presence of a direct path between CM and SO suggests that the homogenizing effects of cross-ownership in other cities in the sample are not due entirely to the fact that the jointly owned media in these cities are characterized by CE, CB, or CS.

Although cross-ownership has effects on story overlap which are not transmitted through CE, CB, or CS, these are nevertheless important intervening variables. The indirect effects of cross-ownership through CE, CB, and CS can be calculated by adding the products of each of the admissible compound paths between CM and SO: the path from CM to CE to SO, the path from CM to CB to SO, the path from CM to CS to SO, and the path from CM to CB to CS to SO. Thus, the indirect effects of cross-ownership on story overlap = (.372)(.087) + (.619)(.090) + (.345)(.189) + (.619)(.137)(.189) = .169 (see Table 21). Since the

---

[22] For further details about the standard assumptions of path analysis, see Kenneth Land, "Principles of Path Analysis," in *Sociological Methodology 1969* (San Francisco: Jossey-Bass, Inc., 1969), ed. by Edgar Borgatta et al., pp. 3-37.

Table 21. Indirect Effects of Cross-Ownership on Story Overlap[a]

Compound Path	Product of Simple Paths	Indirect Effect
CM to CE to SO	(.372) (.087)	.032
CM to CS to SO	(.345) (.189)	.065
CM to CB to SO	(.619) (.090)	.056
CM to CB to CS to SO	(.619) (.137) (.189)	.016
Total indirect effects		.169

Note: CM = cross-media ownership
       CE = cross-employment
       CS = carbon-sharing
       CB = location within same complex of buildings
       SO = story overlap

[a] N = 48

total effects of cross-ownership on story overlap are represented by a standardized b of .357, the indirect effects of cross-ownership through CE, CB, and CS account for nearly one-half of the total effects of cross-ownership on story overlap. In short, these three intervening variables help appreciably to explain how cross-ownership increases story overlap.

Effects of Different Combinations of Cross-Ownership-Related Variables

To capture the effects of different combinations of cross-ownership-related variables, we may regress story overlap on the log of television market size, cross-ownership, carbon-sharing, cross-employment (from a newspaper to a television station), and news organization location (see Table 22). This represents a tabular presentation of a portion of the causal model in Figure 3. As Table 22 indicates, the standardized

Table 22. Effects of Cross-Ownership-Related Variables on Story Overlap, Controlling for the Log of T.V. Market Size

Variable	Standardized b	Unstandardized b	F
Log of T.V. market size (LT)	-.133	-.010	0.83
Cross-media ownership (CM)	+.188	+.036	0.93
Carbon-sharing (CS)	+.189	+.059	1.38
Cross-employment (CE)	+.087	+.021	0.34
Location within same complex of buildings (CB)	+.090	+.024	0.27

Note: Story overlap (SO) = .541 − .010 LT + .036 CM + .059 CS + .021 CE + .024 CB, where CM, CS, CE, and CB each has a value of 1 when the variable is present and 0 when it is not.

[a] N = 48.

b for the carbon-sharing variable (.189) is greater than the standardized b for either the cross-employment variable (.087) or the news organization location variable (.090). Using unstandardized b's, we can translate the standardized b's into more meaningful terms. If SO = story overlap, LT = the log of television market size, CM = cross-media ownership, CS = carbon-sharing, CE = cross-employment (from a newspaper to a television station), and CB = location within the same complex of buildings, then SO = .541 − .010 LT + .036 CM + .059 CS + .021 CE + .024 CB. Substituting the mean value of the log of television market size in the sample (13.34) for LT and the value of 1 when any other variable is present, we can further estimate that, in a market of average size, SO =

.408 + .036 CM + .059 CS + .021 CE + .024 CB. The constant of .408 represents the average story overlap for separately owned media not characterized by CS, CE, or CB in a market where LT = 13.34.

By using the constant of .408 as a basis of comparison, we can estimate the increment in story overlap likely to result from the presence of cross-ownership and any one or more of the cross-ownership-related variables. For example, let us say that a newspaper and a television station are jointly owned and share carbons (but are not characterized by cross-employment or location within the same complex of buildings). If so, then SO = .408 + .036 (1) + .059 (1) + .021 (0) + .024 (0), or SO = .503. Thus, story overlap is likely to increase from .408 to .503 when these two variables (but not the others) are present. In more concrete terms, these two variables by themselves increase story overlap by 23.3% over what it would otherwise be (.095/.408 = 23.3%). Or let us say that a newspaper and a television station are jointly owned, are characterized by cross-employment (from a newspaper to a television station), and are located within the same complex of buildings (but do not share carbons). If so, then SO = .408 + .036 (1) + .059 (0) + .021 (1) + .024 (1), or SO = .489. When these three variables are present (but carbon-sharing is not), story overlap is likely to increase from .408 to 489. In other words, these three variables together increase story overlap by 19.9% over what it would otherwise be (.081/.408 = 19.9%). Because of the relatively small sample size (N = 48), these figures should not be regarded as precise estimates of the effects of particular combinations of variables on story overlap. Nevertheless, they serve as rough indicators of the relative importance of the cross-ownership-related variables.

In particular, they suggest that story overlap is likely to be higher when jointly owned media share carbons than when jointly owned media are characterized by cross-employment and are also located within the same complex of buildings.

Explanatory Power of Cross-Ownership-Related Variables vs. Non-Cross-Ownership-Related Variables

Despite the fact that cross-ownership-related variables clearly have effects on story overlap, it might be argued that these variables do not explain much of the variance in story overlap scores. As Table 23

Table 23. Variance in Story Overlap Explained by the Log of T.V. Market Size and Four Cross-Ownership-Related Variables[a]

Variable	Change in R^2 Attributable to Each Variable	Cumulative R^2
Log of T.V. market size (LT)	.057	.057
Cross-media ownership (CM)	.121	.178
Location within same complex of buildings (CB)	.008	.186
Carbon-sharing (CS)	.023	.210
Cross-employment (CE)	.006	.216

Note: The five independent variables were entered into the regression equation on the basis of their position in the causal model: LT precedes CM which precedes the three intervening variables (CB, CS, and CE). Since the model postulates that CB precedes CS, CB was entered before CS or CE. The latter two variables were entered in accordance with the stepwise inclusion method (the variable which explains the greatest amount of variance in conjunction with preceding variables in the equation is entered before the variables which remain).

[a] $N = 48$.

indicates, the five-variable combination consisting of the four cross-ownership-related variables (CM, CE, CB, and CS) and the log of television market size (LT) explains 21.6% of the variance in story overlap. Whether this is low or high is difficult to judge, in the absence of a basis of comparison. To put the explanatory power of the cross-ownership-related variables in perspective, the proportion of the variance in story overlap explained by CM, CE, CB, CS, and LT can be compared with the proportion explained by LT and four additional variables not caused by cross-ownership.

It is difficult to identify additional variables which are strongly related to story overlap. However, the data do confirm four hypotheses, albeit in a modest manner. First, story overlap varies positively with the size of a television news staff. The larger the television news staff, the greater the probability of contacts between newspaper and television staffs. Such contacts foster cooperation, which tends to increase story overlap. Second, story overlap varies inversely with the size of a newspaper's state capital staff. Since state government news does not make for spicy television coverage (too many "talking heads") and few television stations have their own state capital correspondent, television stations cover fewer state government stories proportionately than newspapers. Consequently, the more committed a newspaper is to covering the statehouse (as reflected in the size of the newspaper's capital staff), the less likely it is to cover the same stories as a television station.[23] Third, story overlap is higher

---

[23] In Sacramento, the only state capital in the sample, a capital staff was defined as the number of people assigned to cover state government.

when the television station's newscasts have higher audience ratings than the newscasts of other television stations in the market. Newspaper reporters and editors pay more attention to newscasts with larger audiences, perhaps because there is a rough positive relationship between program quality and audience size. The more attentive newspaper reporters and editors are to a television station's newscasts, the more likely they are to glean story ideas from the newscasts. Finally, story overlap is higher when the newspaper is published in the morning than when it is published in the afternoon. Morning newspapers are more apt to cover stories which break during an afternoon--stories which television stations often cover on their early evening newscasts-- than afternoon newspapers, which frequently decide that such news is too stale to be covered the following afternoon.

Together with the log of television market size, these four variables (T.V. news staff size, newspaper state capital staff size, T.V. news audience share, and time of newspaper publication) explain only 10.8% of the variance in story overlap (see Table 24). This stands in contrast to the 21.6% of the variance in story overlap explained by the log of television market size and the four cross-ownership variables. In fact, the four cross-ownership variables explain more of the variance, even after controlling for the log of television market size (15.9%), than the other four variables do, in conjunction with the log of television market size.

Effects of Cross-Ownership on Intermedia Relations, by City Size

As has been discussed, nearly one-half of the effects of cross-ownership on story overlap are transmitted through three intervening

Table 24. Variance in Story Overlap Explained by the Log of T.V. Market Size and Four Variables Not Caused by Cross-Ownership[a]

Variable	Change in R^2 Attributable to Each Variable	Cumulative R^2
Log of T.V. market size	.057	.057
Newspaper's state capital staff size	.020	.077
Newspaper's time of publication	.019	.096
T.V. station's news staff size	.007	.102
T.V. station's news audience share	.005	.108

Note: The log of television market size variable was entered first into the regression equation. The remaining variables were entered in accordance with the stepwise inclusion method (the variable which explains the greatest amount of variance in conjunction with preceding variables in the equation is entered before the variables which remain).

[a] $N = 48$.

variables--carbon-sharing, cross-employment (from a newspaper to a television station), and location within the same complex of buildings. By increasing the likelihood that a newspaper-television pair will be characterized by CS, CE, or CB, cross-ownership increases the likelihood that the newspaper and the television station will cover the same stories. To examine the circumstances under which cross-ownership increases the incidence of CS, CE, and CB, we may compare the characteristics of jointly owned and separately owned media in cities of different sizes. For this purpose, cities have been grouped into three categories: cities with populations smaller than 125,000; cities with populations larger than 125,000 but smaller than 1,000,000; and cities with populations larger than 1,000,000.[24]

As Table 25 indicates, cross-ownership fosters carbon-sharing arrangements in cities with populations under 125,000. In these cities,

Table 25. Relationship Between Cross-Ownership and Carbon-Sharing, by City Size[a]

City Size	Proportion of T.V. Stations Owned by a Newspaper Which Receive Newspaper Carbons on an Exclusive Basis	Proportion of T.V. Stations Not Owned by a Newspaper Which Receive Newspaper Carbons on an Exclusive Basis
0-125,000	31.2% (5/16)	5.0% (1/20)
125,000-1,000,000	0 (0/32)	0 (0/53)
1,000,000+	0 (0/5)	0 (0/14)

[a] N = 140.

31.2% of newspaper-owned television stations receive newspaper carbons on an exclusive basis, as opposed to 5.0% of television stations not

---

[24] Instead of arbitrarily choosing the upper and lower reaches of each city size category, cutoff points were empirically determined. Specifically, an effort was made to include jointly owned media characterized by the presence or absence of a particular variable (CS, CE, or CB) in the same city size category. Thus, the cutoff point of 1,000,000 was preferred to 500,000 because the relationship between cross-ownership and cross-employment in cities with populations between 500,000 and 1,000,000 differs from the relationship between cross-ownership and cross-employment in cities with populations over 1,000,000.

owned by a newspaper.[25] There is no evidence of such carbon-sharing arrangements in larger cities. The questionnaire data, of course, may not reveal every example of this practice. Nevertheless, it appears that the practice is confined to cities with populations under 125,000.

As Table 26 indicates, newspaper-owned television stations in cities with populations under 125,000 are more likely than television

Table 26. Relationship Between Cross-Ownership and Cross-Employment, by City Size[a]

City Size	Proportion of T.V. Stations Owned by a Newspaper Which Have Hired a Reporter or Editor Who Worked for the Newspaper Which Owns the T.V. Station	Proportion of T.V. Stations Not Owned by a Newspaper Which Have Hired a Reporter or Editor Who Worked for the Newspaper Which Owns a T.V. Station or for the Only Newspaper in the City
0–125,000	11.8% (2/17)	0 (0/15)
125,000–1,000,000	41.7% (10/24)	10.8% (4/37)
1,000,000+	0 (0/2)	37.5% (3/8)

[a]N = 103.

stations not owned by a newspaper in such cities to have hired a reporter or editor who worked for the newspaper which owns the television station or for the only newspaper in the city. This is also true of cities

---

[25]The single instance where a television station not owned by a newspaper receives newspaper carbons on an exclusive basis is in one of the 14 cities included in the questionnaire survey where there is only one television station and no cross-ownership.

with populations larger than 125,000 but smaller than 1 million. However, cross-ownership does not have positive effects on cross-employment in cities with populations over one million. Indeed, there happens to be more cross-employment between separately owned media in these cities than between jointly owned media. Reporters and editors who work for a newspaper which owns a local television station can usually retain their pension benefits and medical benefits if they transfer to the newspaper-owned television station. In small and medium-sized cities, newsmen contemplating a switch from print journalism to broadcast journalism must be mindful of such mundane concerns. In contrast, broadcasting salaries are so substantial and non-monetary incentives (the promise of instant stardom) are so compelling in large cities that ambitious newspaper reporters and editors may be impervious to such factors as pension benefits and medical benefits.

As Table 27 indicates, newspaper-owned television stations in all three city size categories are more likely than television stations not owned by a newspaper to be located within the same complex of buildings as a newspaper. Thus, the relationship between cross-ownership and the CB variable does not depend on city size as the other relationships do.

To recapitulate, cross-ownership does not increase carbon-sharing in cities with populations over 125,000 and does not increase cross-employment in cities with populations over 1,000,000. Cross-ownership does increase location within the same complex of buildings in all three city size categories. In short, only in cities with populations under 125,000 does cross-ownership have positive effects on all three of the intervening variables which have been established as

Table 27. Relationship Between Cross-Ownership and News Organization Location, by City Size[a]

City Size	Proportion of T.V. Stations Owned by a Newspaper Which Are Located Within Same Complex of Buildings as a Newspaper	Proportion of T.V. Stations Not Owned by a Newspaper Which Are Located Within Same Complex of Buildings as a Newspaper
0-125,000	12.0% (3/25)	3.7% (1/27)
125,000-1,000,000	4.8% (2/42)	0 (0/70)
1,000,000+	20.0% (1/5)	0 (0/14)

[a] N = 180.

influencing story overlap--carbon-sharing, cross-employment (from a newspaper to a television station), and location within the same complex of buildings.

VI

EFFECTS OF CROSS-OWNERSHIP ON
ISSUE TREATMENT AND STORY TREATMENT

Television stations "treat" issues when they broadcast editorials; they fail to treat issues in an important way when they refuse to editorialize. A television station which does not editorialize robs citizens of the opportunity to hear a viewpoint different from that expressed in a local newspaper on the same issue or a viewpoint on another issue altogether. Thus, diversity suffers when a television station refuses to editorialize. Diversity also suffers when a newspaper and a television station treat issues similarly. Newspapers and television stations treat issues similarly when they emphasize ten top issues in the same way (issue ranking similarity). Newspapers and television stations treat issues similarly when they agree on what the top ten issues are (agenda composition similarity).

Similar story treatment is not always harmful to the public, but it can be. Newspapers and television stations treat a story similarly when they underemphasize the same story, overemphasize the same story, or communicate misleading information about the same story. Under such circumstances, similar story treatment is likely to be harmful to the public.

In a democracy, citizens need to be exposed to diverse news and opinions about the issues of the day, as well as diverse opinions (whether explicit or implicit) about the relative importance of various stories and issues. The proper balance between homogeneity and diversity in the flow of news and opinions is that which is struck by journalists making independent decisions, on the basis of the relative merits of stories, issues, and viewpoints.[1] It is important that television stations deal with issues, not only through news coverage but through editorials as well. It is also important that newspaper and television journalists base their issue emphasis on the relative importance of the issues, not on the priorities of one another or the priorities of a common owner. Finally, it is important that newspaper and television journalists base their story treatment on the public's right to know, not on the preferences of one another or the preferences of a common owner.

If cross-ownership reduces the willingness of television stations to editorialize, it is interfering with the public's right to know. If cross-ownership has a homogenizing effect on the issue emphasis of jointly owned newspapers and television stations, it is interfering with the public's interest in diversity. Through the techniques of scientific research or, more specifically, multiple regression analysis, the possibility that cross-ownership influences issue treatment has been examined.

---

[1] Journalistic decisions which are not based on the relative merits of stories, issues, and viewpoints (but which are due to management intervention, pack journalism, economic constraints, or mass media ownership structure) are more easily identified than decisions which are based on a defensible standard of "newsworthiness." However, the individual reporter might determine newsworthiness by considering which human needs are more basic than others and by paying more attention to stories involving the more basic human needs. For a more general discussion of this approach, see Christian Bay, <u>The Structure of Freedom</u> (Stanford: Stanford University Press, 1958).

If cross-ownership results in the suppression or distortion of certain stories, it is interfering with the public's right to know. If cross-ownership results in overemphasis on certain "pet projects" or causes, it is interfering with the public's interest in diversity. Through the techniques of investigative reporting, the possibility that cross-ownership influences story treatment in particular cities has been explored.[2]

It is important to emphasize that the success of investigative reporting depends on numerous factors, including the selection of interviewees, the amount of time devoted to interviews, the persistence and trustworthiness of the interviewer, and the candor of interviewees. Time constraints severely circumscribed the amount of investigative reporting which could be accomplished as part of this project. Also, it is possible--if not likely--that some interviewees were unwilling to volunteer information which might prove embarrassing to their news organization. Nevertheless, a discussion and application of investigative reporting techniques can illustrate both the limitations and possibilities of this approach.

Effects of Cross-Ownership on the Willingness of Television Stations to Editorialize

The F.C.C. encourages--but does not require--editorializing by broadcasting stations. After initially prohibiting editorializing by broadcasting stations, the F.C.C. reversed itself in 1949 and permitted editorializing, with the stipulation that the right to editorialize must

---

[2] Investigative reporting techniques form the basis of most of the examples of "abuses" attributed to cross-ownership in Stephen Barnett, "Cross-Ownership of Mass Media in the Same City: A Report to the John and Mary R. Markle Foundation," unpublished manuscript (Berkeley: September 23, 1974), p. 2.

be "exercised in conformity with the paramount right of the public to hear a reasonably balanced presentation of all responsible viewpoints on particular issues."[3] Since then, the F.C.C. has encouraged broadcasters to editorialize, so that the public might be exposed to as many viewpoints as possible. Indeed, the failure of WHDH-TV to editorialize was one of several factors underlying the F.C.C.'s 1969 decision to award WHDH's license to Boston Broadcasters, Inc., which pledged, among other things, to run frequent editorials.[4]

Despite the F.C.C.'s favorable attitude toward editorializing by broadcasters, a considerable number of television stations still do not editorialize. A recent study, for example, found that 35% of all television stations do not editorialize.[5] There are several reasons why television stations refuse to editorialize, quite apart from any effects which cross-ownership may have. First, editorializing is costly and time-consuming, if taken seriously. Second, some news executives feel that editorializing mars the appearance, if not the reality, of objectivity in news reporting by the station. As one television news director puts it, "For a broadcasting station to editorialize would diminish the credibility of our news reports." Third, broadcast editorials, in contrast to news reports, are subject to personal attack

---

[3] See Walter Emery, _Broadcasting and Government: Responsibilities and Regulations_ (East Lansing: Michigan State University Press, 1971), pp. 330-332.

[4] Sterling Quinlan, _The Hundred Million Dollar Lunch_ (Chicago: J. Philip O'Hara, Inc., 1974), p. 112.

[5] The study, published in 1970, is mentioned in Irving Fang and John Whelan, "Survey of Television Editorials and Ombudsman Segments," _Journal of Broadcasting_ (Summer 1973), pp. 363-371.

rules and the fairness doctrine. Under the personal attack rules, a broadcasting station which attacks the honesty, character, or integrity of an identified person or group must notify the person or group attacked within one week and offer a reasonable opportunity to respond on the air at no cost. Under the fairness doctrine, a broadcasting station must afford a reasonable opportunity for the presentation of contrasting viewpoints on controversial issues.[6] Some news executives regard the paperwork, legal fees, and offers of free air time which the personal attack rules and the fairness doctrine require as too high a price to pay for the privilege of editorializing.

Does cross-ownership have any effects on the willingness of television stations to editorialize? In 1969, Litwin and Wroth found that newspaper-owned broadcasting stations editorialize less frequently than broadcasting stations not owned by a newspaper.[7] However, the Litwin-Wroth conclusions were based on data from only six cities. The questionnaire data we obtained from 117 television stations in several dozen cities provide a better opportunity to examine effects of cross-ownership on the willingness of television stations to editorialize.

As Table 28 indicates, 52.0% of the newspaper-owned television stations do not editorialize at all, as opposed to 25.4% of television stations not owned by a newspaper. The newspaper-owned television

---

[6] Federal Communications Commission, "Public and Broadcasting: Revised Edition," Federal Register (September 5, 1974), p. 32290.

[7] The Litwin-Wroth findings are discussed in Walter Baer et al., "Concentration of Mass Media Ownership: Assessing the State of Current Knowledge," Rand Corporation Report (Santa Monica: September 1974), pp. 127-129, and in Barnett, op. cit., pp. 62-64.

Table 28. Crosstabulation of Cross-Ownership by Editorializing[a]

	T.V. station owned by newspaper	T.V. station not owned by newspaper
Editorializes	24 (48.0%)	50 (74.6%)
Does not editorialize	26 (52.0%)	17 (25.4%)
	50 (100.0%)	67 (100.0%)

N = 117.

station which editorializes is faced with a Hobson's choice. If its editorial viewpoints closely resemble the newspaper's, it invites charges of collusion with the newspaper. On the other hand, if its editorial viewpoints differ from the newspaper's, it is negating the newspaper's editorial efforts. To avoid such a dilemma, many newspaper-owned television stations appear to have decided to avoid editorializing altogether.

The figures in Table 28 suggest a clear behavioral difference between newspaper-owned television stations and other television stations. However, appropriate statistical controls are needed to test whether this difference is due to the confounding influence of other variables. Previous studies have shown that television stations in large markets are more likely to editorialize than television stations in small markets and that network affiliates are more likely to

---

[8]Fang and Whelan, op. cit., pp. 363-371.

editorialize than independents.[8] Since editorializing requires money and manpower, it also seems reasonable to hypothesize that VHF stations (which tend to be more lucrative) are more likely to editorialize than UHF stations and that television stations with large news staffs are more likely to editorialize than television stations with small news staffs.

Through multiple regression analysis, effects of cross-ownership on willingness to editorialize can be measured, after appropriate controls have been applied. Four control variables have been identified: city size, television news staff size, whether a television station is a network affiliate or an independent, and whether a television station is VHF or UHF (frequency). As Table 29 indicates, the standardized b

Table 29. Effects of Cross-Media Ownership on Editorializing, Controlling for City Size, Frequency, Network Affiliation, and T.V. News Staff Size[a]

Independent Variable	Standardized b	F
Cross-media ownership	-.294	11.26[b]
City size	+.210	4.30[c]
Frequency (VHF vs. UHF)	+.185	3.29[c]
Network affiliation (affiliate vs. independent)	+.076	0.45
T.V. news staff size	+.021	0.04

Note: Editorializing is a dichotomous variable indicating whether a television station editorializes or not.

[a] $N = 117$.
[b] $p < .001$.
[c] $p < .01$.

for the regression of editorializing on cross-ownership is -.294 after controls for the four variables have been applied.[9] Clearly, cross-ownership reduces the willingness of television stations to editorialize.

To determine whether this effect is more pronounced in smaller or larger cities, we may compare the editorializing practices of newspaper-owned television stations and other television stations in cities of different sizes. For this purpose, cities have been grouped into three categories: cities with populations smaller than 125,000; cities with populations larger than 125,000 but smaller than 1,000,000; and cities with populations larger than 1,000,000.[10]

As Table 30 indicates, the biggest editorializing gap between newspaper-owned television stations and other television stations is in cities with populations smaller than 125,000. In such cities, 38.9% of the newspaper-owned stations editorialize, as opposed to 77.8% of the other stations. In other words, television stations not owned by a newspaper are twice as likely as newspaper-owned television stations to editorialize in these cities. In cities with populations larger than 125,000 but smaller than 1,000,000, television stations not owned by a newspaper are also more likely to editorialize than newspaper-owned television stations. In such cities, 44.4% of the newspaper-owned stations editorialize, as opposed to 70.7% of the other stations. In cities with populations larger than 1,000,000, newspaper-owned stations are slightly more likely to editorialize than other stations. In these large

---

[9] $p < .001$.

[10] These are the same city size groupings used to examine the effects of cross-ownership on carbon-sharing, cross-employment, and location within the same complex of buildings in cities of different sizes.

Table 30. Relationship Between Cross-Ownership and Editorializing, by City Size[a]

City Size	Proportion of T.V. Stations Owned by a Newspaper Which Editorializes	Proportion of T.V. Stations Not Owned by a Newspaper Which Editorializes
0-125,000	38.9% (7/18)	77.8% (14/18)
125,000-1,000,000	44.4% (12/27)	70.7% (29/41)
1,000,000+	100.0% (4/4)	88.9% (8/9)

[a] N = 117.

cities, 100.0% of the newspaper-owned stations editorialize, as opposed to 88.9% of the other stations.[11] In short, cross-ownership reduces the willingness of television stations to editorialize in cities with populations under 125,000 and in cities with populations between 125,000 and 1,000,000, but not in cities with populations over 1,000,000.

---

[11] It is not altogether clear why newspaper-owned television stations in cities with populations over 1,000,000 are more likely to editorialize than newspaper-owned television stations in smaller cities. However, it may be that newspaper-owned television stations in very large cities have a greater incentive to editorialize to strengthen their case for renewal in the event that a petition to deny or a competing application for their license is filed. In general, television stations in very large cities are more frequent targets of renewal challenges than television stations in smaller cities. Consequently, television stations in very large cities must be more mindful of the criteria the F.C.C. uses in evaluating the performance of an incumbent television licensee. One of these criteria is whether the licensee editorializes or not.

Effects of Cross-Ownership on
Issue Ranking Similarity

Issue ranking similarity refers to the extent to which a newspaper and a television station give the same relative emphasis to an identical set of salient issues.[12] Story overlap and issue ranking similarity are both measures of news homogeneity, but they are discrete concepts. Even if 100% of a television station's state and local news stories also appear in a local newspaper, the issue emphasis of the newspaper and the television station may differ, since a typical newspaper covers many more stories than a television station does, and there is no guarantee that the issue emphasis of a newspaper's non-overlapping stories will be identical to that of its overlapping stories. Furthermore, approximately one-half of a typical television station's state and local news stories are not covered by a given local newspaper, and there is no guarantee that the issue emphasis of a television station's non-overlapping stories will be identical to that of its overlapping stories. Thus, a relationship between cross-ownership and issue ranking similarity cannot be inferred from the fact that there is a relationship between cross-ownership and story overlap.

The same stories used to examine the effects of cross-ownership on story overlap have also been used to examine the effects of cross-ownership on issue ranking similarity.[13] The ten most frequently covered

---

[12] What we have termed an "issue" might be described by others as an "issue type" or "issue area."

[13] The same stories were used for two reasons: first, to control for differences in the number of television stories per newscast and studio location (the stories used to examine the effects of cross-ownership on story overlap contained built-in controls for these two variables); and second, to permit the inclusion of story overlap as an intervening variable between cross-ownership and issue ranking similarity. Because the relationship between story overlap and issue ranking similarity proved to

183

issues for these stories were Law and Order, Elementary & Secondary Education, Transportation, Health, Government Spending, Higher Education, Recession & Unemployment, Environment, Utilities, and Taxes.[14] Each news medium's agenda was determined by ranking these ten issues on the basis of the relative number of stories devoted to each by the news medium. The Spearman's r_s coefficient was used to measure issue ranking similarity for each of the 48 newspaper-television pairs in the sample. This method has been widely used as a means of comparing agendas.[15] Before regressing issue ranking similarity on cross-ownership, city size was included in the model as a control variable.[16] As suggested by the Rand Corporation, T.V. news audience share and newspaper circulation share were also included as control variables.[17] Variables measuring the number of competitors in the market were not included in the model, because of high multicollinearity between these variables and the city size variable.[18]

---

be weak (simple r = .057), story overlap was ultimately not included in the model as an intervening variable between cross-ownership and issue ranking similarity.

[14] These are also the ten most frequently covered issues for all 9,335 coded stories in the sample. In fact, the rank-ordering of issues for both sets of stories is the same, except that the Environment and Utilities issues (tied in the smaller set of stories) are ranked 8th and 9th respectively in the larger set.

[15] See, for example, Maxwell McCombs and Donald Shaw, "The Agenda-Setting Function of Mass Media," Public Opinion Quarterly (Summer 1972), pp. 176-187.

[16] The city size variable was selected, because it is more strongly related to issue ranking similarity than the log of city size, T.V. market size, or the log of T.V. market size.

[17] See Walter Baer et al., "Concentration of Mass Media Ownership: Assessing the State of Current Knowledge," Rand Corporation Report (Santa Monica: September 1974), p. 143.

[18] The simple r between city size and the number of daily newspa-

As Table 31 indicates, the standardized b for the regression of issue ranking similarity on cross-ownership, after controlling for

Table 31. Effects of Cross-Ownership on Issue Ranking Similarity, Controlling for City Size, T.V. News Audience Share, and Newspaper Circulation Share[a]

Variable	Standardized b	F
City size	+.304	3.32[b]
T.V. news audience share	−.028	0.03
Newspaper circulation share	+.107	0.47
Cross-media ownership	+.179	1.42

[a] N = 48

[b] $p < .05$.

city size, T.V. news audience share, and newspaper circulation share, is .179. This is certainly a positive relationship, but it is not statistically significant at an acceptable level. If cross-ownership has some effects on issue ranking similarity, the overall effects are not strong enough to be captured through this kind of analysis.

The picture changes, however, if the effects of a slightly different variable--local cross-ownership--are examined. Local cross-ownership refers to a situation where a newspaper and a television station in the same city have a common owner who is located in that city.

---

pers in a city is .834. The simple r between city size and the number of television stations with newscasts in the market is .893.

The owner may or may not have media interests in other cities as well.[19]

As Table 32 indicates, the standardized b for the regression of issue

Table 32. Effects of Local Cross-Ownership on Issue Ranking Similarity, Controlling for City Size, T.V. News Audience Share, and Newspaper Circulation Share[a]

Variable	Standardized b	F
City size	+.345	4.58[b]
T.V. news audience share	−.062	0.17
Newspaper circulation share	+.122	0.67
Local cross-media ownership	+.336	5.36[c]

[a] $N = 48$.

[b] $p < .01$

[c] $p < .01$.

ranking similarity on local cross-ownership, after controlling for city size, T.V. news audience share, and newspaper circulation share, is .336.[20] In short, local cross-ownership has stronger effects on issue ranking similarity than cross-ownership in general.[21]

---

[19] To illustrate the difference between local and non-local cross-ownership, we may consider the case of Landmark Communications, Inc., which has its headquarters in Norfolk, Virginia. Landmark owns two newspapers and a television station in Norfolk and two newspapers and a television station in Greensboro, North Carolina. Thus, there is local cross-ownership in Norfolk, non-local cross-ownership in Greensboro.

[20] $p < .01$.

[21] The relationship between local cross-ownership and story overlap is also stronger than the relationship between cross-ownership and story overlap. Whereas the standardized b for the regression of story

There are several factors which collectively help to explain the greater homogenizing effects of local cross-ownership. First of all, a local owner's priorities are well known, while the priorities of an absentee owner may not be. If the local owner is actively involved in certain community projects, his involvement may be noted in print or on the air. He may even be interviewed by a reporter. If the local owner has a particular interest in education or health or the environment, he may communicate this interest through his newspaper's editorials or through a personally written column.[22] In short, the local owner tends to be more visible than the absentee owner, and his priorities are easier to discern.

Second, the local owner often plays a role in setting policy for his newspaper. Without issuing direct instructions to reporters, the owner can communicate his preferences through proxies--an executive editor, a managing editor, or others. As Breed has suggested, reporters learn the owner's policy through a process of osmosis: "When the new reporter starts work he is not told what policy is. Nor is he ever told . . . Yet all but the newest staffers know what policy is."[23] The owner may also promote his priorities by hiring and promoting like-minded personnel. Naturally, a local owner can participate more fully in a newspaper's policy-making process and personnel decisions than an

---

overlap on cross-ownership (after controlling for the log of television market size) is .357, the standardized b for the regression of story overlap on local cross-ownership (after controlling for the log of television market size) is .450.

[22] For example, Paul Miller, the chairman of the board of the Gannett Corporation (headquartered in Rochester, New York), writes a weekly column in the Rochester Times-Union.

[23] Warren Breed, "Social Control in the Newsroom: A Functional Analysis," Social Forces (May 1955), pp. 326-335.

absentee owner can.

Third, the local owner of a newspaper-television combination often watches the newscasts of the television station he owns, while the absentee owner cannot. Without directly setting policy for his television station, the local owner may communicate his views indirectly through the station's general manager or news director, with whom he may chat from time to time. Also, the owner may make it clear to television reporters that he watches their newscasts. A reporter for the Gannett Corporation's Rochester television station, WHEC-TV, recalls receiving a memo from Paul Miller complimenting him on a story he had done recently.[24] Such positive reinforcement serves to remind reporters that the owner knows what they are up to. This, in turn, may result in "anticipated reactions"--reporters basing their issue emphasis in part on what they think will please or displease the owner. Such behavior makes sense, of course, only if the owner's awareness of the television station's issue emphasis can be assumed. When the owner is a local owner, this assumption is not unreasonable.

Defenders of cross-ownership often note that most of the owners of newspaper-television combinations in the same city are local owners.[25] The argument is made that local owners take a more active, personal interest in the management of their properties, that they are more keenly aware of their community's needs and problems, and that they are more

---

[24] Miller is chairman of the board of the Gannett Corporation.

[25] Figures compiled by the Rand Corporation indicate that approximately 75% of all newspaper-television combinations in the same city are locally owned. See Walter Baer et al., "Newspaper-Television Station Cross-Ownership: Options for Federal Action," <u>Rand Corporation Report</u> (Santa Monica: September 1974), p. 27.

committed to quality journalism and community service than absentee owners are.[26] Local owners may indeed take a more active, personal interest in the management of their properties than absentee owners, and local owners may have strong beliefs about their community's needs and problems. However, these very characteristics increase the likelihood that the owner's priorities, interests, and concerns will be perceived by news executives and reporters employed by the owner. The figures which appear in Table 32 suggest that local cross-ownership increases the extent to which a newspaper and a television station give similar emphasis to key issues.

Effects of Cross-Ownership on Agenda Composition Similarity

Agenda composition similarity refers to the extent to which a newspaper and a television station agree on what the key issues are. Whereas issue ranking similarity measures the extent to which a newspaper and a television station agree on the relative salience of ten key issues, agenda composition similarity measures the extent to which a newspaper and a television station agree on which ten issues are salient enough to merit more coverage than other issues. As the hypothetical example in Table 33 illustrates, a newspaper and a television station may agree completely on issue ranking without agreeing on agenda composition. Or, as the hypothetical example in Table 34 illustrates, a newspaper and a television station may agree completely on agenda composition without agreeing on issue ranking.

---

[26] An important corollary to this argument is the prediction that the forced divestiture of existing newspaper-television combinations would result in a diminution in local ownership of television stations and an increase in absentee ownership.

Table 33. Issue Emphasis of Hypothetical Newspaper and T.V. Station With Identical Issue Ranking, Different Agenda Composition

Newspaper's Rank-Ordering of the Issues	T.V. Station's Rank-Ordering of the Issues
1. Law & Order*	1. Law & Order*
2. Elementary & Secondary Education*	2. Political Ethics
3. Transportation*	3. Elementary & Secondary Education*
4. Health*	4. Transportation*
5. Government Spending*	5. Wages
6. Higher Education*	6. Health*
7. Recession & Unemployment*	7. Problems of the Elderly
8. Environment*	8. Government Spending*
9. Utilities*	9. Higher Education*
10. Taxes*	10. Housing
11. Consumer Protection	11. Recession & Unemployment*
12. Prison Conditions	12. Agriculture
13. Sanitation	13. Environment*
14. Parks	14. Utilities*
15. Equal Opportunity for Women	15. Taxes*

Note: The issues used in measuring issue ranking similarity are marked by an asterisk. The issues used in measuring agenda composition similarity are the first ten issues on each of the two lists.

Table 34. Issue Emphasis of Hypothetical Newspaper and T.V. Station With Identical Agenda Composition, Different Issue Ranking

Newspaper's Rank-Ordering of the Issues	T.V. Station's Rank-Ordering of the Issues
1. Law & Order*	1. Law & Order*
2. Consumer Protection	2. Higher Education*
3. Elementary & Secondary Education*	3. Recession & Unemployment*
4. Transportation*	4. Consumer Protection
5. Health*	5. Elementary & Secondary Education*
6. Prison Conditions	6. Sanitation
7. Government Spending*	7. Government Spending*
8. Sanitation	8. Transportation*
9. Higher Education*	9. Prison Conditions
10. Recession & Unemployment*	10. Health*
11. Environment*	11. Taxes*
12. Parks	12. Environment*
13. Agriculture	13. Parks
14. Utilities*	14. Utilities*
15. Taxes*	15. Agriculture

Note: The issues used in measuring issue ranking similarity are marked by an asterisk. The issues used in measuring agenda composition similarity are the first ten issues on each of the two lists.

The same stories used to examine the effects of cross-ownership on story overlap and issue ranking similarity have also been used to examine the effects of cross-ownership on agenda composition similarity. To measure agenda composition similarity, each newspaper's top ten issues were compared with the top ten issues of each television station in the same market.[27] If an issue was among a news organization's top ten issues, it received a value of 1; if not, it received a value of 0. By multiplying newspaper and television values for each issue and by adding the products, an agenda composition similarity score was obtained for each of the 48 newspaper-television pairs in the sample. Thus, if two news organizations emphasized the same top ten issues, they were given an agenda composition similarity score of 10, regardless of how they ranked the top ten issues. If two news organizations agreed on nine of the top ten issues, they were given an agenda composition similarity score of 9, regardless of how they ranked the top ten issues. The log of city size was included in the model as a control variable.[28] T.V. news audience share and newspaper circulation share were also included as controls. Variables measuring the number of competitors in the market were not included in the model, because of high multicollinearity between these variables and the log of city size.[29]

---

[27] A total of 36 different issues were coded.

[28] The log of city size was selected, because it is more strongly related to agenda composition similarity than city size, T.V. market size, or the log of T.V. market size.

[29] The simple r between the log of city size and the number of daily newspapers in a city is .812. The simple r between the log of city size and the number of television stations with newscasts in the market is .906.

As Table 35 indicates, the standardized b for the regression of agenda composition similarity on cross-ownership, after controlling for

Table 35. Effects of Cross-Ownership on Agenda Composition Similarity, Controlling for Log of City Size, T.V. News Audience Share, and Newspaper Circulation Share[a]

Variable	Standardized b	F
Log of city size	-.247	3.07[b]
T.V. news audience share	+.394	8.67[c]
Newspaper circulation share	+.117	0.77
Cross-media ownership	+.015	0.01

[a] $N = 48$.
[b] $p < .05$.
[c] $p < .001$.

the log of city size, T.V. news audience share, and newspaper circulation share, is a mere .015. Nor is the relationship between local cross-ownership and agenda composition similarity any stronger. In fact, as Table 36 indicates, the standardized b declines slightly from .015 to -.022 when local cross-ownership is substituted in the equation for cross-ownership.

At first glance, it is puzzling that local cross-ownership should have effects on issue ranking similarity but not on agenda composition similarity. However, these are discrete concepts, as reflected by the fact that the simple r between issue ranking similarity and agenda composition similarity is a relatively low .132. While the issue ranking

Table 36. Effects of Local Cross-Ownership on Agenda Composition Similarity, Controlling for Log of City Size, T.V. News Audience Share, and Newspaper Circulation Share

Variable	Standardized b	F
Log of city size	-.253	3.14[b]
T.V. news audience share	+.400	8.84[c]
Newspaper circulation share	+.120	0.81
Local cross-media ownership	-.022	0.03

[a] $N = 48$.

[b] $p < .05$.

[c] $p < .001$.

measure registers differences between strong emphasis and moderate emphasis on various issues, the agenda composition measure registers differences between moderate-to-strong emphasis and nonexistent-to-weak emphasis on various issues. The fact that local cross-ownership influences issue ranking similarity but not agenda composition similarity suggests that the effects of local cross-ownership on issue emphasis occur at the threshold between moderately salient issues and highly salient issues, but not at a lower threshold. The local owner's strong interest in one or two issues may be reflected in the news outputs of both the newspaper and the television station he owns (in the form of higher issue ranking similarity scores). However, jointly owned newspaper and television news staffs do not adhere slavishly to the local owner's priorities. In particular, they appear to have a great deal of discretion in deciding which issues to downplay or neglect (as indicated by the absence of any effects of local cross-ownership on agenda composition similarity).

These conclusions must be tentative, because issue ranking similarity scores and agenda composition similarity scores cannot be as reliable as story overlap scores involving the same set of stories. One reason for this is that the issue emphasis measures are based only on issue-oriented stories, whereas the story overlap measure is based on issue-oriented and non-issue-oriented stories alike. Another reason is that the issue emphasis measures require the use of at least ten separate categories (some of which contain a small number of stories for a given news medium), whereas the story overlap measure requires only two categories (overlapping vs. non-overlapping). These caveats notwithstanding, local cross-ownership appears to have perceptible but limited homogenizing effects on the issue emphasis of jointly owned newspapers and television stations.

Scientific vs. Journalistic Approaches

Opponents of cross-ownership argue that there is ample evidence that the owners of newspapers and television stations in the same city have abused their power by "whitewashing" certain stories or delaying the disclosure of important information. During oral arguments before the F.C.C., Barnett contended that "there are tons of evidence, in fact, of abuses of media cross-ownership, of harm to the public from concentrations of media control."[30] Startled by Barnett's assertion that abuses attributable to cross-ownership are numerous, Clifford Kirtland, representing the Cox Broadcasting Company, remarked, "I can't think of

---

[30] Stephen Barnett, Oral Argument Before the F.C.C., Comments in Docket 18110 (July 25, 1974), p. 305.

instance number one."[31] Other communications industry spokesmen agreed with Kirtland that evidence of abuses due to cross-ownership is scanty or nonexistent.[32]

To rebut these contentions, Barnett compiled a list of examples which, in his opinion, constitute "concrete evidence of harm from cross-ownership."[33] Some of Barnett's examples cannot be described as "concrete evidence" of harm attributable to cross-ownership. In Spokane, Washington, where the city's two newspapers and KHQ-TV are owned by the same company, it has been alleged (by unidentified sources) that the newspapers and KHQ have "white-washed" local controversies and problems.[34] Even if this is true, have the city's other media outlets performed any better? Do newspapers in comparable cities perform any better? If not, the "white-washing" may be a reflection of torpid journalism, not cross-ownership.

Barnett also notes that a Democratic candidate for Congress in Columbus, Ohio had difficulty securing press coverage in the Columbus Dispatch, a newspaper with Republican leanings. The Dispatch owns a local television station, WBNS-TV. According to the Democratic candidate's press aide, she was told by a Dispatch reporter that her

---

[31]"The Hard Choices of F.C.C. Now Confronts on Crossownership," Broadcasting (August 5, 1974), p. 26.

[32]Among these spokesmen were Lee Loevinger (counsel for the National Association of Broadcasters), R. W. Jennes (counsel for the Washington Post's broadcasting stations), and Theodore Pierson (counsel for Lee Enterprises).

[33]Stephen Barnett, "Cross-Ownership of Mass Media in the Same City: A Report to the John and Mary R. Markle Foundation" (Berkeley: September 23, 1974), p. 2.

[34]Ibid., p. 32.

candidate represented "the wrong political party."[35] Even if this is true, did WBNS also discriminate against the Democratic candidate? Did other Columbus television stations give the candidate the coverage he deserved? If not, this instance of discrimination is irrelevant to a discussion of cross-ownership, unless the assumption is made that jointly owned newspapers and television stations deliberately downplay or suppress the same stories.

In contrast to the Spokane and Columbus examples, other examples cited by Barnett are rather persuasive. In San Francisco, California, where the Chronicle owns KRON-TV, KRON reporters were prohibited by their chief executive officer from covering an impending joint operating agreement between the Chronicle and the city's Hearst newspapers until the newspaper publishers formally announced their decision. KRON's chief executive officer issued these instructions after conferring with his superior, the publisher of the Chronicle. While two other San Francisco television stations informed their viewers of the impending agreement, KRON-TV remained silent prior to the publishers' formal announcement of the decision. Moreover, KRON delayed coverage of the agreement, despite requests by KRON reporters to cover the story before the publishers officially announced their decision.[36]

In Topeka, Kansas, where the Stauffer family owns the State Journal and Capital and WIBW-TV, the Stauffer family's involvement in a company seeking a cable television franchise was obscured by the city's two newspapers until a radio station not owned by the Stauffers broke

---

[35] Ibid., pp. 46-47.

[36] Ibid., pp. 35-37.

the story.[37] In Portland, Oregon, where S. I. Newhouse owns the Oregon Journal, the Oregonian, and 50% of KOIN-TV, important facets of an abortive effort by Newhouse to acquire complete control of KOIN received late or incomplete coverage in the Newhouse newspapers. Other publications, including the Vancouver Columbian and the Oregon Times, were more prompt and thorough in reporting such information as objections raised by two F.C.C. commissioners to any increases in Newhouse's control over Portland's mass media.[38] These examples suggest that cross-ownership has had specific effects on story treatment in San Francisco, Topeka, and Portland. However, it is debatable whether the cross-ownership situations discussed by Barnett are representative of the larger population of cross-ownership stituations. As the Rand Corporation has noted, "To move from specific cases to generalizable patterns requires enough sampling or matched controls to determine whether the examples are indeed representative of the entire set of owners in question."[39] Thus, Barnett's examples do not constitute proof that cross-ownership has "substantial and widespread" effects on story treatment by jointly owned media. The abuses Barnett does document satisfactorily may or may not be typical of cross-ownership situations throughout the country.

In fairness to Barnett, it must be conceded that linkages between cross-ownership and similar story treatment are extremely

---

[37] Ibid., p. 42.

[38] Ibid., pp. 48-51.

[39] Walter Baer et al., "Concentration of Mass Media Ownership: Assessing the State of Current Knowledge," <u>Rand Corporation Report</u> (Santa Monica, California: September 1974), p. 143.

difficult to prove. Also, Barnett is probably correct when he contends that many abuses due to cross-ownership are never disclosed. Since the F.C.C. does not require broadcasters to make tape recordings of their newscasts or copies of their news scripts available for public examination, concerned citizens cannot easily verify suspicions that a particular story has been suppressed or distorted by a newspaper-owned broadcasting station in their community. Newspaper, television, or radio reporters may be aware of such suppression or distortion, but they may be reluctant to reveal what they know, out of loyalty or fear of reprisal. Or the owner and his top news executives may be the only ones who know about the owner's influence, and their lips may be sealed. In short, Barnett's assertion that his examples of abuses represent "only the tip of the iceberg" is as difficult to dispute as it is to prove.[40]

Thus, we have two competing hypotheses, neither of which has been proved. Barnett contends that effects of cross-ownership on story treatment are substantial and widespread. Spokesmen for the communications industry, on the other hand, argue that such effects are rare or nonexistent. We cannot prove or disprove either hypothesis. To do so would require extensive investigative reporting in a large number of cities.[41] Nevertheless, we may add several examples to those Barnett has already assembled--examples which prove very little but which might aid persons interested in exploring possible relationships between

---

[40] Barnett, op. cit., p. 15.

[41] Questionnaires cannot be used to obtain data on something as subtle as story treatment.

cross-ownership and story treatment in greater detail.[42]

Possible Links Between Cross-Ownership and Story Treatment

Cross-ownership appears to have resulted in the suppression of at least one story in Quincy, Illinois, where WGEM-TV is owned by the Herald-Whig. According to a WGEM news staffer, the Herald-Whig ran a series of articles on "positive aspects" of Quincy's economic conditions, including a story portraying local auto sales as good. In his opinion, the series was "Chamber of Commerce puffery" and the auto sales story was seriously misleading. The news staffer reached these conclusions after talking with auto salesmen and loan officers at financial institutions. However, he did not try to set the record straight, since that would have pitted WGEM against the Herald-Whig. "We could have destroyed that story, but didn't, because of the cross-media ownership situation," he explained. "I decided discretion would be the better part of valor and left it alone."

In Dallas Texas, the Morning News and WFAA-TV are owned by the Dealey family, through their holdings in the A. H. Belo Corporation. The chief executive officer of the Belo Corporation and the publisher of the Morning News is Joseph Dealey. Reporters at both the Morning News and WFAA cite instances where stories have been killed, toned down, or otherwise muted. At the Morning News, various stories have been suppressed or altered to suit management--stories ranging from an analysis

---

[42] Some of these examples, like Barnett's, might be more convincing if they explicitly compared the behavior of a newspaper and the newspaper-owned television station with the behavior of other media in the same city.

of the city's "oligarchy" to a comparison of food prices at chain stores (heavy advertisers in the Morning News) and budget stores. At WFAA, certain stories deemed offensive to viewers have been banned from the 6 p.m. newscast and have been handled instead at 10 p.m., in a televised documentary, or not at all. The fact that the Morning News and WFAA are both characterized by management intervention in news decisions does not necessarily mean that cross-ownership has anything to do with such intervention. However, there are two respects in which management intervention has taken a similar form at both the Morning News and WFAA.

First of all, stories involving friends of the Dealey family have received special treatment, in one way or another. A Morning News reporter recalls writing a damaging story about a Dallas investment advisor who was also making money as an advisor to the Securities and Exchange Commission's pension fund. The story ran on the newspaper's front page. Afterward, the reporter learned that the subject of his story was "a friend of Dealey's." According to the reporter, that was enough to preclude subsequent coverage. "The city editor told me 'no more stories' about this particular individual," the reporter recalls. On another occasion, a WFAA reporter put together an unflattering story about a judge who was a friend of publisher Dealey. According to the reporter, his story was aired, but only after "people from across the street" (i.e., the Morning News) viewed it and approved it. The final outcome notwithstanding, such an episode may have had a chilling effect on future coverage involving friends of the Dealey family.

Second, news executives at the Morning News and WFAA have instructed members of their staff to adhere to rather restrictive standards of good taste. In 1974, Bob Miller, city editor of the Morning

News, was told to reduce the use of vulgarisms in print. "The managing editor said there were too many 'damns' and 'hells,'" Miller recalls. "He was probably reflecting top management opinion." Tom Simmons, managing editor of the Morning News, does not remember receiving specific guidelines from publisher Dealey on the difference between good and bad taste. However, he adds, "We know what Dealey likes."

The imposition of narrow standards of good taste has been even more pronounced at WFAA. There, the dominant figure is Michael Shapiro, president of the Belo Broadcasting Corporation and a member of the board of the A. H. Belo Corporation, which Joseph Dealey chairs. According to a WFAA reporter, Shapiro has a "very sensitive stomach" about stories which might upset viewers. On more than one occasion, Shapiro has kept potentially disturbing stories from being aired during the 6 p.m. newscast, when viewers may be dining. These stories have included in-depth looks at such problems as child-beating and prostitution. Despite resistance from some reporters, WFAA, like the Morning News, has adhered to rather restrictive standards of good taste.

In Rock Island, Illinois, where the Argus and WHBF-TV are both owned by the Potter family, WHBF reporters find that the "community-mindedness" of the Potters is contagious. Two WHBF reporters say that they indulge in more boosterism than would otherwise be the case, as a result of the example set by Potter family members. The Potter family's importance as a reference group to WHBF reporters is probably strengthened by the fact that there are bonds of kinship between WHBF's general manager, Edward DeLong, and the Potter family. DeLong is the husband of the former Ann Potter, whose cousin is the current publisher of the Argus, John Potter, III.

According to one WHBF reporter, the Potter family is involved in "just about every community undertaking." These undertakings include fund-raising projects, Chamber of Commerce meetings, Y.M.C.A. activities, and others. "Even though they don't put the pressure on us, we catch the fever a bit," the reporter observes. "We know where their interests are." Another reporter agrees that there is a connection between the Potters' interests and WHBF's attentiveness to civic news. "Because you work for people who are interested in that sort of thing, you feel it would be a good thing to cover," the reporter says. He adds that he and other reporters may view the coverage of certain stories as a matter of "job security."

Boosterism may seem relatively innocuous, but it is important to remember that there is an opportunity cost involved. For every fund-raising drive WHBF covers, it might be covering more issue-oriented stories instead. Thus, boosterism and community service do not necessarily go hand in hand.

In Sacramento, California, where the Bee and KOVR-TV are both owned by the McClatchy Corporation, it is widely known that Bee publisher Eleanor McClatchy is a patron of the arts and a backer of numerous community projects. Bee reporters regard Miss McClatchy as a rather benign figure, but they say that she has a long list of "pet projects" which receive special attention in the Bee because of her interest in them. These include the Eaglet Theater, the State Fair, the Camellia Festival, the Stanford Home for Girls, the Central Valleys Science Fair, and the Ella McClatchy Library.

A particular favorite of Miss McClatchy's is the Music Circus--a tent theater where famous Hollywood stars perform in the summertime.

The Music Circus is partially underwritten by the McClatchy Corporation. In May of 1975, the Bee was making plans to publish a special tabloid on the Music Circus as a supplement in the newspaper. The suggestion to do this was relayed by the McClatchy Corporation's public relations department to managing editor Frank McCulloch. McCulloch acknowledges that Miss McClatchy's interest in such activities as the Music Circus has "some influence" on the Bee's decisions.

The McClatchy organization also passed along a request for special coverage of the Music Circus to KOVR-TV's program department, which suggested the idea of a television special on the Music Circus to news director Norm Hartman. Hartman agreed to do a half-hour special on the Music Circus, and he assigned a reporter to travel to Los Angeles to interview some of the stars who would be performing in the Music Circus. Whether KOVR gave the Music Circus too much attention is a matter of judgment. However, as one KOVR reporter put it, "I'm sure we give it more attention than the other stations."

A final possibility--that cross-ownership has homogenizing effects on story treatment by increasing cross-employment--is also worth considering. In Fresno, California, where the Bee and KMJ-TV are jointly owned, a reporter for KMJ-TV (Mike Hartman) used to work for the Bee, and a reporter for the Bee (Lanny Larson) used to work for KMJ. On at least two occasions, Hartman has covered stories concerning the Bee's involvement in a controversy.[43] On at least one occasion, Larson has written a story concerning KMJ's involvement in a controversy.[44]

---

[43] On March 4 and 6, 1975, Hartman covered court decisions stemming from the refusal of two Bee reporters--Joseph Rosato and William Patterson--to reveal the identity of a source.

[44] See Lanny Larson, "U.S. Attempts to Sever Bee, Three KMJ Stations," The Fresno Bee (November 2, 1974).

The Bee has been in the news ever since two Bee reporters defied a court order to divulge the identity of the source of a sealed grand jury transcript, excerpts of which were published in the Bee. Because the San Joaquin Communications Corporation and the Justice Department have acted to prevent the renewal of KMJ's license, KMJ has also been in the news.

Whether a former Bee employee is objective enough to cover a controversial story about the Bee is problematic. Whether a former KMJ employee is objective enough to cover a controversial story about KMJ is equally problematic. By increasing cross-employment, cross-ownership is likely to increase the probability that such dilemmas will arise.

An Unresolved Question

The investigative reporting approach has yielded several new examples of possible effects of cross-ownership on story treatment. These examples, like Barnett's, are best described as inconclusive but suggestive. Together with Barnett's examples, they seem to belie arguments that cross-ownership has negligible effects on story treatment. And yet, if effects of cross-ownership on story treatment were rife, as Barnett seems to believe, one would expect the reporter's net to have brought larger and uglier fish to the surface.

In criticizing Barnett's approach, the Rand Corporation has noted that "there is case evidence showing abuses by media owners with both concentrated and nonconcentrated holdings."[45] However, there are some "abuses" of which owners with "nonconcentrated holdings" are

---

[45] Walter Baer et al., op. cit., p. 143.

incapable. The newspaper owner who owns no broadcasting properties cannot instruct both newspaper and television employees to handle a certain story (or a certain kind of story) in the same way. He cannot hire and promote like-minded people at both the newspaper and the television station. He cannot trigger similar responses at both news organizations by making known the identity of his friends and his enemies, his likes and his dislikes, his special interests and his blind spots. In contrast, the owner of a newspaper and a television station in the same city is capable of these things. The potential for serious abuses is greater in his case.

It is clear that cross-ownership interferes with diversity in the flow of opinions by reducing the willingness of television stations to editorialize. It also appears that local cross-ownership has limited but perceptible homogenizing effects on the issue emphasis of jointly owned media. However, the extent to which cross-ownership--local or otherwise--results in similar story treatment by jointly owned media is still an open question.

VII

PUBLIC POLICY RECOMMENDATIONS

In January 1975, the Federal Communications Commission adopted a rule concerning the joint ownership of a daily newspaper and a broadcasting station in the same market. Although the F.C.C.'s pronouncement marked a crucial turning point in the cross-ownership controversy, it was not necessarily the last word on the subject. Consequently, an evaluation of the F.C.C.'s cross-ownership decision can form the basis for policy recommendations for the future.

The newspaper-television provisions of the F.C.C.'s cross-ownership rule may be summarized as follows: first, the F.C.C. "grandfathered" the overwhelming majority of newspaper-television combinations in the same market; second, the F.C.C. ordered the divestiture of newspaper-television "monopolies" in seven cities where only one television station places a city-grade signal[1] over a city served by only one daily newspaper;[2] third, the F.C.C. prohibited the formation of new newspaper-

---

[1] The definition of a "city-grade signal" differs for television stations assigned to different channels. Television stations assigned to channels 2-6 place a city-grade signal over a city if their signal has a field strength of 74 dBu's (decibels above one microvolt per meter) in the city.

[2] By defining a television market in a particular way, the F.C.C. can constrict or expand the scope of an order. The number of television stations in a market tends to increase as the definition of a market changes from city of license to area over which television stations place a city-grade signal to area over which television stations place a grade A signal to area over which television stations place a grade B signal. Thus, had the F.C.C. defined a market as the city of license, a larger

television combinations in the same market (defined as a market where the television station places a grade A signal[3] over the city where the newspaper is published); fourth, the F.C.C. prohibited the transfer of newspaper-television combinations in the same market (one where the television station places a grade A signal over the city where the newspaper is published); fifth, the F.C.C. identified conditions under which affected parties could obtain waivers of the rule; sixth, the F.C.C. said that petitions to deny renewal of a television license on the grounds of cross-ownership would not be designated for a hearing unless the petitioner could demonstrate "economic monopolization" forbidden by the Sherman Act; and seventh, the F.C.C. deferred a decision on the appropriate weight to be given the cross-ownership factor in license renewal hearings involving competing applicants for a television license.[4]

An F.C.C. ruling is more irrevocable than an ambitious politician's declaration of non-candidacy but more reversible than a home place umpire's "strike three" call. F.C.C. decisions are sometimes reversed by the courts, as when the D.C. Court of Appeals struck down the Commission's policy statement concerning comparative license

---

number of cities would have been designated as newspaper-television "monopolies." Had the F.C.C. defined a market as the area over which television stations place a grade A signal, a smaller number of cities would have been designated as newspaper-television monopolies.

[3] The definition of a "grade A signal" differs for television stations assigned to different channels. Television stations assigned to channels 2-6 place a grade A signal over a city if their signal has a field strength of 68 dBu's (decibels above one microvolt per meter) in the city.

[4] See the Federal Communications Commission, Second Report and Order in Docket 18110, adopted January 28, 1975.

renewal hearings.[5] F.C.C. decisions are also occasionally reversed by the Commission itself. In 1975, for example, the F.C.C. ruled that "equal time" requirements do not apply to debates involving candidates for federal office--a reversal of the position taken by the Commission in 1962.[6]

There are several circumstances under which the F.C.C.'s cross-ownership ruling of January 1975 could be modified or reversed. First, the D.C. Court of Appeals might strike down portions of the F.C.C.'s ruling and remand the cross-ownership matter to the F.C.C. Second, new information might persuade the F.C.C. to modify its decision. At the very least, new information might help the F.C.C. to decide what weight to give the cross-ownership factor in comparative license renewal hearings. Third, new commissioners--with different values--might reach different conclusions about cross-ownership, should the Commission revisit the matter at some future date. Consequently, new information can be useful not only in evaluating the F.C.C.'s decision of January 1975 but in recommending modifications of that decision for the future.

The Case for Divestiture

The case for divestiture ultimately rests on the assumption that diversity in the flow of news and opinion is indispensable to successful self-government. If democracy is to work, the public needs to know the

---

[5] In June 1971, the D.C. Court of Appeals struck down an F.C.C. policy statement which provided for the renewal of broadcasting licenses if the incumbent licensee was "substantially attuned" to the needs and interests of his community. See Citizens Communications Center vs. F.C.C., 447 F. 2d 1201 (1971).

[6] "League of Women Voters Takes Advantage of New Ruling on Section 315," Broadcasting (February 9, 1976), pp. 36-38.

truth—about events, problems, trends, issues, candidates for office, public officials, etc. But what is the truth? In a democracy, we hesitate to articulate a societal orthodoxy. Rather, we assume, as Milton and Mill did, that the perception of truth depends on the airing of diverse viewpoints.[7] This is not a universally held assumption, but it is one which sets our political system apart from totalitarian systems. When a newspaper or a television station editorializes against capital punishment, it is obviously expressing a viewpoint. When a newspaper or a television station covers a story, it is also (but less obviously) expressing a viewpoint—namely, that the story is more important than others which might have been covered. Public awareness of a problem or an opportunity is so crucial in a democracy that a news organization's decision to cover some stories rather than others is laden with political significance. For this reason, diversity in the flow of news is as important as diversity in the flow of opinions.

Some proponents of divestiture have argued that a relationship between media pluralism (i.e., separate ownership) and message pluralism should be assumed. F.C.C. Commissioner Glen Robinson, for example, has contended that "a competitive, unconcentrated ownership structure is prima facie in the public interest" and that "the vices of cross-ownership" need not be proved to justify divestiture.[8] In a similar

---

[7] See John Milton, "Areopagitica," in John Milton: Complete Poems and Major Prose, ed. by Merritt Hughes (New York: The Odyssey Press, 1957), pp. 716-749; also see John Stuart Mill, On Liberty, ed. by Alburey Castell (New York: Appleton-Century-Crofts, Inc., 1947).

[8] Glen Robinson, Statement Accompanying the Federal Communications Commission's Second Report and Order in Docket 18110, pp. 20-21.

vein, the National Citizens Committee for Broadcasting has maintained that "the assumed benefits of diversification" are properly treated as "a presumption" and that the burden of proof must be borne by those who oppose divestiture.[9]

As the N.C.C.B. has noted, an assumed connection between media pluralism and message pluralism undergirds a number of previous F.C.C. decisions, including prohibitions against the joint ownership of two broadcasting stations of the same type (two AM, two FM, or two TV) in the same market and prohibitions against the ownership of more than five VHF television stations by a single company.[10] However, the case for divestiture need not rest on untested assumptions about the homogenizing effects of mass media ownership concentration.

As our research indicates, the joint ownership of a newspaper and a television station in the same city interferes with diversity in the flow of news by reducing the de facto independence of jointly owned newspapers and television stations. There are at least three ways in which this occurs. First, newspaper-owned television stations are more likely than comparable television stations to receive newspaper carbons on an exclusive basis. Carbon-sharing not only represents an institutionalized flow of information between newspaper and television news staffs, but it also legitimizes other more informal exchanges of information. Second, newspaper-owned television stations are more likely

---

[9] The National Citizens Committee for Broadcasting, <u>Petition for Review of the Federal Communications Commission's Second Report and Order in Docket 18110</u>, p. 34.

[10] Ibid., pp. 4-12. The assumed connection between media pluralism and message pluralism also formed the basis of the F.C.C.'s 1970 proposal to order the divestiture of all newspaper-television combinations in the same market within a five-year period.

than comparable television stations to hire a reporter or editor who has worked for the newspaper which owns the television station or for the only newspaper in town. Cross-employment transforms some relationships between newspaper and television news staffers into relationships between former colleagues, linked by bonds of friendship and respect. Third, newspaper-owned television stations are more likely than comparable television stations to be located within the same complex of buildings as a newspaper. This increases opportunities for interaction between newspaper and television news staffs and thereby facilitates cooperation between them.

The motives of newspaper and television reporters who exchange information may be no different than those of neighbors who borrow and lend lawn-mowers, can-openers, or sugar. Nevertheless, such exchanges can be harmful to the public. No matter how innocuous they seem, effects of cross-media ownership on intermedia relations have additional effects which undermine message pluralism in the mass media. Newspapers and television stations characterized by carbon-sharing, cross-employment, or location within the same complex of buildings tend to cover more of the same stories as a result.[11] Overall, cross-ownership increases story overlap between newspapers and television stations by 16.7%.[12]

---

[11] Approximately one-half of the effects of cross-ownership on story overlap can be explained by these three variables.

[12] An average of 40.8% of the stories of television stations not owned by a newspaper are covered by a newspaper in the same city with which the television station is being compared. In contrast, an average of 47.6% of the stories of newspaper-owned television stations are covered by a newspaper in the same city which owns the television station and with which the television station is being compared. Thus, cross-ownership increases story overlap by 16.7% (.068/.408 = 16.7%).

When newspaper and television news staffs cover the same story because they have independently decided that the story is worth covering, the public may be well served. However, when newspaper and television news staffs cover the same story because they are taking cues from one another, the public may be harmed. By covering more of the same stories, jointly owned news organizations are apt to give the public an exaggerated sense of the importance of certain stories. By covering more of the same stories, jointly owned news organizations forego the opportunity to cover other stories of potentially greater importance. By covering more of the same stories, jointly owned news organizations increase the probability that persons exposed to the outputs of both will receive redundant information.

In addition to its homogenizing effects on news content, cross-ownership constricts the flow of opinions in the mass media. Cross-ownership does this by reducing the willingness of television stations to editorialize. Whereas 25.4% of television stations not owned by a newspaper never editorialize, 52.0% of newspaper-owned television stations never editorialize. The refusal of a television station to editorialize increases the dependence of the public on newspapers for viewpoints on local issues of importance.

Cross-ownership itself does not appear to have homogenizing effects on issue emphasis. However, local cross-ownership (as opposed to absentee cross-ownership) apparently increases the extent to which a newspaper and a television station give the same relative emphasis to ten key issues. In view of studies which suggest that the mass media "set the agenda" for the public, the apparent homogenizing effects of local cross-ownership on the issue emphasis of newspapers and television stations must be regarded as a cause for concern.[13]

The Case Against Divestiture

Opponents of divestiture have argued that divestiture would cause financial injury to the owners of newspaper-television combinations in the same city. Although such an argument is highly speculative, it is certainly conceivable that divestiture might result in a decline of the market value of newspaper-owned television stations.[14] However, the fact remains that the Federal Communications Commission's primary responsibility is to serve the public interest, not to maximize the profits of incumbent broadcasting licensees. Furthermore, the F.C.C. could reduce financial harm to the owners of newspaper-television combinations in the same city by issuing tax certificates to them.[15]

Arguments against divestiture are more compelling when they attempt to link harm to the owners of newspaper-television combinations with harm to the public. Opponents of divestiture have contended, for

---

[13] For studies of the agenda-setting power of the mass media, see Maxwell McCombs and Donald Shaw, "The Agenda-Setting Function of Mass Media," Public Opinion Quarterly (Summer 1971), pp. 176-187; also see G. Ray Funkhouser, "The Issues of the 60's: An Exploratory Study in the Dynamics of Public Opinion," Public Opinion Quarterly (Spring 1973), pp. 62-75.

[14] A study by Frazier and Gross (commissioned by the American Newspaper Publishers Association) estimated that across-the-board divestiture would lead to a 10 to 20 percent decline in the value of television stations. However, the Rand Corporation found serious flaws in this study. See Walter Baer et al., "Concentration of Mass Media Ownership: Assessing the State of Current Knowledge," Rand Corporation Report (Santa Monica: September 1974), pp. 115-118.

[15] The F.C.C. has already indicated a willingness to issue tax certificates in cases where it has required divestiture. See The Second Report and Order in Docket 18110, p. 45.

example, that divestiture would cause the collapse of a number of newspapers, since some newspapers use profits from their broadcasting properties to remain solvent.[16] Competing newspapers are practically an endangered species, and a reduction in the number of newspapers would be a serious matter. However, divestiture would not require newspaper owners to get out of the broadcasting business. By trading a television station in the city where his newspaper is published for a television station in another city (with a supplementary cash transaction, if appropriate), a newspaper owner would be in full compliance with a divestiture order. Or, if he preferred, he could sell the television station and invest the money in other profitable enterprises to keep his newpaper afloat. In short, divestiture need not result in the demise of additional newspapers.

Another argument against divestiture is that it would result in the sale of locally owned television stations to absentee owners, who (it is said) are apt to be less knowledgeable about the community and less committed to serving the community (as opposed to making profits). Approximately 75% of all newspaper-television combinations in the same city are locally owned. If newspaper owners traded their broadcasting properties with one another to comply with a divestiture order, local ownership would almost certainly be diminished. However, as we have seen, local cross-ownership apparently has homogenizing effects on issue emphasis which absentee cross-ownership does not. Local owners may indeed take a more active, personal interest in the management of

---

[16] The precedent most frequently cited by opponents of divestiture is the WHDH case. Shortly after the F.C.C. ordered the Boston Herald-Traveler to divest itself of WHDH-TV, the Herald-Traveler went out of business. Whether the Herald-Traveler could have survived, had it been permitted to retain WHDH, is unclear.

their properties than absentee owners, and local owners may have strong beliefs about their community's needs and problems. But these very factors increase the probability that the local owner's priorities and concerns will be perceived and pursued by news executives and reporters employed by the local owner. If local ownership has advantages for the public, it also has special disadvantages for the public, when associated with cross-ownership.

One of the most significant arguments against divestiture is the contention that newspaper-owned television stations provide "better" service than other television stations. According to opponents of divestiture, newspaper owners, whose business is informing the public, have a stronger commitment to the news and public affairs components of broadcasting than owners of insurance companies or banks. An F.C.C. staff study lends some support to this argument. After controlling for frequency, network affiliation, group ownership, station revenue, the number of minutes broadcast per week, and the number of commercial television stations in the market, the Commission's staff found that newspaper-owned television stations provided 6% more local news, 9% more local non-entertainment, and 12% more total local (including entertainment) programming than other television stations.[17]

These findings are suggestive, but they cannot be regarded as conclusive. Television stations in the nation's top seven markets were omitted from the analysis "because previous work by the staff indicated that the stations in these markets behave somewhat differently than stations in other markets and would weight the results because of

---

[17] The staff study appears in Appendix C of the Federal Communications Commission's Second Report and Order in Docket 18110.

their large size."[18] This omission may have biased the results in favor of newspaper-owned television stations, since some of the "best" television stations in the nation (using the F.C.C.'s criteria) are television stations not owned by a newspaper which happen to be located in the top seven markets which were excluded from analysis by the F.C.C.'s staff.[19] Moreover, the staff study is at odds with a previous study by Levin, who found that ownership by a newspaper does not affect the amount of news or the amount of local programming provided by television stations. Levin, like the F.C.C., found that newspaper ownership has a "very small positive effect" on the amount of public affairs programming provided by television stations. However, he also found that newspaper ownership has a "small negative effect" on the amount of local programming provided by television stations in markets served by only one VHF station.[20]

If newspaper ownership has positive effects on the amount of local non-entertainment programming provided by television stations, such effects need to be considered along with effects on intermedia

---

[18] Ibid., p. C3.

[19] The National Black Media Coalition has ranked 138 VHF network affiliates in the nation's top 50 television markets according to a number of criteria, including amounts of local news and local public affairs programming. An analysis of these rankings reveals that four non-newspaper-owned television stations in the top seven markets (those excluded from analysis by the F.C.C.'s staff) are in the top 10 for local news programming (KGO-TV, San Francisco; WCVB-TV, Boston; KABC-TV, Los Angeles; and KNBC-TV, Los Angeles) and that two are in the top 10 for local public affairs programming (WNAC-TV, Boston; and WPVI-TV, Philadelphia). For further details, see David Honig, "Broadcasting in America--1975," Access (December 1, 1975), pp. 7-12.

[20] Levin presented these findings to the F.C.C. in May 1974. Levin's findings have been summarized by Commissioner Robinson in his Statement Accompanying the Federal Communications Commission's Second Report and Order in Docket 18110, pp. 18-19.

relations, story overlap, and the willingness of television stations to editorialize. However, until differences between the F.C.C. staff study and the Levin study are reconciled, the evaluation of public policy choices cannot be based on either study.[21]

Ethics and Policy Choice

Before prescribing public policy choices, we need to specify the system of values which undergirds our recommendations. Most policy choices are complex enough to require the ordering or weighing of values, and this is certainly true of choices concerning cross-ownership. The normative foundations of our public policy recommendations need to be made explicit. In keeping with MacRae's suggestion, we have adopted an ethical system which is "clear, consistent, and general."[22] Our ethical system is based on Rawls' Theory of Justice, which we have extended so that it is applicable to communications policy choices.[23]

Rawls' preliminary argument is that normative principles are as fair as the groundrules for choosing them. With this in mind, Rawls has introduced a mechanism for choosing "just" principles, which he calls "the original position." In the original position, parties are behind a "veil of ignorance." They do not know how intelligent or talented or wealthy they are. They do not even know to which generation

---

[21] There is much to be said for a reanalysis of the F.C.C.'s staff study. Since cross-ownership may have different effects in different kinds of markets, such a reanalysis should include a breakdown by city size or (better yet) by the number of local television stations per city.

[22] Duncan MacRae, Jr., "Scientific Communication, Ethical Argument, and Public Policy," American Political Science Review (March 1971), p. 40.

[23] See John Rawls, A Theory of Justice (Cambridge, Massachusetts: The Belknap Press, 1971).

they belong. Under such conditions, Rawls asserts, parties would resort to a "maximin" strategy--i.e., they would "adopt the alternative the worst outcome of which is superior to the worst outcomes of the others."[24]

According to Rawls, two principles would be chosen in the original position. The principles are lexically ordered--or, in other words, the first must be fully satisfied before the second is even considered. The two principles have been summarized by Rawls as follow:

> First Principle--Each person is to have an equal right to the most extensive total system of equal basic liberties compatible with a similar system of liberty for all. Liberty can be restricted only for the sake of liberty. A less extensive liberty must strengthen the total system of liberty shared by all. A less than equal liberty must be acceptable to those with the lesser liberty.
>
> Second Principle--Social and economic inequalities are to be arranged so that they are:
>
> a) attached to offices and positions open to all under conditions of fair equality of opportunity; and
>
> b) to the greatest benefit of the least advantaged.[25]

By basic liberties, Rawls means the liberties we tend to associate with the rights of citizenship. Specifically, he mentions "political liberty (the right to vote and to be eligible for public office) together with freedom of speech and assembly; liberty of conscience and freedom of thought; freedom of the person along with the right to hold (personal) property; and freedom from arbitrary arrest and seizure as defined by the concept of the rule of law."[26]

---

[24] Ibid., pp. 152-153.

[25] Ibid., pp. 302-303.

[26] Ibid., p. 61.

If the right to vote is to be meaningful, citizens must have the opportunity to inform themselves about political issues and processes, the qualifications of candidates for office, the performance of public officials, etc. As Rawls notes, "All citizens should have the means to be informed about political issues. They should be in a position to assess how proposals affect their well-being and which policies advance their conception of the public good."[27] Thus, as a corollary to the right to vote, it is reasonable for individuals in the original position to establish a right for citizens to know as much as possible about public affairs. A right to know must be affirmed to institutionalize the pursuit of truth and guarantee the worth of the right to vote.

As applied to communications policy, then, the Rawlsian position is that the public has a right to know which takes precedence over considerations involving the distribution of benefits in society. This is not to say that such values as competition (the Justice Department's concern) and stability (the broadcasting industry's concern) are unimportant. However, such values should be considered only if the public's right to know is not at stake.

Does cross-ownership pose a threat to the public's right to know? Previously, it was only clear that cross-ownership involved a potential threat to the public's right to know. It is now clear that cross-ownership interferes with diversity in the flow of news by promoting carbon-sharing, cross-employment, and the location of a newspaper and a television station within the same complex of buildings. It is

---

[27] Ibid., p. 225.

also clear that cross-ownership interferes with diversity in the flow of opinions by reducing the willingness of television stations to editorialize. Insofar as cross-ownership is associated with these effects, it does pose a threat to the public's right to know.

A Critical Evaluation of the
F.C.C.'s Cross-Ownership Decision

Any retrospective analysis of a policy decision must begin with an acknowledgement of the fact that access to new information gives the critic an advantage over those who had to make a decision without the benefit of such information. In January 1975, when the F.C.C. announced its decision, effects of cross-ownership on intermedia relations, news content, and the willingness of television stations to editorialize were unclear. Had the F.C.C. been privy to facts which are now known, its decision might have been different. Thus, if the F.C.C.'s decision is found wanting in the light of new information, that does not preclude the possibility that the F.C.C. made the best decision it could at the time.

The F.C.C.'s prohibition against the formation of new newspaper-television combinations or the transfer of existing combinations from one owner to another was based on an assumption which we now know to be correct--namely, that there is a relationship between media pluralism and message pluralism. Since a prospective ban against cross-ownership did not entail the involuntary sale of a television station or a newspaper (which might cause financial injury to some incumbent licensees), the F.C.C. had no reservations about such a ban. The F.C.C. justified

---

[28] The Federal Communications Commission, Second Report and Order in Docket 18110, pp. 33-36.

the ban on the grounds that diversity could be fostered without harming incumbent licensees or causing unnecessary disruption.[28] We find ourselves in agreement with this aspect of the F.C.C.'s decision.

In contrast, we cannot support the F.C.C.'s decision to leave the overwhelming majority of newspaper-television combinations intact. First of all, the Commission appears to have accepted the arguments of communications industry spokesmen that jointly owned newspapers and television stations maintain genuinely independent news staffs. In the Commission's words: "Various combination owners have stressed that their two media interests--print and broadcast--are operated separately . . . Were it otherwise and the two operated jointly, it might have been necessary for the Commission to require divestiture in many more situations."[29]

Some jointly owned newspapers and television stations are indeed operated separately. In Dayton, for example, the jointly owned newspaper and television news staffs have been careful to maintain an arm's length relationship. However, other jointly owned newspapers and television stations have not been so careful. In Portland, Maine, where the jointly owned newspapers and television station share carbons, the news staffs can hardly be described as independent. In Quincy, Illinois, where the jointly owned newspaper and television station exchange information on a routine basis over the telephone, the news staffs can hardly be described as independent. In short, some jointly owned newspaper and television news staffs are genuinely independent, but others are not.

Second, the Commission appears to have decided that the homogenizing effects of cross-ownership on programming content must be not only

---

[29] Ibid., p. 49.

clear but substantial to warrant the divestiture of newspaper-television combinations, except where newspaper-television "monopolies" exist.[30] As the Commission put it, "Divestiture has a substantial impact, and should be required only when we can determine that it is required by the public interest. We agree that it is not necessary to have proof of abuses before we can act, and we recognize that trading of stations would tend to lessen concern based on financial losses or investment uncertainty. However, we do not think that these considerations are a substitute for the requirement of a stronger showing than we have of the need for such a severe remedy on a broader basis."[31]

This is a curious position indeed, in view of the Commission's assurance that "our primary concern is diversity in programming service."[32] If diversity in programming service is the Commission's primary concern, how can it condone the continuation of cross-ownership in Portland, Maine, where cross-ownership has clear homogenizing effects on the flow of news? There is not a newspaper-television monopoly in Portland, but the newspaper-owned television station is one of only

---

[30] The Commission's position is difficult to pinpoint because of confusing language in the Second Report and Order in Docket 18110--language which may reflect subtle differences of opinion among the commissioners themselves. On p. 37, the Commission rejects the option of across-the-board divestiture on the grounds that "a mere hoped for gain in diversity is not enough." This suggests that the Commission was not convinced that cross-ownership has homogenizing effects. However, on p. 38, the Commission concedes that "it is unrealistic to expect true diversity from a commonly owned station-newspaper combination." This suggests that the Commission did not doubt that cross-ownership has homogenizing effects but rather doubted whether those effects are serious enough to justify divestiture in a substantial number of markets.

[31] The Federal Communications Commission, Second Report and Order in Docket 18110, p. 39.

[32] Ibid., p. 38.

two Portland television stations. If diversity in programming service is in fact the Commission's primary concern (as opposed to financial protection for incumbent licensees), then divestiture is appropriate in Portland, by the Commission's own standards.

The Commission is certainly correct that the "number of voices available to the people of a given area" ought to be examined as part of "the diversity approach."[33] If cross-ownership had similar homogenizing effects on news content in cities with different numbers of local television stations, such effects would pose a greater threat to the public's right to know in cities with only one local television station than in cities with two, a greater threat in cities with two local television stations than in cities with three. However, the mere presence of a second television station in a city where cross-ownership exists is not sufficient to establish that the public's right to know is not at stake. Similarly, the absence of a second television station in a city where cross-ownership exists would be of no concern if we could be sure that cross-ownership had no harmful effects in such a market. In short, a "diversity approach" ought to take into account both the number of local television stations in a city and the extent to which cross-ownership has homogenizing effects in cities with different numbers of local television stations.

Third, the Commission used a standard for determining the number of local television stations in a city (namely, the number of television stations placing a city-grade signal over the city) which rendered the Commission's definition of what constitutes a newspaper-

---

[33] Ibid., p. 38.

television "monopoly" unrealistic. According to the Commission's definition, there are only eight "true monopoly situations" involving newspaper-television combinations in the same city.[34] However, even if two or more television stations place a city-grade signal over a particular city, there may be only one television station with a studio located in that city. Studio location is a crucial factor in the coverage of local issues, because a television station tends to pay more attention to a city if it has a studio there (and less attention if it does not). In three of three cases we have examined, the television station with a studio in a particular city devoted a higher percentage of its news stories to that city than other stations in the same market which do not have a studio in that city.[35]

---

[34] According to the Commission's definition, there are newspaper-television monopolies in only eight cities: Anniston, Alabama, Albany, Georgia, Mason City, Iowa, Meridian, Mississippi, Hickory, North Carolina, Watertown, New York, Texarkana, Texas, and Bluefield, West Virginia. The Commission ordered divestiture in seven of these eight cities. The Commission exempted Hickory from its requirement on the grounds that the newspaper-owned television station there (a UHF independent with a small audience) would be very difficult to sell.

[35] In the Quincy-Hannibal market, KHQA-TV, with a studio in Hannibal, devotes a higher percentage of its news stories to Hannibal than WGEM-TV, which does not have a studio in Hannibal. In the Quad Cities market, WQAD-TV, with a studio in Moline, devotes a higher percentage of its news stories to Moline than WHBF-TV, which does not have a studio in Moline. In the Sacramento-Stockton market, KOVR-TV, with a studio in Stockton, devotes a higher percentage of its news stories to Stockton than KCRA-TV or KXTV-TV, which do not have studios in Stockton. Studio location is closely related to a television station's city of license. A television station must have a studio in its city of license; it can have a studio elsewhere too. The effects of television news viewing on public awareness are apt to depend on studio location, as they do on a television station's city of license. According to Lucas and Possner, regular television news viewing has positive effects on the public's knowledge of local officials and understanding of local issues in a television station's city of license but not in adjacent towns. See William Lucas and Karen Possner, "Television News and Local Awareness: A Retrospective Look," _Rand Corporation Report_ (Santa Monica, California: October 1975).

In Rock Island, Illinois, where the Argus owns WHBF-TV, WHBF is the only television station with a studio in that city. WQAD-TV, with a studio in nearby Moline, places a city grade signal over Rock Island, but WQAD devotes a higher percentage of its news stories to Moline than WHBF and WHBF devotes a higher percentage of its news stories to Rock Island than WQAD. Consequently, the Rock Island television viewer who seeks to maximize his exposure to news about his own city has no real alternative to WHBF. In reality, Rock Island has only one "local" television station. And yet, according to the Commission's definition, Rock Island does not constitute a newspaper-television monopoly situation. If the number of local television stations in a city is defined as the number of television stations which have a studio in that city and which air local newscasts, the number of newspaper-television monopolies is 15, not 8 (see Table 37).

Overall, the F.C.C.'s ruling of January 1975 must be described as an inadequate response to problems caused by newspaper-television cross-ownership. By confining its divestiture order to seven newspaper-television monopoly situations, the Commission allowed newspaper-television combinations to remain intact in a number of cities where cross-ownership has effects serious enough to interfere with the public's right to know. In Portland, Maine and Quincy, Illinois, for example, cross-ownership has effects on intermedia relations and news content which undermine diversity in the flow of news. Even the Commission's decision to break up newspaper-television monopolies (a decision which is entirely justified if cross-ownership has homogenizing effects in such cities) suffers from the fact that the Commission's definition of what constitutes a monopoly is unduly narrow.

Table 37. Newspaper-Television Monopolies

City	Newspaper(s)	T.V. Station
1. Anniston, Alabama	Star	WHMA
2. Albany, Georgia	Herald	WALB
3. Rock Island, Illinois	Argus	WHBF
4. Mason City, Iowa	Globe-Gazette	KGLO
5. Columbus, Mississippi	Commercial Dispatch	WCBI
6. Meridian, Mississippi	Star	WTOK
7. Hastings, Nebraska	Tribune	KHAS
8. Watertown, New York	Times	WWNY
9. Greensboro, North Carolina	News, Record	WFMY
10. Hickory, North Carolina	Record	WHKY
11. Akron, Ohio	Beacon Journal	WAKR
12. Johnstown, Pennsylvania	Tribune-Democrat	WJAC
13. Temple, Texas	Telegram	KCEN
14. Texarkana, Texas	Gazette, News	KTAL
15. Bluefield, West Virginia	Telegraph	WHIS

Note: A newspaper-television monopoly exists when a city is served by only one newspaper company and only one local television station, both of which are jointly owned. We have defined a local television station as one which has a studio in the city and which airs local newscasts.

In rejecting the option of across-the-board divestiture of newspaper-television combinations in the same city, the F.C.C. did not necessarily act improperly. As we have observed, cross-ownership appears to have no homogenizing effects in certain cities. Since the public's right to know is not at stake in these cities, other factors can be considered. Where the public's right to know is not at stake, the merits of divestiture are difficult to determine. Divestiture might eliminate unfair advantages which newspaper-owned television stations enjoy over their competitors in certain cities.[36] On the other hand, divestiture might cause substantial financial harm to incumbent licensees. Divestiture might result in lower newspaper or television advertising rates and attendant savings to the consumer.[37] On the other hand, divestiture might deprive the public of the continuity of service which is one component of "quality" broadcasting.

The F.C.C. may have been correct in rejecting across-the-board divestiture as an "overkill" strategy. The F.C.C. may have also been correct in assigning a greater value (implicitly) to stability than to competition. However, the Commission erred in deciding that newspaper-television cross-ownership needs to be abolished in only seven cities. Newspaper-television cross-ownership interferes with diversity in the flow of news and opinion in other cities as well. In a democracy, such effects are too serious to be ignored.

Rulemaking vs. Case-by-Case Approaches

If reliable data on the effects of cross-ownership in individual cities were easily obtained and considerations of political and

---

[36] In St. Louis, Missouri, for example, the Post-Dispatch, which owns KSD-TV, has apparently given KSD (channel 5) a special boost by mentioning its program offerings first in the newspaper's television listings, despite the fact that other local stations have lower channel numbers. See Stephen Barnett, "Cross-Ownership of Mass Media in the Same City: A Report to the John and Mary R. Markle Foundation" (Berkeley: September 23, 1974), p. 56.

[37] Owen found evidence to support this hypothesis, but his study has been challenged by others. See Walter Baer et al., "Concentration of Mass Media Ownership: Assessing the State of Current Knowledge," Rand Corporation Report (Santa Monica: September 1974), pp. 82-92.

administrative feasibility were irrelevant, case-by-case approaches to problems caused by cross-ownership might be preferable to a rulemaking approach. Case-by-case approaches are appealing in that they would single out for remedial action those situations where cross-ownership actually has harmful effects. Case-by-case approaches have the advantage of protecting owners of newspaper-television combinations from injury in cities where cross-ownership poses no threat to the public's right to know.

However, case-by-case approaches have several important drawbacks, both general and specific. First of all, the case-by-case method would be time-consuming, tedious, and possibly unproductive. In the words of Commissioner Robinson, it would involve "problems of managerial nuisance."[38] This would be especially true if the F.C.C. attempted to determine whether the owner of a newspaper-television combination deliberately distorted the news.[39] Furthermore, even a full-scale F.C.C. inquiry might leave crucial questions unresolved. As Robinson puts it, the Commission could find itself trying to evaluate "largely unreliable and anecdotal information."[40]

Second, the F.C.C. is reluctant to examine the news content of a broadcasting station (or a newspaper) for fear of treading on the First Amendment. In Commissioner Hooks' opinion, for example, the case-by-case method would require the F.C.C. to deal with program content and with "a whole thicket of things we ought not to be dealing

---

[38] Personal interview with Glen Robinson, March 12, 1976.

[39] The F.C.C. attempted to do this in the Chronicle case. See Barnett, op. cit., pp. 34-41.

[40] Interview with Robinson, op. cit.

with."[41] Commissioner Robinson, who agrees with Hooks, notes that other commissioners feel the same way: "They're not going to get into a case-by-case journalistic analysis of content unless there is some extrinsic evidence of abuse."[42] According to Commissioner Quello, an example of an abuse which might warrant an inquiry would be the "deliberate suppression of stories."[43] Except in such an egregious case, the Commission would probably eschew an examination of the news content of jointly owned newspapers and television stations.

In addition to these general problems, there are more specific problems with particular case-by-case approaches. For example, the Justice Department could file antitrust suits against newspaper-television combinations in various markets, but such suits would probably be extremely difficult to win. In markets where the newspaper-television combination resulted from a merger or acquisition, Section 7 of the Clayton Act would apply. In these markets, the Justice Department might win its case by demonstrating that the newspaper-television combination controlled 30% of the relevant market.[44] However, in markets where the newspaper-television combination resulted from an original license application, Section 7 of the Clayton Act would apparently not apply. In these markets, the Justice Department would probably have

---

[41] "Commission Hears Last Word on Crossownership, Gets Ready to Draft Rule," Broadcasting (July 29, 1974), pp. 5-6.

[42] Interview with Robinson, op. cit.

[43] Personal interview with James Quello, March 8, 1976.

[44] The 30% concentration standard is found in United States vs. Philadelphia National Bank (1963). In its petitions to deny the renewals of various newspaper-owned television stations, the Justice Department has applied the 30% standard to the share of local advertising revenues controlled by newspaper-broadcasting combinations.

to rely on Section 2 of the Sherman Act, which prohibits economic "monopolization." According to Barnett, "many" current newspaper-broadcasting combinations resulted from an original license application rather than a merger or acquisition.[45] In such markets, antitrust suits might not be viable.

A more satisfactory case-by-case approach would be to deal with cross-ownership through license renewal mechanisms. However, the efficacy of the license renewal process for this purpose depends on the willingness of interested parties to file a petition to deny or a competing application for a license in a particular case. It also depends on the willingness of the F.C.C. to designate a petition to deny for a hearing[46] or to give substantial weight to the cross-ownership factor in a comparative license renewal hearing.[47] If no group came forward to challenge the license renewal application of WGEM-TV in Quincy, nothing would be done about cross-ownership there. Even if a group did file a petition to deny the television station's license, the F.C.C. would not be obligated to designate the petition for a hearing. Even if a hearing were held, the F.C.C. would not be obligated to give substantial weight to the cross-ownership factor.

---

[45] Barnett, op. cit., p. 4.

[46] Although many petitions to deny have been filed, the F.C.C. has designated very few of them for a hearing. According to James Brown of the F.C.C.'s Renewal and Transfer Division, 337 petitions to deny were filed between 1969 and May 1976. According to Frank Lloyd of the Citizens Communications Center, only 14 of these petitions have been designated for a hearing by the F.C.C.

[47] The D.C. Court of Appeals has ruled that the F.C.C. must give some weight to the cross-ownership factor in a license renewal hearing. See Citizens Communications Center vs. F.C.C., 447 F. 2d 1201 (1971).

Moreover, the license renewal bill passed by the House in 1974 would have prohibited the F.C.C. from considering cross-ownership at renewal time.[48] The license renewal bill passed by the Senate later in the same year would not have prohibited the F.C.C. from considering cross-ownership at renewal time but would have limited such consideration to "unique cases" where the concentration of mass media is "compelling enough" to warrant attention.[49] If Congress were to approve legislation comparable to that which has already passed the House, the F.C.C. would be barred from considering cross-ownership during license renewal proceedings altogether.

A rule which cuts a broad swath through existing newspaper-television combinations (requiring divestiture in some cities where newspaper-television cross-ownership has no demonstrable homogenizing effects) might seem unfair to those "innocent" licensees who suffer financial harm as a result. However, such a rule is the only feasible solution to problems caused by newspaper-television cross-ownership. Financial harm caused to "innocent" licensees is regrettable, but the public's right to know must take precedence over this concern.

This is not only the Rawlsian position; it is also the position of the U.S. Supreme Court. As the Supreme Court has declared, "It is the right of the viewers and listeners, not the right of the broadcasters, which is paramount."[50] The Supreme Court has also stressed that a

---

[48] Broadcast License Renewal Act, Congressional Record--House (May 1, 1974), pp. H3413-H3433.

[49] "Renewal Relief Takes Another Step Forward," Broadcasting (September 30, 1974), pp. 22-23.

[50] Red Lion Broadcasting Company vs. F.C.C., 395 U.S. 390 (1969).

broadcasting license is a public trust and that renewal is to be granted or denied on the basis of the public interest, not on the basis of the economic well-being of the incumbent licensee. In the Court's own language, "Licenses to broadcast do not confer ownership of designated frequencies, but only the temporary privilege of using them."[51]

A Proposed Rule

No conceivable rule can perfectly distinguish between cities where divestiture is needed and cities where it is not needed. Nevertheless, a rule can be designed to isolate as much as possible those cities where cross-ownership poses a threat to the public's right to know. To determine where cross-ownership interferes the most with message pluralism, we need to decide how cities should be grouped, so that the homogenizing effects of cross-ownership can be compared in different kinds of cities. If cross-ownership had identical homogenizing effects in cities with different numbers of local television stations, these effects would pose a greater threat to the public's right to know in cities served by a smaller number of local television stations.[52] Since the number of local television stations per city is a variable worth considering in its own right, we have grouped cities into four categories according to the number of local television stations per city: one, two, three, or more than three. In each group of cities, we have examined the relationship between cross-ownership and four variables which interfere with diversity in the flow of news or opinion: carbon-

---

[51] Red Lion Broadcasting Company vs. F.C.C., 395 U.S. 394 (1969).

[52] We have defined a local television station as one which has a studio in the same city as that in which the newspaper is published and which airs local newscasts.

sharing (CS), cross-employment (CE), location within the same complex of buildings (CB), and the refusal of a television station to editorialize (RE). For each of the four variables, we have subtracted the percentage of non-newspaper-owned television stations associated with the variable from the percentage of newspaper-owned television stations associated with the variable. By summing these differences, we have obtained a measure of the cumulative homogenizing effects of cross-ownership in each group of cities.

As Table 38 indicates, cross-ownership has effects on CS, CE, and RE but not CB, in cities with only one local television station. Whereas 33.3% of the newspaper-owned television stations receive carbons on an exclusive basis, 9.1% of the non-newspaper-owned television stations do. Whereas 18.2% of the newspaper-owned television stations have hired a reporter or editor who worked for the newspaper which owns the television station, none of the non-newspaper-owned television stations has hired a reporter or editor who worked for the newspaper which owns the television station or for the only newspaper in town. Whereas 75.0% of the newspaper-owned television stations never editorialize, 30.0% of the non-newspaper-owned television stations never editorialize. In these cities, there are no instances where a newspaper and a television station are located within the same complex of buildings.

In cities served by two local television stations, cross-ownership has effects on CS, CE, CB, and RE, although it should be noted that the effects on CE are very small (see Table 39). Whereas 13.3% of the newspaper-owned television stations are characterized by carbon-sharing, none of the non-newspaper-owned television stations is. Whereas 16.7% of the newspaper-owned television stations are character-

Table 38. Effects of Cross-Ownership on Four Variables Which Limit Diversity, in Cities with One Local Television Station

Variable	T.V. Station Owned By Paper (A)	T.V. Station Not Owned By Paper (B)	Difference Between Percentages (A-B)
Carbon-sharing	33.3%	9.1%	24.2%
Cross-employment	18.2%	0.0%	18.2%
Location within same complex of buildings	0.0%	0.0%	0.0%
Refusal to editorialize	75.0%	30.0%	45.0%
Sum of differences			87.4%

Note: A local television station has been defined as one which has a studio in the same city as that in which the newspaper is published and which airs local newscasts. There are 15 newspaper-owned television stations in cities with one local television station: WHMA (Anniston, Alabama), WALB (Albany, Georgia), WHBF (Rock Island, Illinois), KGLO (Mason City, Iowa), WCBI (Columbus, Mississippi), WTOK (Meridian, Mississippi), KHAS (Hastings, Nebraska), WWNY (Watertown, New York), WFMY (Greensboro, North Carolina), WHKY (Hickory, North Carolina), WAKR (Akron, Ohio), WJAC (Johnstown, Pennsylvania), KCEN (Temple, Texas), KTAL (Texarkana, Texas), and WHIS (Bluefield, West Virginia).

ized by cross-employment, 11.1% of the non-newspaper-owned television stations are. Whereas 22.2% of the newspaper-owned television stations are located within the same complex of buildings as the newspaper which owns them, 5.6% of the non-newspaper-owned television stations are located within the same complex of buildings as a newspaper. Whereas 50.0% of the newspaper-owned television stations never editorialize, 10.0% of the non-newspaper-owned television stations never editorialize.

In cities served by three local television stations, cross-ownership has effects on CE and RE but not CS or CB (see Table 40).

Table 39. Effects of Cross-Ownership on Four Variables Which Limit Diversity, in Cities with Two Local Television Stations

Variable	T.V. Station Owned By Paper (A)	T.V. Station Not Owned By Paper (B)	Difference Between Percentages (A-B)
Carbon-sharing	13.3%	0.0%	13.3%
Cross-employment	16.7%	11.1%	5.6%
Location within same complex of buildings	22.2%	5.6%	16.6%
Refusal to editorialize	50.0%	10.0%	40.0%
Sum of differences			75.5%

Note: A local television station has been defined as one which has a studio in the same city as that in which the newspaper is published and which airs local newscasts. There are 18 newspaper-owned television stations in cities with two local television stations: WFLA (Tampa, Florida), KIFI (Idaho Falls, Idaho), WCIA (Champaign, Illinois), WGEM (Quincy, Illinois), WSBT (South Bend, Indiana), WTHI (Terre Haute, Indiana), KCRG (Cedar Rapids, Iowa), KCCI (Des Moines, Iowa), WIBW (Topeka, Kansas), WPSD (Paducah, Kentucky), WGAN (Portland, Maine), KYTV (Springfield, Missouri), WHIO (Dayton, Ohio), WFMJ (Youngstown, Ohio), WSEE (Erie, Pennsylvania), WTPA (Harrisburg, Pennsylvania), WGAL (Lancaster, Pennsylvania), and WTAR (Norfolk, Virginia).

Whereas 35.7% of the newspaper-owned television stations are characterized by cross-employment, 15.0% of the non-newspaper-owned television stations are. Whereas 56.2% of the newspaper-owned television stations never editorialize, 31.8% of the non-newspaper-owned television stations never editorialize. In these cities, there are no known instances of carbon-sharing and no instances where a newspaper and a television station are located within the same complex of buildings.

Table 40. Effects of Cross-Ownership on Four Variables Which Limit Diversity, in Cities with Three Local Television Stations

Variable	T.V. Station Owned By Paper (A)	T.V. Station Not Owned By Paper (B)	Difference Between Percentages (A-B)
Carbon-sharing	0.0%	0.0%	0.0%
Cross-employment	35.7%	15.0%	20.7%
Location within same complex of buildings	0.0%	0.0%	0.0%
Refusal to editorialize	56.2%	31.8%	24.4%
Sum of differences			45.1%

Note: A local television station has been defined as one which has a studio in the same city as that in which the newspaper is published and which airs local newscasts. There are 26 newspaper-owned television stations in cities with three local television stations: WAPI (Birmingham, Alabama), KMJ (Fresno, California), WTOP (Washington, D.C.), WMAL (Washington, D.C.), WBRZ (Baton Rouge, Louisiana), KSLA (Shreveport, Louisiana), WBAL (Baltimore, Maryland), WMAR (Baltimore, Maryland), WWJ (Detroit, Michigan), WCCO (Minneapolis, Minnesota), WJTV (Jackson, Mississippi), KTVI (St. Louis, Missouri), KSD (St. Louis, Missouri), KETV (Omaha, Nebraska), KORK (Las Vegas, Nevada), WBEN (Buffalo, New York), WHEC (Rochester, New York), WSYR (Syracuse, New York), WDAY (Fargo, North Dakota), WCPO (Cincinnati, Ohio), WBNS (Columbus, Ohio), WKY (Oklahoma City, Oklahoma), WFBC (Greenville, South Carolina), WMC (Memphis, Tennessee), KSL (Salt Lake City, Utah), and KHQ (Spokane, Washington).

As Table 41 indicates, cross-ownership has effects on CE and CB but not CS or RE, in cities served by over three local television stations.[53] Whereas 50.0% of the newspaper-owned television stations are characterized by cross-employment, 13.6% of the non-newspaper-owned

---

[53]In these cities, there is a very slight negative relationship between cross-ownership and refusal to editorialize.

Table 41. Effects of Cross-Ownership on Four Variables Which Limit Diversity, in Cities with More Than Three Local Television Stations

Variable	T.V. Station Owned By Paper (A)	T.V. Station Not Owned By Paper (B)	Difference Between Percentages (A-B)
Carbon-sharing	0.0%	0.0%	0.0%
Cross-employment	50.0%	13.6%	36.4%
Location within same complex of buildings	15.4%	0.0%	15.4%
Refusal to editorialize	22.2%	23.1%	-0.9%
Sum of differences			50.9%

Note: A local television station has been defined as one which has a studio in the same city as that in which the newspaper is published and which airs local newscasts. There are 13 newspaper-owned television stations in cities with more than three local television stations: KOVR (Sacramento, California), KRON (San Francisco, California), WSB (Atlanta, Georgia), WFLD (Chicago, Illinois), WGN (Chicago, Illinois), WHAS (Louisville, Kentucky), WPIX (New York, New York), WEWS (Cleveland, Ohio), KOIN (Portland, Oregon), WFAA (Dallas, Texas), KDFW (Dallas, Texas), KPRC (Houston, Texas), and WTMJ (Milwaukee, Wisconsin).

television stations are. Whereas 15.4% of the newspaper-owned television stations are located within the same complex of buildings as the newspaper which owns them, none of the non-newspaper-owned television stations is located within the same complex of buildings as a newspaper. In these cities, there are no known instances of carbon-sharing, and the relationship between cross-ownership and refusal to editorialize (negative in these cities) is negligible.

If we compare the cumulative effects of cross-ownership on CS, CE, CB, and RE in the four different groups of cities, we discover that cross-ownership has greater homogenizing effects in cities served by one or two local television stations than in cities served by three or more local television stations (see Figure 4). It is not self-evident that each of the four variables (CS, CE, CB, and RE) should be weighted equally in determining the cumulative effects of cross-ownership. It might be argued, for example, that carbon-sharing (CS) should be weighted twice as heavily as either cross-employment (CE) or location within the same complex of buildings (CB), since our causal model indicated that the effects of CS on story overlap are approximately twice as great as those of either CE or CB.[54] If we were to weight CS twice as heavily as each of the other three variables, the gap between cities with fewer than three local television stations and cities with more than two local television stations would become even wider, since cross-ownership has effects on carbon-sharing in cities with one or two local television stations but not in other cities. Thus, such a weighting scheme would make the case for divestiture in cities with only one or two local television stations even stronger.

The case for divestiture in cities with one or two local television stations is further strengthened if we remind ourselves that homogenizing effects of identical magnitudes would be more serious in cities served by one or two local television stations than in cities served by more than two local television stations. In Rawlsian terms, citizens who live in cities served by only one or two local television

---

[54]The effects of CS on story overlap are represented by a standardized b of .189. The combined effects of CE and CB on story overlap (both direct and indirect) are represented by a standardized b of .203. The effects of CB on story overlap are slightly greater than the effects of CE.

FIGURE 4. CUMULATIVE EFFECTS OF CROSS-OWNERSHIP ON FOUR
VARIABLES WHICH LIMIT DIVERSITY, BY NUMBER OF
LOCAL T.V. STATIONS PER CITY

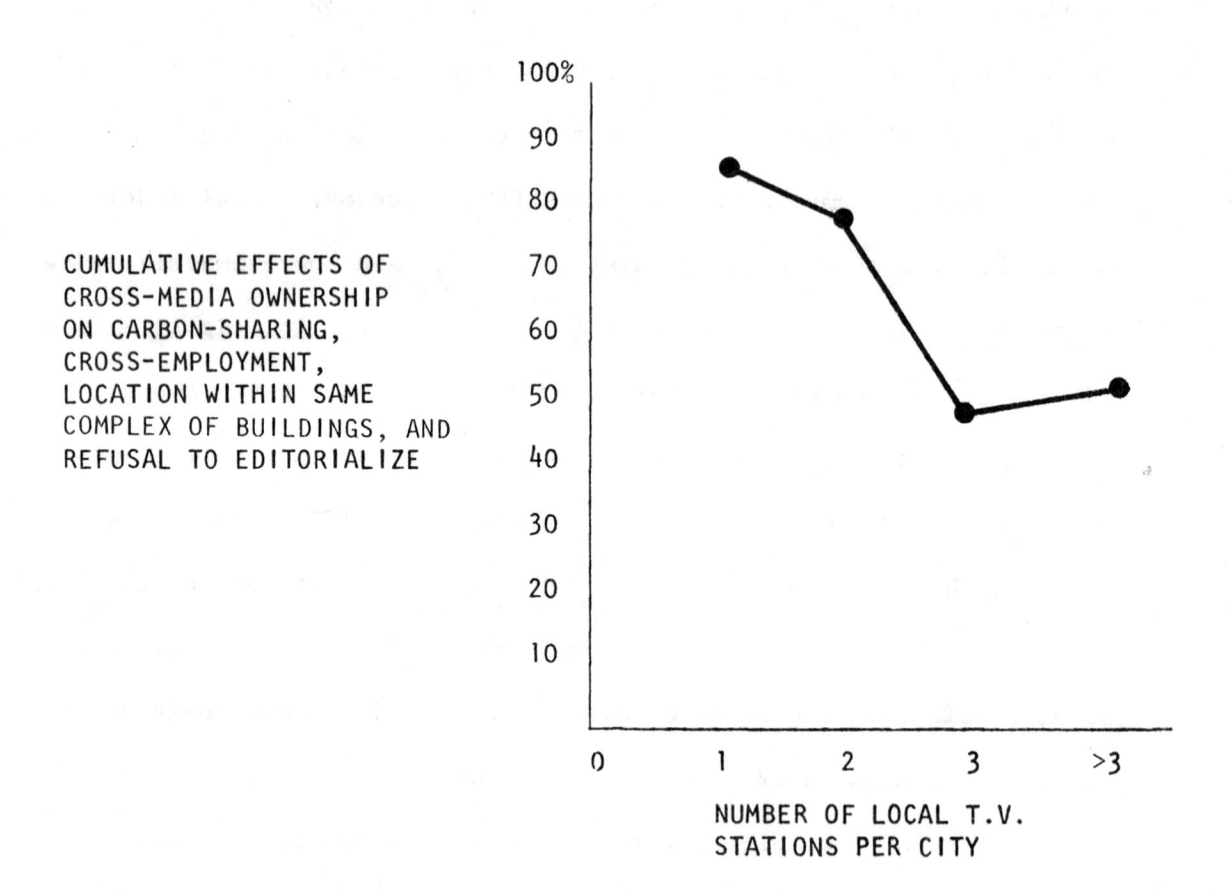

CUMULATIVE EFFECTS OF
CROSS-MEDIA OWNERSHIP
ON CARBON-SHARING,
CROSS-EMPLOYMENT,
LOCATION WITHIN SAME
COMPLEX OF BUILDINGS, AND
REFUSAL TO EDITORIALIZE

NUMBER OF LOCAL T.V.
STATIONS PER CITY

Note: A local television station has been defined as one which has a studio in the same city as that in which the newspaper is published and which airs local newscasts.

stations, one of which is owned by a local newspaper, are the "least advantaged" in two senses: first, they live in cities where cross-ownership has greater homogenizing effects; and second, they have access to fewer local television stations to counter such effects. Thus, we are led to propose that newspaper-television cross-ownership be eliminated in cities served by only one or two local television stations (where a local television station is defined as one which has a studio in the same city as that in which the newspaper is published and which airs local newscasts). We cannot state conclusively that a rule based on our proposal would be preferable to across-the-board divestiture.[55] That judgment depends on the relative merits of competition (a value emphasized by the Justice Department) and stability (a value emphasized by the communications industry). However, we are prepared to argue that divestiture is necessary in cities served by only one or two local television stations to eliminate dangerous impediments to diversity in the flow of news and opinion.

Our proposed rule, which would leave 39 newspaper-television combinations intact, differs from a rule suggested by Commissioner Robinson which would leave 10 newspaper-television combinations intact.[56]

___

[55] Were it necessary to choose between the status quo and across-the-board divestiture, we believe that the primacy of the public's right to know would require that the latter alternative be chosen.

[56] Robinson's suggestion represents an application of the 30% concentration standard for divestiture (as articulated in U.S. vs. Philadelphia National Bank) to data on circulation/audience shares controlled by a newspaper-television combination. Specifically, Robinson would require divestiture in cases where the newspaper controlled over 30% of the circulation of daily newspapers published within the newspaper's home city and where the television station controlled over 30% of the prime-time audience of television stations licensed to the city. Robinson would also find across-the-board divestiture an acceptable solution. See Glen Robinson, Statement Accompanying the Federal Communications Commission's Second Report and Order in Docket 18110,

Our proposal also differs from the rule adopted by the F.C.C., which left 65 newspaper-television combinations intact.[57] We agree with the F.C.C. that divestiture is required in cities where newspaper-television monopolies exist, but we find the F.C.C.'s definition of what constitutes a monopoly too narrow. We agree with the F.C.C. that the number of local television stations in a city is a legitimate consideration in determining the appropriate scope of a divestiture order, but we do not regard the number of local television stations as the only relevant measure of diversity. Finally, we agree with the F.C.C. that the financial well-being of incumbent licensees is a value worth considering, but we believe that it pales in comparison to the public's right to know. In cities served by only one or two local television stations, we believe that newspaper-television cross-ownership poses a threat to the public's right to know and needs to be eliminated.

Supplementary Proposals

A rule requiring the divestiture of newspaper-television combinations in cities served by fewer than three local television stations

---

pp. 30-31. For the data Robinson used, see Walter Baer et al., "Newspaper-Television Station Cross-Ownership: Options for Federal Action," *Rand Corporation Report* (Santa Monica: September 1974), pp. 13-15 and Tables 8-9. Robinson's 30% rule would leave 10 newspaper-television combinations in the same city intact: the Sacramento Bee and KOVR, the San Francisco Chronicle and KRON, the Washington Star and WMAL, the Washington Post and WTOP, the Chicago Tribune and WGN, the Chicago Daily News & Sun-Times and WFLD, the Baltimore News American and WBAL, the St. Louis Post-Dispatch and KSD, the St. Louis Globe Democrat and KTVI, and the New York Daily News and WPIX. Robinson's 30% rule would also leave the Ogden Standard-KUTV combination intact, but we have not treated that combination as a genuine example of cross-ownership in the same city, since KUTV does not have a studio in Ogden, Utah, where the Standard is published.

[57] The F.C.C. ordered the divestiture of only seven newspaper-television combinations.

should be regarded as a first step but not a final step. If divestiture in a particular city would actually undermine the public's right to know in that city, a waiver of the rule would be appropriate. If, for example, divestiture would bring about the demise of either the newspaper or the television station, a waiver would be warranted.[58] If the presence of a third local television station could be demonstrated in one of the cities we have earmarked for divestiture, a waiver might also be appropriate.[59] However, the public's right to know is too important to justify a waiver simply because divestiture would cause financial harm to a particular licensee. And we have concluded that the public's right to know is at stake in cities served by fewer than three local television stations, one of which is owned by a local newspaper.

Just as waivers are warranted in cities where our proposed rule goes too far, supplementary approaches are needed in cities where our proposed rule does not go far enough. As one step, the F.C.C. might adopt a policy statement or rule affirming the need for "the operational separation of commonly owned newspaper-television and newspaper-radio combinations," as suggested by Commissioner Quello.[60] Or the F.C.C.

---

[58] Thus, we agree with the reasoning behind the F.C.C.'s decision not to require divestiture in Hickory, North Carolina, where the F.C.C. anticipates that the newspaper-owned television station could not be sold to another buyer. See the Second Report and Order in Docket 18110, pp. 45-46.

[59] Questionnaires mailed to all television stations with studios in cities where cross-ownership exists sought to determine which television stations aired local newscasts. In cases where the questionnaire was not returned, we assumed that the television station did not air local newscasts if the station did not have a news director listed in Television Factbook: Stations Volume. That assumption may have been incorrect in particular cases, or the situation may have changed in other cases.

[60] James Quello, Statement Accompanying the Federal Communications Commission's Second Report and Order in Docket 18110. Commissioner

might be more specific--proscribing carbon-sharing between newspapers and broadcasting stations[61] and prohibiting the location of a newspaper and a television station within the same complex of buildings.[62] However, the F.C.C. has shown a reluctance to interfere with the news-gathering methods of broadcasting stations. Also, measures restricting the freedom of newspapers to communicate as they wish with television stations might be deemed unconstitutional by the courts.

The license renewal approach may be cumbersome, but it represents the best available mechanism for dealing with harmful effects of cross-ownership in cities where divestiture has not been required by rulemaking. Although the F.C.C. can deny the renewal of a broadcasting license on its own authority, challenges by outside parties are more frequent. Such challenges may take the form of a petition to deny the license (where the challenger does not seek the license for himself) or a competing application for the license (where the challenger does seek the license for himself).

In the Second Report and Order, the F.C.C. stated that petitions to deny which raise objections to the concentration of mass media ownership would not be designated for a hearing unless the petitioner could show "economic monopolization" prohibited by the Sherman Act.[63] This

---

Benjamin Hooks has also expressed support for such a policy statement or rule. See Benjamin Hooks, Statement Accompanying the Federal Communications Commission's Second Report and Order in Docket 18110.

[61] Although our questionnaire data suggest that carbon-sharing is confined to cities with fewer than three local television stations, there may be instances of carbon-sharing in other cities as well.

[62] If it proved too difficult to operationalize the concept of "location within the same complex of buildings," the F.C.C. might simply prohibit location within the same building.

[63] Second Report and Order in Docket 18110, p. 49.

unduly restricts the ability of petitioners to argue that the renewal of the license of a particular newspaper-owned television station would not be in the public interest. If a petitioner can demonstrate that the public's right to know is at stake in a particular city, the petition to deny ought to be designated for a hearing. Furthermore, the F.C.C. should eliminate the "Catch 22" which bedevils many of those who file petitions to deny. As the National Citizens Committee for Broadcasting explains it, "To get a hearing you need discovery and subpoena tools to obtain the facts; but you cannot get discovery until the Commission designates the matter for hearing."[64] To facilitate an intelligent judgment on the question of whether a hearing is warranted in the first place, the F.C.C. should enable petitioners to obtain documents pertaining to the performance of incumbent licensees--documents which could help to clarify what effects (if any) cross-ownership has in a particular city.

Indeed, the F.C.C. should require broadcasting stations to make tape recordings of their news and editorial presentations available at a nominal fee to interested parties, whether they have filed a petition to deny or not.[65] Without access to such materials, concerned citizens may find themselves relying on fleeting impressions of what was covered

---

[64] The National Citizens Committee for Broadcasting, <u>Petition for Review of the Federal Communications Commission's Second Report and Order in Docket 18110</u>, p. 66.

[65] The F.C.C. currently requires broadcasting stations to make copies of their program logs available "provided the party making the request shall pay the reasonable costs of machine reproduction." See F.C.C. "Public and Broadcasting, Revised Edition," <u>Federal Register</u> (September 5, 1974), p. 32296. However, program logs reveal only the categories of programs aired, not the actual content of these programs.

(or how a particular story was handled) by the newspaper-owned television station in their city. If they had reliable data on the television station's news and editorial content, they would be in a better position to judge whether cross-ownership has homogenizing effects on the news outputs of the jointly owned newspaper and television station in their city. This knowledge could help them to decide whether any harmful effects attributable to cross-ownership in their city were serious enough to warrant the filing of a petition to deny.

The weight to be assigned the cross-ownership factor in comparative license renewal hearings (i.e., hearings involving competing applicants for a license) has not yet been decided by the F.C.C.[66] It is our view that the cross-ownership factor should be weighted on the basis of the extent to which it interferes with the public's right to know in a particular city. In comparative license renewal hearings (or other hearings, for that matter), the F.C.C. ought to evaluate all available evidence--especially any evidence which addresses the question of whether cross-ownership has homogenizing effects on news or editorial content in the city involved. It would be a mistake for the F.C.C. to investigate programming content with an eye toward distinguishing between "good" and "bad" ideas. However, to consider whether there is a relationship between media pluralism and message pluralism in a particular city is merely to test an assumption which has guided the F.C.C. in a number of policy-making deliberations.

Other factors which need to be considered in license renewal hearings are the extent to which the jointly owned news staffs function

---

[66]<u>Second Report and Order in Docket 18110</u>, pp. 47-49.

independently of one another, the number of local television stations in the city, whether the newspaper-owned television station editorializes, and the amount of local news and public affairs programming provided by the newspaper-owned television station. If a newspaper-owned television station in a particular city provides more local news and public affairs programming than comparable television stations, that certainly ought to count in its favor.[67]

License renewal machinery is, admittedly, cumbersome. However, reliance on such machinery (or something comparable) is a necessary adjunct to any rule which falls far short of across-the-board divestiture, as is true of our proposed rule. Newspaper-television cross-ownership may pose a threat to the public's right to know in certain cities served by more than three local television stations. The rights of citizens in these cities cannot be abrogated for the sake of administrative convenience.

Conclusion

In certain cities, cross-ownership may involve the deliberate distortion or suppression of the same stories by jointly owned newspapers and television stations (the equivalent of a "smoking pistol"). However, the effects of cross-ownership on news content which we have discovered are more subtle. By contributing to "pack journalism,"

---

[67] We have neither accepted nor rejected the F.C.C.'s argument that newspaper-owned television stations provide more local news and public affairs programming than comparable television stations. We believe the F.C.C.'s data ought to be reanalyzed and broken down by the number of local television stations per city. Negative effects of cross-ownership vary with the number of local television stations per city. If cross-ownership has certain positive effects, these may also vary with the number of local television stations per city.

cross-ownership interferes with diversity in the flow of news. By reducing the willingness of television stations to editorialize, cross-ownership interferes with diversity in the flow of opinions. The homogenizing effects of cross-ownership which we have identified are so circuitous as to be invisible to the casual observer. Nevertheless, homogenizing effects of cross-ownership need not be blatant, deliberate, or spectacular to warrant remedial action.

Remedial action which takes the form of divestiture may cause financial harm to incumbent licensees. However, as the late Justice Frankfurter observed, "Truth and understanding are not wares like peanuts or potatoes. And so, the incidence of restraints upon the promotion of truth through denial of access to the basis for understanding calls into play considerations very different from comparative restraints in a cooperative enterprise having merely a commercial aspect."[68]

Ultimately, the quality of decisions which citizens make depends on their access to a wide variety of information and opinions pertaining to the issues of the day, the qualifications of candidates for office, the performance of public officials, and socioeconomic trends. Impediments to diversity in the flow of news and opinions (message pluralism) undermine the search for truth. To the extent that cross-media ownership interferes with message pluralism, it is interfering with a prerequisite to successful self-government. As Meiklejohn has suggested, that is no small matter: "When men decide to be self-governed, to take control of their behavior, the search for truth is not merely one of a number of interests which may be

---

[68] *Associated Press vs. U.S.*, 326 U.S. 28 (1945).

'balanced' on equal terms, against one another. In that enterprise, the attempt to know and to understand has a unique status, a unique authority, to which all other activities are subordinated."[69] Cross-ownership may not involve Machiavellian abuses of power, but it does pose a threat to the public's right to know. In a democracy, the public's right to know is more important than the financial well-being of private entrepreneurs.

---

[69] Alexander Meiklejohn, Free Speech and Its Relation to Self-Government (New York: Harper & Brothers, 1948), pp. 68-69.

APPENDIX A

Jointly Owned Daily Newspapers and
Television Stations in the Same City

City	Newspaper(s)	T.V. Station	Number of Dailies in the City	Number of T.V. Stations in the City[a]
1. Anniston, Alabama	Star	WHMA	1	1
2. Birmingham, Alabama	News	WAPI	2	3
3. Fresno, California	Bee	KMJ	1	3
4. Sacramento, California	Bee	KOVR	2	4
5. San Francisco, California	Chronicle	KRON	2	4
6. Washington, D.C.	Post	WTOP	2	3
7. Washington, D.C.	Star	WMAL	2	3
8. Tampa, Florida	Tribune, Times	WFLA	2	2
9. Albany, Georgia	Herald	WALB	1	1
10. Atlanta, Georgia	Constitution, Journal	WSB	2	4
11. Idaho Falls, Idaho	Post Register	KIFI	1	2
12. Champaign, Illinois	News Gazette	WCIA	2	2

APPENDIX A (continued)

City	Newspaper(s)	T.V. Station	Number of Dailies in the City	Number of T.V. Stations in the City[a]
13. Chicago, Illinois	News, Sun-Times	WFLD	6	6
14. Chicago, Illinois	Today, Tribune	WGN	6	6
15. Quincy, Illinois	Herald-Whig	WGEM	1	2
16. Rock Island, Illinois	Argus	WHBF	1	1
17. South Bend, Indiana	Tribune	WSBT	1	2
18. Terre Haute, Indiana	Star, Tribune	WTHI	2	2
19. Cedar Rapids, Iowa	Gazette	KCRG	1	2
20. Des Moines, Iowa	Register, Tribune	KCCI	2	2
21. Mason City, Iowa	Globe, Gazette	KGLO	1	1
22. Topeka, Kansas	Capital, State Journal	WIBW	2	2
23. Louisville, Kentucky	Courier-Journal, Times	WHAS	2	4
24. Paducah, Kentucky	Sun-Democrat	WPSD	1	2
25. Baton Rouge, Louisiana	Advocate, State-Times	WBRZ	2	3
26. Shreveport, Louisiana	Journal	KSLA	2	3

250

APPENDIX A (continued)

City	Newspaper(s)	T.V. Station	Number of Dailies in the City	Number of T.V. Stations in the City[a]
27. Portland, Maine	Press Herald, Express	WGAN	2	2
28. Baltimore, Maryland	News American	WBAL	2	3
29. Baltimore, Maryland	Sun	WMAR	2	3
30. Detroit, Michigan	News	WWJ	2	3
31. Minneapolis, Minnesota	Tribune, Star	WCCO	2	3
32. Columbus, Mississippi	Commercial Dispatch	WCBI	1	1
33. Jackson, Mississippi	Clarion-Ledger, News	WJTV	2	3
34. Meridian, Mississippi	Star	WTOK	1	1
35. St. Louis, Missouri	Globe-Democrat	KTVI	2	3
36. St. Louis, Missouri	Post-Dispatch	KSD	2	3
37. Springfield, Missouri	News, Leader & Press	KYTV	2	2
38. Hastings, Nebraska	Tribune	KHAS	1	1
39. Omaha, Nebraska	World Herald	KETV	1	3
40. Las Vegas, Nevada	Review-Journal	KORK	2	3

APPENDIX A (continued)

City	Newspaper(s)	T.V. Station	Number of Dailies in the City	Number of T.V. Stations in the City[a]
41. Buffalo, New York	News	WBEN	2	3
42. New York, New York	Daily News	WPIX	3	6
43. Rochester, New York	Democrat & Chronicle, Times-Union	WHEC	2	3
44. Syracuse, New York	Post-Standard, Herald-Journal	WSYR	2	3
45. Watertown, New York	Times	WWNY	1	1
46. Greensboro, North Carolina	News, Record	WFMY	2	1
47. Hickory, North Carolina	Record	WHKY	1	1
48. Fargo, North Dakota	Forum	WDAY	1	3
49. Akron, Ohio	Beacon Journal	WAKR	1	1
50. Cincinnati, Ohio	Post & Times-Star	WCPO	2	3
51. Cleveland, Ohio	Press	WEWS	2	5
52. Columbus, Ohio	Dispatch	WBNS	2	3
53. Dayton, Ohio	Journal Herald, News	WHIO	2	2

252

APPENDIX A (continued)

City	Newspaper(s)	T.V. Station	Number of Dailies in the City	Number of T.V. Stations in the City[a]
54. Youngstown, Ohio	Vindicator	WFMJ	1	2
55. Oklahoma City, Oklahoma	Oklahoman, Times	WKY	3	3
56. Portland, Oregon	Oregonian, Oregon Journal	KOIN	3	4
57. Erie, Pennsylvania	News, Times	WSEE	2	2
58. Harrisburg, Pennsylvania	Patriot, News	WTPA	2	2
59. Johnstown, Pennsylvania	Tribune-Democrat	WJAC	1	1
60. Lancaster, Pennsylvania	Intelligencer Journal, New Era	WGAL	2	2
61. Greenville, South Carolina	News, Piedmont	WFBC	2	3
62. Memphis, Tennessee	Commercial Appeal, Press-Scimitar	WMC	2	3
63. Dallas, Texas	Morning News	WFAA	2	4
64. Dallas, Texas	Times-Herald	KDFW	2	4
65. Houston, Texas	Post	KPRC	2	4
66. Temple, Texas	Telegram	KCEN	1	1

253

APPENDIX A (continued)

City	Newspaper(s)	T.V. Station	Number of Dailies in the City	Number of T.V. Stations in the City[a]
67. Texarkana, Texas	Gazette, News	KTAL	2	1
68. Salt Lake City, Utah	Deseret News	KSL	2	3
69. Norfolk, Virginia	Virginian-Pilot, Ledger-Star	WTAR	2	2
70. Spokane, Washington	Spokesman-Review, Chronicle	KHQ	2	3
71. Bluefield, West Virginia	Telegraph	WHIS	1	1
72. Milwaukee, Wisconsin	Journal, Sentinel	WTMJ	2	4

Sources: Broadcasting International Yearbook 1975, Editor and Publisher International Yearbook 1975, Television Factbook: Stations Volume (1974-1975), and Broadcasting Magazine.

[a]To avoid including television stations which cover no state and local news or very little state and local news, the number of television stations has been defined as the number of television stations which have a studio in the city and which air at least one regular newscast dealing primarily with state and local news.

APPENDIX B

Average Daily Circulation of Television Stations Owned by Newspapers in the Same City

Television Market Area	Estimated Number of Television Households Reached Daily by Newspaper-Owned Television Stations
1. Anniston, Alabama	31,700
2. Birmingham, Alabama	294,700
3. Fresno, California	162,700
4. Sacramento-Stockton, California	397,100
5. San Francisco, California	913,700
6. Washington, D.C.	664,800
7. Tampa-St. Petersburg, Florida	477,700
8. Albany, Georgia	138,000
9. Atlanta, Georgia	566,000
10. Idaho Falls-Pocatello, Idaho	41,400
11. Champaign-Decatur-Springfield, Illinois	203,900
12. Chicago, Illinois	1,429,300
13. Quincy, Illinois-Hannibal, Missouri	94,100
14. Rock Island, Illinois-Davenport, Iowa-Moline, Illinois	216,000
15. South Bend-Elkhart, Indiana	178,700
16. Terre Haute, Indiana	136,300
17. Cedar Rapids, Iowa	172,600
18. Des Moines, Iowa	194,600
19. Mason City, Iowa	87,100
20. Topeka, Kansas	117,200

APPENDIX B (continued)

Television Market Area	Estimated Number of Television Households Reached Daily by Newspaper-Owned Television Stations
21. Louisville, Kentucky	305,200
22. Paducah, Kentucky-Cape Girardeau, Missouri-Harrisburg, Illinois	201,000
23. Baton Rouge, Louisiana	182,600
24. Shreveport, Louisiana-Texarkana, Texas	227,100
25. Portland-Poland Spring, Maine	166,500
26. Baltimore, Maryland	619,700
27. Detroit, Michigan	1,073,900
28. Minneapolis-St. Paul, Minnesota	583,800
29. Columbus, Mississippi	71,000
30. Jackson, Mississippi	167,900
31. Meridian, Mississippi	68,700
32. Joplin, Missouri-Pittsburg, Kansas	130,100
33. St. Louis, Missouri	627,700
34. Springfield, Missouri	163,500
35. Lincoln-Kearney-Hastings, Nebraska	57,800
36. Omaha, Nebraska	237,200
37. Las Vegas, Nevada	71,300
38. Buffalo, New York	411,100
39. New York, New York	1,824,300
40. Rochester, New York	235,500
41. Syracuse, New York	267,700
42. Watertown-Carthage, New York	52,100

APPENDIX B (continued)

Television Market Area	Estimated Number of Television Households Reached Daily by Newspaper-Owned Television Stations
43. Greensboro-Winston Salem-High Point, North Carolina	287,300
44. Hickory, North Carolina	1,000
45. Fargo, North Dakota	121,300
46. Cincinnati, Ohio	499,200
47. Cleveland-Akron, Ohio	865,800
48. Columbus, Ohio	424,300
49. Dayton, Ohio	403,600
50. Youngstown, Ohio	185,700
51. Oklahoma City, Oklahoma	335,100
52. Portland, Oregon	398,600
53. Erie, Pennsylvania	76,700
54. Harrisburg-York-Lancaster-Lebanon, Pennsylvania	345,100
55. Johnstown-Altoona, Pennsylvania	353,200
56. Greenville-Spartanburg-Anderson, South Carolina-Asheville, North Carolina	339,800
57. Memphis, Tennessee	373,100
58. Dallas-Fort Worth, Texas	625,800
59. Houston, Texas	512,800
60. Temple-Waco, Texas	104,100
61. Salt Lake City, Utah	265,700
62. Norfolk-Portsmouth, Virginia	287,900
63. Spokane, Washington	186,600

APPENDIX B (continued)

Television Market Area	Estimated Number of Television Households Reached Daily by Newspaper-Owned Television Stations
64. Bluefield-Beckley-Oak Hill, West Virginia	92,700
65. Milwaukee, Wisconsin	421,800
Total	22,862,200

Source: Television Factbook: Stations Volume (1974-1975).

Note: There are 65,243,900 television households in the U.S.

APPENDIX C

Questionnaire for Newspaper Managing Editors

INTERMEDIA RELATIONS PROJECT

1. a) How many reporters on your staff are involved in the writing of state or local news stories?

   b) How many editors on your staff are involved in the assigning or editing of state or local news stories?

2. Please identify (by title) each reporter or editor on your staff who has worked for a television station, along with the television station(s) for which each has worked.

Person's Title (reporter, editor)	T.V. Station (call letters)	City of T.V. Station
a)		
b)		
c)		
d)		
e)		

3. Which television station do you think most members of your state and local news staff (reporters and editors) prefer for televised state and local news reports?

4. a) As far as you know, does any member of your staff (a reporter or an editor) monitor a state and local television news broadcast on a regular basis to obtain information or get ideas for stories?

   b) If so, which television station does he (she) usually monitor?

5. a) Do you ever furnish copies of your state or local news stories to a television station for background or for use on the air in some form?

   b) If so, which television station(s)?

APPENDIX C (continued)

6. In general, how would you rate the state and local news broadcasts of each television station in your area? (Check one box for each television station in your area.)

T.V. Station (call letters)	Excellent	Good	Fair	Poor
a)				
b)				
c)				
d)				

7. Has the owner of your newspaper ever offered formal or informal guidelines or comments on newsgathering procedures or decisions? If so, please indicate briefly the nature of these guidelines or comments.

8. Do you regard newspaper reporters and television reporters as belonging to one journalistic profession? Please elaborate.

9. How often would you say you interact with television personnel on a professional basis (e.g., at a news event or a meeting)? (Circle one.)

   Regularly   Occasionally   Rarely   Never

   b) How often would you say you interact with television personnel on a social basis (e.g., over lunch or drinks)? (Circle one.)

   Regularly   Occasionally   Rarely   Never

THANKS VERY MUCH FOR YOUR COOPERATION.

Feel free to use an additional sheet of paper if necessary.

APPENDIX D

Questionnaire for Television News Directors

INTERMEDIA RELATIONS PROJECT

NOTE: DOES YOUR TELEVISION STATION EVER BROADCAST A NEWS PROGRAM DEALING TO SOME EXTENT WITH STATE OR LOCAL NEWS? IF SO, PLEASE PROCEED WITH THIS QUESTIONNAIRE. IF NOT, PLEASE PLACE A BLANK SHEET OF PAPER IN THE ENCLOSED ENVELOPE AND DROP IT IN THE MAIL. THANK YOU.

1. a) Does your television station regularly broadcast at least one news program dealing primarily with state and local news?

   b) If so, how many nights a week?

2. a) How many reporters on your staff are involved in the writing of state or local news stories?

   b) How many editors on your staff are involved in the assigning or editing of state or local news stories?

3. Please identify (by title) each reporter or editor on your staff who has worked for a newspaper, along with the newspaper(s) for which each has worked.

Person's Title (reporter, editor)	Newspaper (name of newspaper)
a)	
b)	
c)	
d)	
e)	

4. Which newspaper do you think most members of your state and local news staff (reporters and editors) prefer for printed state and local news reports?

APPENDIX D (continued)

5. a) As far as you know, does any member of your staff (a reporter or an editor) monitor a newspaper's state and local news reports on a regular basis to obtain information or get ideas for stories?

   b) If so, which newspaper does he (she) usually monitor?

6. a) Do you ever furnish copies of your state or local news stories to a newspaper for background or for use in print in some form?

   b) If so, which newspaper(s)?

7. Does your television station broadcast editorials? (Circle one.)

   Daily   Weekly   Occasionally   Never

8. In general, how would you rate the state and local news reports of each daily newspaper in your area? (Check one box for each daily newspaper in your area.)

Newspaper (identify)	Excellent	Good	Fair	Poor
a)				
b)				
c)				
d)				

9. Has the owner of your television station ever offered formal or informal guidelines or comments on newsgathering procedures or decisions? If so, please indicate briefly the nature of these guidelines or comments.

10. Do you regard newspaper and television reporters as belonging to one journalistic profession? Please elaborate.

APPENDIX D (continued)

11. a) How often would you say you interact with newspaper personnel on a professional basis (e.g., at a news event or a meeting)? (Circle one.)

    Regularly   Occasionally   Rarely   Never

b) How often would you say you interact with newspaper personnel on a social basis (e.g., over lunch or drinks)?

    Regularly   Occasionally   Rarely   Never

THANKS VERY MUCH FOR YOUR COOPERATION.

Feel free to use an additional sheet of paper if necessary.

APPENDIX E

Questionnaire Cover Letter

INSTITUTE FOR RESEARCH
IN SOCIAL SCIENCE

UNIVERSITY OF NORTH CAROLINA • CHAPEL HILL • 27514

January 20, 1975

I am a former reporter and a current Ph.D. candidate at the University of North Carolina, where I am gathering data for my dissertation. As an integral part of my dissertation research, I am sending questionnaires to managing editors and news directors in over 80 cities. The purpose of the questionnaire is to explore relations between newspaper and television news organizations.

I am sure you must be extremely busy. However, I would greatly appreciate it if you could take a few minutes to complete the enclosed questionnaire, which can be sent to me in the enclosed stamped envelope.

Responses to the questionnaire will be used in a statistical analysis of conditions affecting relations between newspapers and television stations. The responses will also be used to lay the groundwork for more detailed research in a sample of cities.

I have already typed your return address on the enclosed envelope, so that I can identify your questionnaire for internal purposes. I will then be able to link your responses to conditions in your city. I will not be identifying you, your news organization, or your city by name, on the basis of your responses to the questionnaire. In short, your personal responses will be incorporated into my dissertation, but will be considered confidential.

Thanks in advance for your cooperation. If you have any questions, please call me at (919) 933-3061.

Sincerely,

William Gormley, Director
Intermedia Relations Project

Enclosures

A SELECTED BIBLIOGRAPHY

Books

Allison, Graham. *Essence of Decision: Explaining the Cuban Missile Crisis.* Boston: Little, Brown & Company, 1971.

Almond, Gabriel and Verba, Sidney. *Civic Culture.* Boston: Little, Brown & Company, 1965.

Argyris, Chris. *Behind the Front Page.* San Francisco: Jossey-Bass Publishers, 1974.

Bagdikian, Ben. *The Effete Conspiracy and Other Crimes by the Press.* New York: Harper & Row, Inc., 1972.

Barnard, Chester. *The Functions of the Executive.* Cambridge, Massachusetts: Harvard University Press, 1968.

Barron, Jerome. *Freedom of the Press for Whom? The Right of Access to Mass Media.* Bloomington, Indiana: Indiana University Press, 1973.

Bay, Christian. *The Structure of Freedom.* Stanford: Stanford University Press, 1958.

Berelson, Bernard et al. *Voting.* Chicago: University of Chicago Press, 1954.

Berns, Walter. *Freedom, Virtue and the First Amendment.* Baton Rouge: Louisiana State University Press, 1957.

Bernstein, Carl and Woodward, Bob. *All the President's Men.* New York: Simon and Schuster, 1974.

Berry, Jason. *Amazing Grace: With Charles Evers in Mississippi.* New York: Saturday Review Press, 1973.

Blalock, Hubert. *Social Statistics.* New York: McGraw-Hill, Inc., 1972.

Blau, Peter. *Exchange and Power in Social Life.* New York: John Wiley & Sons, Inc., 1964.

Budd, Richard et al. *Content Analysis of Communications.* New York: The MacMillan Company, 1967.

Cantril, Hadley. *The Invasion from Mars*. Princeton: Princeton University Press, 1952.

Cater, Douglass. *The Fourth Branch of Government*. New York: Random House, Inc., 1959.

Cobb, Roger and Elder, Charles. *Participation in American Politics: The Dynamics of Agenda-Building*. Boston: Allyn and Bacon, Inc., 1972.

Cohen, Bernard. *The Press and Foreign Policy*. Princeton: Princeton University Press, 1963.

Crouse, Timothy. *The Boys on the Bus*. New York: Random House, 1973.

Dahl, Robert. *Polyarchy: Participation and Opposition*. New Haven: Yale University Press, 1971.

DeVries, Walter and Tarrance, V. Lance. *The Ticket-Splitter*. Grand Rapids, Michigan: Eerdmans Publishing Company, 1972.

Dewey, John. *Liberalism and Social Action*. New York: Capricon Books, 1963.

Downs, Anthony. *An Economic Theory of Democracy*. New York: Harper and Brothers, 1957.

Downs, Anthony. *Inside Bureaucracy*. Boston: Little, Brown & Company, 1967.

Dunn, Delmer. *Public Officials and the Press*. Reading, Massachusetts: Addison-Wesley Publishing Company, 1969.

Easton, David. *A Systems Analysis of Political Life*. New York: John Wiley & Sons, Inc., 1965.

Edelman, Murray. *The Symbolic Uses of Politics*. Urbana: University of Illinois Press, 1964.

Emery, Edwin. *The Press and America: An Interpretative History of the Mass Media*. Englewood Cliffs, New Jersey: Prentice-Hall, Inc., 1972.

Emery, Walter. *Broadcasting and Government: Responsibilities and Regulations* East Lansing: Michigan State University Press, 1971.

Frankena, William. *Ethics*. Englewood Cliffs, New Jersey: Prentice-Hall, Inc., 1963.

Gerald, J. Edward. *The Social Responsibility of the Press*. Minneapolis: University of Minnesota Press, 1963.

Hecht, Ben and MacArthur, Charles. *The Front Page*. New York: Samuel French, 1950.

Holsti, Ole. *Content Analysis for the Social Sciences and Humanities*. Reading, Massachusetts: Addison-Wesley Publishing Company, 1969.

Hovland, Carl et al., *The Order of Presentation in Persuasion*. New Haven: Yale University Press, 1957.

Jones, Charles. *An Introduction to the Study of Public Policy*. Belmont, California: Wadsworth Publishing Company, Inc., 1970.

Katz, Elihu and Lazarsfeld, Paul. *Personal Influence*. New York: The Free Press, 1964.

Key, V. O., Jr. *Public Opinion and American Democracy*. New York: Alfred Knopf Company, 1961.

Key, V. O., Jr. *The Responsible Electorate*. New York: Vintage Books, 1966.

Krasnow, Erwin and Longley, Lawrence. *The Politics of Broadcast Regulation*. New York: St. Martin's Press, Inc., 1973.

Lazarsfeld, Paul, et al. *The People's Choice*. New York: Columbia University Press, 1944.

Levin, Harvey. *Broadcast Regulation and Joint Ownership of Media*. New York: New York University Press, 1960.

Liebling, A. J. *The Press*. New York: Ballantine Books, 1964.

Lindblom, Charles. *The Intelligence of Democracy*. New York: The Free Press, 1965.

Lindblom, Charles. *The Policy-Making Process*. Englewood Cliffs, New Jersey: Prentice-Hall, Inc., 1968.

Long, Norton. *The Polity*. Chicago: Rand McNally and Company, 1962.

MacNeil, Robert. *The People Machine: The Influence of Television on American Politics*. New York: Harper & Row, 1968.

March, James and Simon, Herbert. *Organizations*. New York: John Wiley & Sons, Inc., 1958.

Meiklejohn, Alexander. *Free Speech and Its Relation to Self-Government*. New York: Harper & Brothers, 1948.

Mencken, H. L. *A Gang of Pecksniffs*, ed. by Theo Lippman, Jr. New Rochelle, New York: Arlington House Publishers, 1975.

Merrill, John. *The Imperative of Freedom: A Philosophy of Journalistic Autonomy*. New York: Hastings House Publishers, 1974.

Milbrath, Lester. *Political Participation*. Chicago: Rand McNally and Company, 1965.

Mill, John Stuart. *On Liberty*, ed. by Alburey Castell. New York: Appleton-Century-Crofts, Inc., 1947.

Mills, C. Wright. *The Power Elite*. New York: Oxford University Press, 1956.

Milton, John. *John Milton: Complete Poems and Major Prose*, ed. by Merritt Hughes. New York: The Odyssey Press, 1957.

Noll, Roger et al. *Economic Aspects of Television Regulation*. Washington, D.C.: Brookings Institution, 1973.

Olson, Mancur. *The Logic of Collective Action*. New York: Schocken Books, 1971.

Price, David. *Who Makes the Laws?* Cambridge, Massachusetts: Schenkman Publishing Company, 1972.

Quinlan, Sterling. *The Hundred Million Dollar Lunch*. Chicago: J. Philip O'Hara, Inc., 1974.

Rae, Douglas and Taylor, Michael. *The Analysis of Political Cleavages*. New Haven: Yale University Press, 1970.

Rawls, John. *A Theory of Justice*. Cambridge, Massachusetts: The Belknap Press, 1971.

Riesman, David. *The Lonely Crowd*. New Haven: Yale University Press, 1961.

Rivers, William. *The Adversaries: Politics and the Press*. Boston: Beacon Press, 1970.

Rucker, Bryce. *The First Freedom*. Carbondale, Illinois: Southern Illinois University Press, 1968.

Schattschneider, E. E. *The Semi-Sovereign People*. New York: Holt, Rinehart, and Winston, 1960.

Siebert, Fred et al. *Four Theories of the Press*. Urbana, Illinois: University of Illinois Press, 1956.

Sigal, Leon. *Reporters and Officials: The Organization and Politics of Newsmaking*. Lexington, Massachusetts: D. C. Heath & Company, 1973.

Truman, David. *The Governmental Process*. New York: Alfred Knopf, 1962.

Veblen, Eric. *The Manchester Union Leader in New Hampshire Elections*. Hanover, New Hampshire: University Press of New England, 1975.

Watson, James. *The Double Helix*. New York: Mentor Books, 1969.

White, Theodore. *The Making of the President 1972*. New York: Atheneum Publishers, 1973.

Wicker, Tom. *Facing the Lions*. New York: Viking Press, 1973.

Articles and Reports

Abel, John et al. "Station License Revocations and Denials of Renewal 1934-1969." *Journal of Broadcasting* (Fall 1970), pp. 411-421.

Anderson, James. "The Alliance of Broadcast Stations and Newspapers: The Problem of Information Control." *Journal of Broadcasting* (Winter 1971-1972), pp. 51-63.

Anderson, James. "Broadcast Stations and Newspapers: The Problem of Information Control: A Content Analysis of Local News Presentations." *Broadcast Research Center Report* (Athens, Ohio: June 1971).

Anderson, James et al. "Economic Issues Relating to the F.C.C.'s Proposed 'One-to-a-Customer' Rule." *Journal of Broadcasting* (Summer 1969), pp. 241-252.

Baer, Walter et al. "Concentration of Mass Media Ownership: Assessing the State of Current Knowledge." *Rand Corporation Report* (Santa Monica, California: September 1974).

Baer, Walter et al. "Newspaper-Television Station Cross-Ownership: Options for Federal Action." *Rand Corporation Report* (Santa Monica, California: September 1974).

Bagdikian, Ben. "Congress and the Media: Partners in Propaganda." *Columbia Journalism Review* (January/February, 1974), pp. 3-10.

Bagdikian, Ben. "The Myth of Newspaper Poverty." *Columbia Journalism Review* (March/April 1973), pp. 19-25.

Bagdikian, Ben. "Newspapers: Learning (Too Slowly) to Adapt to TV," *Columbia Journalism Review* (November/December 1973), pp. 44-51.

Bagdikian, Ben. "The Politics of American Newspapers." *Columbia Journalism Review* (March/April 1972), pp. 8-13.

Bagdikian, Ben. "Shaping Media Content: Professional Personnel and Organizational Structure." *Public Opinion Quarterly* (Winter 1973-1974), pp. 569-579.

Baldridge, Paul. "Group and Non-Group Owner Programming: A Comparative Analysis." *Journal of Broadcasting* (Spring 1967), pp. 125-130.

Barnett, Stephen. "Cross-Ownership of Mass Media in the Same City: A Report to the John and Mary R. Markle Foundation." Unpublished Manuscript (Berkeley: September 23, 1974).

Barnett, Stephen. "The F.C.C.'s Nonbattle Against Media Monopoly." *Columbia Journalism Review* (January/February 1973), pp. 43-50.

Baxter, William. "Regulation and Diversity in Communications Media." *American Economic Review* (May 1974), pp. 392-399.

Bay, Christian. "Politics and Pseudopolitics." *American Political Science Review* (March 1965), pp. 39-51.

Bishop, Robert. "The Rush to Chain Ownership." *Columbia Journalism Review* (November/December 1972), pp. 10-19.

Bogart, Leo. "How the Challenge of Television News Affects the Prosperity of Daily Newspapers." *Journalism Quarterly* (Autumn 1975), pp. 403-410.

Bogart, Leo. "The Management of Mass Media: An Agenda for Research." *Public Opinion Quarterly* (Winter 1973-1974), pp. 580-589.

Breed, Warren. "Social Control in the Newsroom: A Functional Analysis." *Social Forces* (May 1955), pp. 326-335.

Brenner, Daniel. "Toward a New Balance in License Renewals." *Journal of Broadcasting* (Winter 1972-1973), pp. 63-76.

Brown, Steve et al. "Dallas News Eats Its Words." *Texas Journalism Review* (Spring 1975), pp. 10-11.

Buckalew, James. "News Elements and Selection by TV News Editors." *Journal of Broadcasting* (Winter 1969-1970), pp. 47-54.

Carmody, John and Kilpatrick, Carroll. "A Replacement for Burch: Wiley Named F.C.C. Chairman." *The Washington Post* (February 23, 1974), p. B1.

Chandler, Marsha et al. "Policy Analysis and the Search for Theory." *American Politics Quarterly* (January 1974), pp. 107-118.

Clarke, Peter and Ruggels, Lee. "Preferences Among News Media for Coverage of Public Affairs." *Journalism Quarterly* (Autumn 1970), pp. 464-471.

Clyde, Robert and Buckalew, James. "Inter-Media Standardization: A Q-Analysis of News Editors." *Journalism Quarterly* (Summer 1969), pp. 349-351.

Cnudde, Charles. "Public Opinion and State Politics." *State Politics*, ed. by Robert Crew (Belmont, California: Wadsworth Publishing Company, 1968), pp. 165-184.

Coase, R. H. "The Market for Goods and the Market for Ideas." *American Economic Review* (May 1974), pp. 384-391.

"The Continuing Study of Newspaper Reading." Conducted by the Advertising Research Foundation in Cooperation with the Bureau of Advertising of the American Newspaper Publishers Association.

Donohew, Lewis. "Newspaper Gatekeepers and Forces in the News Channel." *Public Opinion Quarterly* (Spring 1967), pp. 61-68.

Donohue, George et al. "Mass Media and the Knowledge Gap: A Hypothesis Reconsidered." *Communication Research* (January 1975), pp. 3-24.

Downs, Anthony. "Up and Down with Ecology--The Issue-Attention Cycle." *The Public Interest* (Summer 1972), pp. 38-50.

Duncan, Graeme and Lukes, Steven. "Democracy Restated." *Frontiers of Democratic Theory*, ed. by Henry Kariel (New York: Random House, 1970), pp. 188-213.

Eversole, Pam. "Concentration of Ownership in the Communications Industry." *Journalism Quarterly* (Summer 1971), pp. 251-268.

Fang, Irving and Whelan, John. "Survey of Television Editorials and Ombudsman Segments." *Journal of Broadcasting* (Summer 1973), pp. 363-371.

Flegel, Ruth and Chaffee, Steven. "Influences of Editors, Readers, and Personal Opinions on Reporters." *Journalism Quarterly* (Winter 1971), pp. 645-651.

Foley, Joseph. "Broadcast Regulation Research: A Primer for Non-Lawyers." *Journal of Broadcasting* (Spring 1973), pp. 147-157.

Funkhouser, G. Ray. "The Issues of the 60's: An Exploratory Study in the Dynamics of Public Opinion." *Public Opinion Quarterly* (Spring 1973), pp. 62-75.

Gormley, William. "Newspaper Agendas and Political Elites." *Journalism Quarterly* (Summer 1975), pp. 304-308.

Halberstam, David. "CBS: The Power and the Profits, Part II." *The Atlantic Monthly* (February 1976), pp. 52-91.

Harris, Mark. "The Last Article." New York Times Magazine (October 6, 1974), pp. 20-34.

Hogan, Paul. "Ohio: Printing the Obscenity." Columbia Journalism Review (July/August 1975), pp. 15-17.

Honig, David. "Broadcasting in America--1975." Access (December 1, 1975), pp. 7-23.

Hooper, Michael. "Party and Newspaper Endorsement as Predictors of Voter Choice." Journalism Quarterly (Summer 1969), pp. 302-305.

"How Portland, Oregon Adults Use TV and Radio for News," News Research for Better Newspapers, Vol. 6, ed. by Galen Rarick, pp. 12-39.

Huntington, Samuel. "Postindustrial Politics: How Benign Will It Be?" Comparative Politics (January 1974), pp. 163-191.

Huston, Luther. "F.C.C. Weighs Arguments on Cross-Ownership Rights." Editor and Publisher (August 3, 1974), pp. 9-28.

Johnson, Nicholas. "The Media Barons and the Public Interest." The Atlantic Monthly (June 1968), pp. 43-51.

Johnstone, John et al. "The Professional Values of American Newsmen." Public Opinion Quarterly (Winter 1972-1973), pp. 522-540.

Kentera, George. "F.C.C. Rule Limits Newspaper Ownership of T.V. and Radio." The Detroit News (January 29, 1975), p. 7.

Kuralt, Charles. "All Those Pretty TV News Anchormen." The Quill (October 1975), pp. 9-10.

Kuttner, Bob. "F.C.C. Decision Urged." The Washington Post (July 25, 1974), p. 4.

Lambeth, Edmund and Weinberg, Steve. "The Looking Glass: How Dailies Covered Themselves on Cross-Ownership and Divestiture." Mass Communication Review (July 1975), pp. 3-8.

Land, Kenneth Land. "Principles of Path Analysis." Sociological Methodology 1969, ed. by Edgar Borgatta et al. (San Francisco: Jossey-Bass, Inc., 1969), pp. 3-37.

Lemert, James. "Content Duplication by the Networks in Competing Evening Newscasts." Journalism Quarterly (September 1974), pp. 238-244.

Lichty, Lawrence. "Members of the Federal Radio Commission and Federal Communications Commission 1927-1961." Journal of Broadcasting (Winter 1961-1962), pp. 23-34.

Long, Norton. "Bureaucracy and Constitutionalism." *American Political Science Review* (September 1952), pp. 808-818.

Lucas, William and Possner, Karen. "Television News and Local Awareness: A Retrospective Look." *Rand Corporation Report* (Santa Monica, California: October 1975).

McBee, Susanna. "Justice Department Move on Media Surprised White House." *The Washington Post* (January 21, 1974), p. 2.

McCombs, Maxwell. "Editorial Endorsements: A Study of Influence." *Journalism Quarterly* (Autumn 1967), pp. 545-548.

McCombs, Maxwell. "Mass Media in the Marketplace." *Journalism Monographs* (August 1972).

McCombs, Maxwell and Shaw, Donald. "The Agenda-Setting Function of Mass Media." *Public Opinion Quarterly* (Summer 1972), pp. 176-187.

McLeod, Jack et al. "Another Look at the Agenda-Setting Function of the Press," *Communication Research* (April 1974), pp. 131-165.

MacRae, Duncan, Jr. "Scientific Communication, Ethical Argument, and Public Policy." *American Political Science Review* (March 1971), pp. 38-50.

Molotch, Harvey and Lester, Marilyn. "News as Purposive Behavior: On the Strategic Use of Routine Events, Accidents, and Scandals." *American Sociological Review* (February 1974), pp. 101-112.

Mueller, John. "Choosing Among 133 Candidates." *Public Opinion Quarterly* (Fall 1970), pp. 395-402.

"A National Survey of the Content and Readership of the American Newspaper." Published by the Newspaper Advertising Bureau (New York: December 1972).

Nestvold, Karl. "Diversity in Local Television News." *Journal of Broadcasting* (Summer 1973), pp. 345-352.

Newman, W. Russell. "Patterns of Recall Among Television News Viewers." *Public Opinion Quarterly* (Spring 1976), pp. 115-123.

Nixon, Raymond and Jones, Robert. "The Content of Non-Competitive vs. Competitive Newspapers." *Journalism Quarterly* (Summer 1956), pp. 299-314.

Pincus, Walter. "Media Monopolies: Is Bigness a Curse?" *New Republic* (January 26, 1974), pp. 11-14.

Powell, Lew and Meek, Edwin. "Mississippi's WLBT: After the License Challenge." Columbia Journalism Review (May/June 1973), pp. 50-55.

Powers, Ron and Oppenheim, Jerrold. "Is T.V. Too Profitable?" Columbia Journalism Review (May/June 1972), pp. 7-13.

Rarick, Galen and Hartman, Barrie. "The Effects of Competition on One Daily Newspaper's Content." Journalism Quarterly (Autumn 1966), pp. 459-463.

Rarick, Galen. "Newspaper Item Readership and Prior Exposure Via Electronic Media." News Research for Better Newspapers, Vol. 2, ed. by Chilton Bush, pp. 29-31.

Richardson, Jack. "Television News as Pop Religion." Harper's (December 1975), pp. 34-38.

Sasser, Emery and Russell, John. "The Fallacy of News Judgment." Journalism Quarterly (Summer 1972), pp. 280-284.

Scanlon, Thomas. "A Theory of Freedom of Expression." Philosophy and Public Affairs (Winter 1972), pp. 204-226.

Shifrin, Carole. "Bars Set on Media Owners." The Washington Post (January 29, 1975), p. D9.

Singer, Peter. "Philosophers Are Back on the Job." New York Times Magazine (July 7, 1974), pp. 6-20.

Smith, Griffin, Jr. "Deadline in Dallas." Texas Monthly (June 1974), pp. 52-81.

Smith, Mike. "They Chase News--and TV Ratings." The Norfolk Virginian-Pilot (August 18, 1974), p. F1.

Stempel, Guido, III. "Effects on Performance of a Cross-Media Monopoly." Journalism Monographs (June 1973).

Sterling, Christopher. "Newspaper Ownership of Broadcast Stations, 1920-1968." Journalism Quarterly (Summer 1969), pp. 227-254.

Stern, Andrew. "Recall for Television News Found to Be Low." News Research for Better Newspapers, Vol. 6, ed. by Galen Rarick, pp. 40-41.

Stokes, Donald. "Compound Paths: An Expository Note." American Journal of Political Science (February 1974), pp. 191-214.

"That Monopoly of Opinion." The Masthead (Fall 1974), pp. 8-30.

Thomas, Jack. "Did Boston's 'Herald Traveler' Have to Fail?" Columbia Journalism Review (July/August 1972), pp. 41-44.

Tipton, Leonard. "Media Agenda-Setting in City and State Election Campaigns." *Journalism Quarterly* (Spring 1975), pp. 15-22.

Wackman, Daniel et al. "Chain Newspaper Autonomy as Reflected in Presidential Campaign Endorsements." *Journalism Quarterly* (Autumn 1975), pp. 411-420.

Walker, Jack. "A Critique of the Elitist Theory of Democracy." *American Political Science Review* (June 1966), pp. 285-295.

Wilensky, Harold. "The Professionalization of Everyone?" *American Journal of Sociology* (September 1964), pp. 137-158.

Government Documents and Court Cases

Associated Press vs. U.S., 326 U.S. 1 (1945).

Broadcast License Renewal Act, *Congressional Record* (May 1, 1974), pp. H3413-H3433.

Broadcast License Renewal Hearings Before the Subcommittee on Communications and Power of the Committee on Interstate and Foreign Commerce of the House of Representatives (March, April, May, and September 1973).

Citizens Communications Center vs. F.C.C., 447 F. 2d 1201 (1971).

Columbus Broadcasting Coalition vs. F.C.C., 505 F. 2d 320 (1974).

Federal Communications Commission, *First Report and Order in Docket 18110* (March 25, 1970).

Federal Communications Commission, *Memorandum Opinion and Order in Docket 18110* (May 28, 1975).

Federal Communications Commission, *Memorandum Opinion and Order in Docket 20559* (January 21, 1976).

Federal Communications Commission, *Petition for Review of a Report and Order of the Federal Communications Commission (Second Report and Order in Docket 18110)*: Brief for Respondent (February 17, 1976).

Federal Communications Commission, "Public and Broadcasting: Revised Edition," *Federal Register* (September 5, 1974).

Federal Communications Commission, *Rules and Regulations*, Vol. III (September 1972).

Federal Communications Commission, <u>Second Report and Order in Docket 18110</u> (January 28, 1975).

Federal Communications Commission, Thirty-Eighth Annual Report/Fiscal Year 1972.

National Citizens Committee for Broadcasting, <u>Petition for Review of a Report and Order of the Federal Communications Commission (Second Report and Order in Docket 18110)</u>: Brief for Petitioner (October 1, 1975).

National Citizens Committee for Broadcasting, <u>Petition for Review of a Report and Order of the Federal Communications Commission (Second Report and Order in Docket 18110)</u>: Reply Brief for Petitioner (May 20, 1976).

<u>Office of Communication of the United Church of Christ vs. F.C.C.</u>, 359 F. 2d 994 (1966).

<u>Red Lion Broadcasting Company vs. F.C.C.</u>, 395 U.S. 367 (1969).

<u>United States Code</u>, Title 47, Articles 307-309.

<u>U.S. vs. Carolene Products Company</u>, 304 U.S. 144 (1938).

PN 4745 .G66

PN 4745 .G66